Selected as an Amazon Best Books of 2015 in the Cookbooks and Food Writing Category
AMAZON ON *THE COMPLETE VEGETARIAN COOKBOOK*

"An exceptional resource for novice canners, though preserving veterans will find plenty here to love as well."
LIBRARY JOURNAL (STARRED REVIEW) ON
FOOLPROOF PRESERVING

"The editors at America's Test Kitchen, known for their meticulous recipe testing and development, are back at it again. This time, they've trained their laser-eyed focus on reduced-sugar baking. . . . Cooks with a powerful sweet tooth should scoop up this well-researched recipe book for healthier takes on classic sweet treats."
BOOKLIST ON *NATURALLY SWEET*

"A beautifully illustrated, 318-page culinary compendium showcasing an impressive variety and diversity of authentic Mexican cuisine."
MIDWEST BOOK REVIEW ON *THE BEST MEXICAN RECIPES*

"A terrifically accessible and useful guide to grilling in all its forms that sets a new bar for its competitors."
PUBLISHERS WEEKLY (STARRED REVIEW) ON
MASTER OF THE GRILL

"Another winning cookbook from ATK. . . . The folks at America's Test Kitchen apply their rigorous experiments to determine the facts about these pans."
BOOKLIST ON *COOK IT IN CAST IRON*

"The 21st-century *Fannie Farmer Cookbook* or *The Joy of Cooking*. If you had to have one cookbook and that's all you could have, this one would do it."
CBS SAN FRANCISCO ON *THE NEW FAMILY COOKBOOK*

"The sum total of exhaustive experimentation . . . anyone interested in gluten-free cookery simply shouldn't be without it."
NIGELLA LAWSON ON *THE HOW CAN IT BE GLUTEN-FREE COOKBOOK*

"This book upgrades slow cooking for discriminating, 21st-century palates—that is indeed revolutionary."
THE DALLAS MORNING NEWS ON *SLOW COOKER REVOLUTION*

"Some 2,500 photos walk readers through 600 painstakingly tested recipes, leaving little room for error."
ASSOCIATED PRESS ON *THE AMERICA'S TEST KITCHEN COOKING SCHOOL COOKBOOK*

"A one-volume kitchen seminar, addressing in one smart chapter after another the sometimes surprising whys behind a cook's best practices. . . . You get the myth, the theory, the science, and the proof, all rigorously interrogated as only America's Test Kitchen can do."
NPR ON *THE SCIENCE OF GOOD COOKING*

"This book is a comprehensive, no-nonsense guide . . . a well-thought-out, clearly explained primer for every aspect of home baking."
THE WALL STREET JOURNAL ON *THE COOK'S ILLUSTRATED BAKING BOOK*

"The go-to gift book for newlyweds, small families, or empty nesters."
ORLANDO SENTINEL ON *THE COMPLETE COOKING FOR TWO COOKBOOK*

"There are pasta books . . . and then there's this pasta book. Flip your carbohydrate dreams upside down and strain them through this sieve of revolutionary, creative, and also traditional recipes."
SAN FRANCISCO BOOK REVIEW ON *PASTA REVOLUTION*

"The perfect kitchen home companion. . . . The practical side of things is very much on display . . . cook-friendly and kitchen-oriented, illuminating the process of preparing food instead of mystifying it."
THE WALL STREET JOURNAL ON *THE COOK'S ILLUSTRATED COOKBOOK*

"Further proof that practice makes perfect, if not transcendent. . . . If an intermediate cook follows the directions exactly, the results will be better than takeout or Mom's."
THE NEW YORK TIMES ON *THE NEW BEST RECIPE*

VEGAN FOR EVERYBODY

Foolproof Plant-Based Recipes for
Breakfast, Lunch, Dinner, and In-Between

THE EDITORS AT
AMERICA'S TEST KITCHEN

Library of Congress Cataloging-in-Publication Data
Names: America's Test Kitchen (Firm)
Title: Vegan for everybody : foolproof plant-based recipes
    for breakfast, lunch, dinner, and in-between /
    by the editors at America's Test Kitchen.
Other titles: America's test kitchen (Television program)
Description: Brookline, MA : America's Test Kitchen, [2017] |
    Includes index.
Identifiers: LCCN 2016049179 | ISBN 9781940352862
Subjects: LCSH: Vegan cooking. | LCGFT: Cookbooks.
Classification: LCC TX771 .V377 2017 | DDC 641.5/636--dc23
LC record available at https://lccn.loc.gov/2016049179

AMERICA'S TEST KITCHEN
17 Station Street, Brookline, MA 02445

AMERICA'S
TEST KITCHEN ®

Manufactured in Canada
10 9 8 7 6 5 4 3 2 1

Distributed by Penguin Random House Publisher Services
Tel: 800–733–3000

CHIEF CREATIVE OFFICER: Jack Bishop
EDITORIAL DIRECTOR, BOOKS: Elizabeth Carduff
EXECUTIVE EDITOR: Julia Collin Davison
EXECUTIVE EDITOR: Adam Kowit
EXECUTIVE FOOD EDITOR: Suzannah McFerran
SENIOR EDITORS: Stephanie Pixley and Anne Wolf
ASSOCIATE EDITORS: Leah Colins, Nicole Konstantinakos,
  and Sacha Madadian
TEST COOKS: Afton Cyrus, Joseph Gitter, and Katherine Perry
ASSISTANT TEST COOK: Esther Reynolds
EDITORIAL ASSISTANT: Alyssa Langer
ART DIRECTOR, BOOKS: Carole Goodman
ASSOCIATE ART DIRECTORS: Allison Boales and
  Jen Kanavos Hoffman
PRODUCTION DESIGNER: Reinaldo Cruz
GRAPHIC DESIGNER: Katie Barranger
PHOTOGRAPHY DIRECTOR: Julie Cote
SENIOR STAFF PHOTOGRAPHER: Daniel J. van Ackere
STAFF PHOTOGRAPHER: Steve Klise
ASSISTANT PHOTOGRAPHY PRODUCER: Mary Ball
FEATURE PHOTOGRAPHY: Keller + Keller and Carl Tremblay
FOOD STYLING: Catrine Kelty, Kendra McKnight, Marie Piraino,
  Maeve Sheridan, Elle Simone Scott, and Sally Staub
PHOTOSHOOT KITCHEN TEAM:
  SENIOR EDITOR: Chris O'Connor
  TEST COOKS: Daniel Cellucci and Matthew Fairman
  ASSISTANT TEST COOK: Mady Nichas
PRODUCTION DIRECTOR: Guy Rochford
SENIOR PRODUCTION MANAGER: Jessica Lindheimer Quirk
PRODUCTION MANAGER: Christine Walsh
IMAGING MANAGER: Lauren Robbins
PRODUCTION AND IMAGING SPECIALISTS: Heather Dube,
  Sean MacDonald, Dennis Noble, and Jessica Voas
COPY EDITOR: Cheryl Redmond
PROOFREADER: Ann-Marie Imbornoni
INDEXER: Elizabeth Parson

Pictured on front cover: Black Bean Burgers (page 114),
Crispy Onions (page 121), Quick Pickled Radishes
(page 121), Pub-Style Burger Sauce (page 120).
Pictured on back cover: Basmati Rice Bowl with Spiced
Cauliflower and Pomegranate (page 168), Hearty Vegetable
Lasagna (page 190), Sesame Soba Noodles with Snow Peas,
Radishes, and Cilantro (page 238), Cauliflower Steaks with
Salsa Verde (page 202), Dark Chocolate Cupcakes (page 282).

contents

Welcome to America's Test Kitchen

This book has been tested, written, and edited by the folks at America's Test Kitchen, a very real 2,500-square-foot kitchen located just outside of Boston. It is the home of *Cook's Illustrated* magazine and *Cook's Country* magazine and is the Monday-through-Friday destination for more than 60 test cooks, editors, and cookware specialists. Our mission is to test recipes over and over again until we understand how and why they work and until we arrive at the "best" version.

We start the process of testing a recipe with a complete lack of preconceptions, which means that we accept no claim, no technique, and no recipe at face value. We simply assemble as many variations as possible, test a half-dozen of the most promising, and taste the results blind. We then construct our own recipe and continue to test it, varying ingredients, techniques, and cooking times until we reach a consensus. As we like to say in the test kitchen, "We make the mistakes so you don't have to." The result, we hope, is the best version of a particular recipe, but we realize that only you can be the final judge of our success (or failure). We use the same rigorous approach when we test equipment and taste ingredients.

All of this would not be possible without a belief that good cooking, much like good music, is based on a foundation of objective technique. Some people like spicy foods and others don't, but there is a right way to sauté, there is a best way to cook a pot roast, and there are measurable scientific principles involved in producing perfectly beaten, stable egg whites. Our ultimate goal is to investigate the fundamental principles of cooking to give you the techniques, tools, and ingredients you need to become a better cook. It is as simple as that.

To see what goes on behind the scenes at America's Test Kitchen, check out our social media channels for kitchen snapshots, exclusive content, video tips, and much more. You can watch us work (in our actual test kitchen) by tuning in to *America's Test Kitchen* or *Cook's Country from America's Test Kitchen* on public television or on our websites. Listen to test kitchen experts on public radio (SplendidTable.org) to hear insights that illuminate the truth about real home cooking. Want to hone your cooking skills or finally learn how to bake—with an America's Test Kitchen test cook? Enroll in one of our online cooking classes. If the big questions about the hows and whys of food science are your passion, join our *Cook's Science* experts for a deep dive. However you choose to visit us, we welcome you into our kitchen, where you can stand by our side as we test our way to the best recipes in America.

facebook.com/AmericasTestKitchen

twitter.com/TestKitchen

youtube.com/AmericasTestKitchen

instagram.com/TestKitchen

pinterest.com/TestKitchen

google.com/+AmericasTestKitchen

AmericasTestKitchen.com

CooksIllustrated.com

CooksCountry.com

CooksScience.com

OnlineCookingSchool.com

Introduction

"Eating vegan" is no longer the polarizing concept it once was, and it's not just full-time vegans who are interested in plant-based meals. Veganism appeals to some from a health perspective—there's ever-growing evidence of the benefits of eating fewer animal products. For others, environmental or political beliefs drive their choice.

But there are many reasons why you may choose to prepare a vegan recipe, even just occasionally. Maybe you're baking a birthday cake for a loved one. Maybe you want to add more whole grains and vegetables to your diet, so you try eating vegan once a week, or for a month. Or maybe you're simply intrigued by the ingredients and flavors in vegan cuisine. We were, and that's why we've published our first vegan cookbook, one that suits the needs of everyone—whether you're a strict vegan or not. In doing so, we developed recipes (with no animal products—period) that wowed us in terms of flavor and texture, showing that veganism isn't about making sacrifices or substitutions but about celebrating a new way to eat.

Cooking vegan challenged us to rethink the way we look at mealtime, reinventing rather than replicating dishes. Animal products tend to have an obscuring presence; it's easy to define a dish by the meat component or the cheesy filling rather than as the sum of all its parts. When we stripped away those ingredients, we were sometimes disappointed (we sampled many bland tofu dishes). But more often, when we experimented with new techniques, we learned that a hearty vegetable, seared until charred and daubed with a bright sauce, can be your steak—but fresher. A nut-and-vegetable-based pasta sauce can have all the richness and savor of a cheese-based cream sauce—but less leaden. And so we were able to create some of our most interesting and unique recipes to date—like Baja-Style Cauliflower Tacos, which feature crispy coconut-coated cauliflower paired with spicy mango slaw and cilantro cream.

Two misconceptions about vegan cooking—that it's expensive and requires a slew of specialty ingredients—were happily dispelled during the development process. As we show in the pages that follow, all you really need beyond the norm is supersavory nutritional yeast, umami-rich miso paste, and some dairy-free milk. When it came to processed items like vegan cheese, we ended up buying minimally; in fact, we didn't use a single store-bought cheese (learn why on page 26). And we created a lineup of DIY recipes that are valuable additions to your cooking—from a nut-and-spice blend called *dukka* that you'll want to sprinkle on everything to a creamy, dreamy vegan mayo that tastes like the real thing.

Developing baked goods without using dairy and eggs is an undeniable challenge. After all, these are the building blocks of most traditional desserts. And many of the vegan baked goods we sampled were dry, pale, and crumbly. But after rigorous testing (we made more than 100 batches of our Blueberry Muffins), we were amazed at the treats we were able to create: tender cakes, browned pastries, and even ultracreamy ice cream. These are desserts you'd be proud to serve to vegans and nonvegans alike. How did we do it? Instead of just swapping in substitutes for any animal products, we altered our techniques and combined ingredients in surprising (but simple) ways that allowed us to deliver beloved muffins, cakes, cookies, brownies, and pies. They might not be made exactly like your traditional favorites, but they'll satisfy your cravings just the same.

At the end of our testing and development process, we'd created recipes that will remain a part of our day-to-day cooking. These are recipes we've come to crave and that we feel good about eating. Writing this cookbook made us better appreciate the potential of ingredients that had been there all along.

the vegan kitchen

Test Kitchen Secrets to Optimizing a Vegan Diet

Here's a summary of some of the most interesting tips, tricks, and tidbits the test kitchen discovered through rigorous testing along the way. You'll learn more about these topics as the introduction progresses.

Wake Up. . . with Tofu

We re-created egg dishes using tofu, as its texture can be similar to that of eggs cooked any style. Scrambled tofu breaks into curds. Squares of simmered tofu take on the silky interior of a poached egg in Tofu Ranchero (page 44). It even blends into a homogeneous mixture to create a firm but creamy frittata. We discuss the power protein on page 14.

Cauliflower: An Unlikely Hero

What we once thought of as a pleasant but unassuming vegetable is truly a powerhouse ingredient in the test kitchen. Cauliflower has a nutty flavor that makes it great in soups and even cut into steaks for a meal's centerpiece. It was also our secret weapon in creating creamy sauces—without cream. We blended cooked cauliflower with nuts to create a silky-smooth sauce that has body but that isn't too thick or nutty for indulgent pasta dishes. See how we make cauliflower a star on page 6.

Get Flavor with a Shake

Wouldn't it be nice to have magic dust that you could just sprinkle on foods to give them savor? Enter nutritional yeast (street name: nooch). Available at some movie theaters, this yeast is more than just for popcorn. We used the stuff to provide soup, pasta, dressing, and more with depth. What is nutritional yeast exactly? Turn to page 20 for the 411.

Miso Makes Things Marvelous

Miso is packed with glutamates so it gives foods umami depth. You'd be hard-pressed to tell that our vegan risotto doesn't include butter or Parmesan—a base of miso mimics the flavor and creaminess of both. Miso went from a favorite ingredient to one we just can't live without. Learn more on page 20.

Achieving Cheesy Flavor without Cheese

Dairy-free cheeses exist, but they're nothing like the real thing. That doesn't mean you have to go without the robust flavor cheese provides dishes. We even made our own Vegan Parmesan Substitute from nuts (you'll want to serve the stuff with everything) and a creamy cashew ricotta. Find the recipes on page 27.

Marinate—without the Meat

Marinating isn't just for cuts of meat. We've found that when left to bathe in an acidic elixir, tempeh softens, loses its bitter edge, and becomes intense in flavor. It's a go-to protein when you want a lively meal with bold flavors. We talk tempeh on page 15.

Aquafaba Is a Fab Egg Replacement

Aquawhatta? Aquafaba is the liquid that comes in a can of chickpeas—and you don't want to throw it away. This starchy liquid binds and whips just like eggs and is one of our secrets for superlative baked goods you'd never know are vegan. We did a lot of research on this humble ingredient. Find it starting on page 34.

Cream of Tartar Helps You Whip It Good

Cream of tartar is the stuff you forget at the back of the cabinet. But this acidic powder lowers baked goods' pH and contributes structure, and it helps whipped aquafaba hold peaks just like whipped egg whites. See it in action on page 35.

Browning without Butter

Vegan treats are notoriously pale because they lack the milk proteins of buttery baked goods. We often found ourselves choosing oat milk for the liquid in our baking. It's naturally higher in sugar than other alternatives so recipes made with it baked up golden and appetizing.

VEGANIZING THE KITCHEN

The biggest challenge when diving into vegan cooking isn't determining what's in and what's out—we've made that easy in this introduction. Instead, it's replacing your nonvegan meals with nutritious alternatives. That's why we've broken down the vegan diet into ingredient categories, with an emphasis on vegetables, grains, legumes, and protein sources. We think you'll find that many naturally vegan foods are those you already love to eat, like fresh, vibrantly colored produce and chewy, sweet, nutty-tasting whole grains. We're here to teach you how to prepare, combine, and, most importantly, reimagine these foods, maximizing their flavor. That said, animal products can sneak into foods you assumed were naturally vegan, and we've listed those in this chart. Your best line of defense when buying any product is to read the ingredient list.

Foods That Might Not Be Vegan

1 Sugar

Most white sugar is filtered through animal bone char to bleach it. Some companies turn to granular carbon to do this job, but it's impossible to be sure, so conventional sugar is out for strict vegans. The same goes for brown sugar since it's made by adding molasses to white sugar. (If you're not a strict vegan, feel free to use conventional sugars in our recipes.)

Where sugar hides Ketchup (the test kitchen's favorite ketchup, Heinz Organic Tomato Ketchup, is vegan), sandwich bread, bread crumbs, shredded coconut, chocolate (for information on chocolate, see page 31), and jams, jellies, and preserves.

Choose instead Organic granulated, brown, and confectioners' sugar are never processed with bone char. (For more information on organic sugar, see page 31). If you're strict, look for organic products and condiments.

2 Pasta and Noodles

We've found pastas of all varieties, from spaghetti to lasagna noodles, with eggs in the ingredient lists.

Choose instead Most of our favorite pastas are vegan, including spaghetti (De Cecco Spaghetti No. 12), elbow noodles (Barilla Elbows), whole-wheat spaghetti (Bionaturae Organic 100% Whole Wheat Spaghetti), and fettuccine (Garofalo Fettucce). For no-boil lasagna noodles, we used Prince Oven Ready Lasagna.

3 Wine

Wine fining agents include casein, albumin, gelatin, and isinglass (fish bladder), and traces of these items can end up in the wine. But many producers are now using bentonite clay or activated charcoal, which are vegan. Check labels for a vegan demarcation or ask a store clerk.

Other Nonvegan Ingredients to Look Out For

Albumin, casein, gelatin, lactose, and whey Do you ever see these ingredients and wonder what they are? They're all animal products. Albumin is an animal protein (most notably found in eggs) that is used as a binder. Casein is a protein found in milk that gives some nondairy cheeses meltability. Gelatin is used as a thickener, especially in desserts, and is made from animal bones and skin. (Agar-agar is a vegan alternative.) Lactose is a milk sugar found in many confections. And whey, a byproduct of cheese making, is found in snack foods and even breads. Be careful too with anything that contains colorings: Many red dyes are made from crushed insects.

Rediscovering Vegetables

"Eat your veggies." No matter what your diet is, Mom's words were wise. Eating a wide variety of vegetables means you're getting a wide variety of nutrients. But health isn't the only reason to embrace vegetables when you're eating vegan. When you strip away animal products, you can better appreciate vegetables' earthy, nuanced flavors—you'll actually enjoy them, even crave them. We've reimagined the way we think about vegetables; instead of categorizing them by variety or season, we've considered what they contribute to your meal, so that it's special and, most importantly, satisfying.

MEATY MEAL-MAKERS

Relegated to side dishes and salads, vegetables often deserve center-of-the-plate status. Different preparation methods can expand vegetables' potential, making them main dish–friendly. The following vegetables, with their hearty textures and deep flavors, are particularly well suited for taking the place of meat on your plate. These are our veggie stars.

Mighty Mushrooms

Mushrooms are a familiar vegetable-as-meat ingredient because of the ubiquity of portobello cap burgers. But we've found that it's not just size, shape, and texture that make mushrooms a stellar meat substitute; their umami-packed flavor and versatility also make them mighty. For example, to elevate our charred Grilled Portobello Burgers (page 118) from the "vegan option" to the best option, we marinate the raw caps in a mixture of oil, vinegar, and garlic. Scoring the caps before adding them to the marinade exposes more surface area and lets the mushrooms absorb more flavor, faster.

But mushrooms aren't just burger kings. Pulsing them in the food processor and then browning them gives them a texture and flavor similar to that of ground meat. They pull the most weight in our Spaghetti and Meatless Meatballs (page 192): Combined with protein crumbles, bread crumbs, aquafaba (for more information on aquafaba, see page 34), and eggplant, ground-and-browned 'shrooms form meatballs with the classic deep flavor and chew.

Cauliflower Is Everything

Cauliflower is a surprising workhorse, shining in dishes associated with cuts of meat; for example, crispy coated florets stand in for chunks of chicken in Buffalo Cauliflower Bites (page 262). But the most dramatic reimagining, visually and conceptually, is as steak. Our Cauliflower Steaks with Salsa Verde (page 202) feature a plate-size cross-section of deeply browned cauliflower. A superhot oven yields tender, meaty, and caramelized cauliflower—perfect for brushing with fragrant salsa verde as you would a thick-cut beef steak.

Preparing Portobello Caps for Grilling

Cut 1/16-inch-deep slits on the top side of the mushroom caps, spaced 1/2 inch apart, in a crosshatch pattern.

Cutting Cauliflower Steaks

1 Halve the cauliflower lengthwise through the core.

2 Cut one 1½-inch-thick slab from each cauliflower half.

Squash as Steak

Cauliflower isn't the only vegetable that makes great steaks. Necks of butternut squash have lots of surface area for browning, and the sweet vegetable stands up nicely to a bold rub and a creamy sauce, as in our Chile-Rubbed Butternut Squash Steaks with Ranch Dressing (page 205). We roast and then sear the squash for a substantial yet tender texture—and even give the steaks a crosshatched crust.

Beet Burgers Can't Be Beat

While portobello burgers are familiar, you don't as often see a beet burger. When shredded and combined with beans and grains in our Pinto Bean–Beet Burgers (page 117), the beet becomes tender during cooking and melds seamlessly into the burger, adding an unbeatable earthy flavor and slight sweetness that make for a fun alternative to the norm.

Preparing Butternut Squash Steaks

1 Cut each neck in half lengthwise.

2 Cut one ¾-inch-thick slab lengthwise from each squash half.

3 Cut ¹⁄₁₆-inch-deep slits on both sides of the steaks, spaced ½ inch apart, in a crosshatch pattern.

GETTING YOUR GREENS

When you're eating vegan, you want to optimize your vegetables. That's why for salads and bowls, we typically favor filling, fiber-full, and nutrient-dense dark greens over light, frilly lettuce varieties. Kale is the star of a vegan Kale Caesar Salad (page 142) that is so satisfying it can be a meal. Spinach fills grain salads and bowls like our Farro Bowl with Tofu, Mushrooms, and Spinach (page 172). Swiss chard is a hearty filling for Pinto Bean and Swiss Chard Enchiladas (page 201).

ADDING INTRIGUE

Vegan cooking is all about balance—of flavors, textures, and heartiness. Certain vegetables can add a strong backbone of flavor to long-cooked dishes or act as the perfect finishing touch, contributing that missing crunch, freshness, or pizzazz to a meal.

Can-Do Carrots

Carrots' best qualities, their crunch and sweetness, make them the right addition to dishes that need that special something. Grated, they pair with chickpeas in our Mediterranean-inspired Chickpea Salad with Carrots, Arugula, and Olives (page 163), providing a sweet counterpart to a lemony dressing and briny kalamata olives. Lightly pickled, they add to the rainbow of fresh veggie toppings on our Spicy Peanut Rice Noodle Bowl (page 175). Not used often enough in stir-fries, tender-crisp carrots caramelize and liven up our Stir-Fried Tempeh, Napa Cabbage, and Carrots (page 220).

Slice-'em-Up Radishes

Radishes have a unique flavor that's spicy and sweet, and a crisp texture that gives dishes refreshing bite in a hurry. Try them sliced thin on top of warm grain bowls. A generous amount gives Sesame Soba Noodles with Snow Peas, Radishes, and Cilantro (page 238) a cooling crunch.

Stellar Sandwich Topper

Alfalfa sprouts need no treatment to provide fresh crunch. They're a fitting topping for burgers and sandwiches like our Chickpea Salad Sandwiches (page 122). Paired with rich avocado, they give dishes West Coast flair.

Always-Welcome Herbs

Chopped herbs or whole leaves are a quick way to boost freshness. The unique aroma and pleasant grassiness of basil and cilantro brighten the flavor of robust dishes like Hearty Vegetable Lasagna (page 190) and highlight that of lighter ones like Sizzling Saigon Crêpes (page 130).

Quick-Pickled Vegetables

When given a vinegar brine soak, these veggies are a go-to accompaniment throughout this book—and there's no canning necessary. Our Quick Pickled Radishes (page 121) require only 15 minutes of pickling, and they're one of our favorite burger toppings, adding spicy brightness to rich, earthy veggie or bean burgers. Quick Sweet-and-Spicy Pickled Red Onions (page 121) can be stored for sandwiches for a week. A medley of quick pickles is an essential component of both our Tofu Banh Mi (page 125), where the vegetables balance the rich crispy tofu and creamy sauce, and our Korean Rice Bowl with Tempeh (page 180), where they mingle with other toppings to create a multiflavored and multitextured dish.

Great Grains

Packed with nutrients, vitamins, minerals, fiber, and protein (not to mention low in fat and affordable), grains are an essential food group in the vegan diet. Grains can be the foundation of a main dish, salad, or bowl. Or they can be added to soups for heft or to burgers for substance. The following are the grains we build meals around in this book.

Oats

Wheat Berries

Freekeh

Cornmeal

BARLEY

While barley might be most familiar as a key ingredient in beer, it's a nutritious high-fiber, high-protein cereal grain with a nutty flavor similar to that of brown rice. It's great in soups and salads and can be used to make risotto. Hulled barley, which is sold with the hull removed and the fiber-rich bran intact, is considered a whole grain. Pearl (or pearled) barley is hulled barley that's been polished to remove the bran. There is also quick-cooking barley, which is available as kernels or flakes. Hulled barley takes a long time to cook and should be soaked prior to cooking. We use pearl barley in our recipes; it cooks much more quickly, making it a more versatile choice.

BULGUR

Bulgur is made from parboiled or steamed wheat kernels/berries that are then dried, partially stripped of their outer bran layer, and coarsely ground. The result is a relatively fast-cooking, highly nutritious grain. Medium-grind bulgur is perfect for tabbouleh and salads because it requires little more than a soak (we like to use a flavorful liquid like lemon juice) to become tender. Coarse-grind bulgur, which requires simmering, is our top choice for making pilaf. (Cracked wheat, often sold alongside bulgur, is not precooked and cannot be substituted for bulgur.) Be sure to rinse bulgur to remove excess starches that can turn the grain gluey.

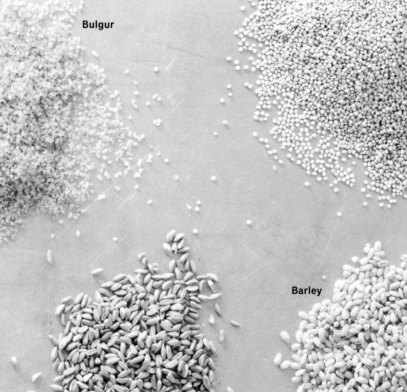

Bulgur

Quinoa

Barley

Rice

Farro

CORNMEAL

Different recipes require different grinds and types of cornmeal, so make sure to read carefully. Conventional cornmeal, with its fine grains, does the trick when used as a breading for tofu or vegetables. But for dishes like Creamy Breakfast Grits with Chives (page 52), you need a more specialized product: old-fashioned grits. The nomenclature is a bit confusing: Grits, too, are ground-up corn, but they tend to have a thicker grind.

FARRO

These hulled whole-wheat kernels boast a sweet, nutty flavor and a chewy bite. In Italy, the grain is available in three sizes—farro

piccolo, farro *medio*, and farro *grande*; the midsize type is most common in the U.S. Farro, when boiled, becomes tender but has al dente chew. Cooking times vary by brand.

FREEKEH

Sometimes spelled *frikeh* or *farik*, freekeh is a nutrient-packed grain that's used in eastern Mediterranean and North African pilafs, salads, and more. It has a nutty, slightly smoky flavor. Freekeh is made from durum wheat, which is harvested while immature and then fire-roasted and rubbed to remove the chaff, or husk (*freekeh* means "to rub" in Arabic). It can then be left whole or cracked into smaller pieces. *(continued)*

the vegan kitchen

11

OATS

From breakfast table to cookie jar, this cereal grass is a staple. Old-fashioned oats are made by hulling, cleaning, steaming, and rolling whole oats. We love them for their toasty flavor and hearty chew in cookies and in toppings for crisps. Steel-cut oats are partially cooked and then cut into pieces with steel blades. These chewy, buttery oats are our choice for oatmeal, but because they take much longer to cook and do not soften, they cannot be used in baked goods. We don't use quick or instant oats.

QUINOA

Quinoa originated in the Andes Mountains. While it's treated like a grain, it's actually the seed of the goosefoot plant. Sometimes referred to as a "super grain," quinoa is high in protein, and its protein is complete; it possesses all of the amino acids our bodies require. We love quinoa for its almost crunchy texture, nutty taste, and ease of preparation. Cooked as a pilaf, it can be ready in about 20 minutes. Unless labeled "prewashed," quinoa should be rinsed before cooking to remove its bitter protective layer (called saponin). White quinoa is the most common but red and black are increasingly available. (They cannot be used interchangeably.)

RICE

A grain of rice is made up of endosperm, germ, bran, and husk. Brown rice is simply husked; white rice also has the germ and bran removed. This makes the rice cook faster and softer, but it also removes nutrients as well as flavor. In addition to fluffy long-grain white rice, clumpier medium-grain rice, and sticky-soft short-grain brown and white rices, there's basmati rice, which has a sweet aroma; nutritious red rice, which has a red coat; and black rice, which has an antioxidant-rich black hull.

WHEAT BERRIES

Wheat berries are whole, unprocessed kernels of wheat. Since none of the grain has been removed, chewy wheat berries are an excellent source of nutrition. Compared with more refined forms of wheat, wheat berries require a relatively long cooking time.

Grain Cooking Chart

TYPE OF GRAIN	COOKING METHOD	AMOUNT OF GRAIN	AMOUNT OF WATER	AMOUNT OF SALT	COOKING TIME
Pearl Barley	Pilaf-Style	1 cup	1⅔ cups	¼ teaspoon	20 to 40 minutes
	Boiled	1 cup	4 quarts	1 tablespoon	20 to 40 minutes
Bulgur (medium- to coarse-grind)	Pilaf-Style*	1 cup	1½ cups	¼ teaspoon	16 to 18 minutes
	Boiled	1 cup	4 quarts	1½ teaspoons	5 minutes
	Microwave	1 cup	1 cup	¼ teaspoon	5 to 10 minutes
Farro	Boiled	1 cup	4 quarts	1 tablespoon	15 to 30 minutes
Freekeh	Boiled	1 cup	4 quarts	1 tablespoon	30 to 45 minutes
Long-Grain Brown Rice	Pilaf-Style	1 cup	1¾ cups	¼ teaspoon	40 to 50 minutes
	Boiled	1 cup	4 quarts	1 tablespoon	25 to 30 minutes
	Microwave	1 cup	2 cups	¼ teaspoon	25 to 30 minutes
Quinoa	Pilaf-Style	1 cup	1 cup plus 3 tablespoons	¼ teaspoon	18 to 20 minutes
	Microwave	1 cup	2 cups	¼ teaspoon	5 minutes on medium, then 5 minutes on high
Wheat Berries	Boiled	1 cup	4 quarts	1½ teaspoons	1 hour to 1 hour 10 minutes

* For pilaf, do not rinse, and skip the toasting step, adding the grain to the pot with the liquid.

Legume Love

Legumes are the category of plant whose seeds grow in long pods, and they include beans, lentils, peanuts, peas, and soybeans. Inexpensive, healthful legumes are a major source of protein and are therefore a key part of vegan cooking.

DO THE CANCAN

There are some long-cooked recipes, like our Ultimate Vegan Chili (page 105), where using dried beans makes sense. But most of the time, we prefer the ease of already-cooked canned beans. We've found them to be more consistently creamy and flavorful, too.

LOVELY LENTILS

Lentils (always dried) come in different sizes and colors, and the variation in texture is considerable—making for variation in a vegan diet.

Brown and Green Lentils

These larger, all-purpose lentils are what you'll find in every supermarket. They are a uniform drab brown or green. They have a mild yet light and earthy flavor and a creamy texture. They hold their shape well when cooked.

Lentilles du Puy

These olive-green French lentils are smaller than the common brown and green varieties. We love them for their rich, peppery, complex flavor and firm yet tender texture. They're perfect where the lentils take center stage.

Red and Yellow Lentils

These small, split orange-red or golden-yellow lentils completely disintegrate when cooked, breaking down into a thick puree for velvety soups and curries.

Black Lentils

Like lentilles du Puy, black lentils are on the small side. They have a deep black hue similar to that of caviar, so some markets refer to them as beluga lentils. They have a robust, earthy flavor and hold their shape well.

EAT YOUR EDAMAME

Edamame are immature soybeans that are cooked and served, sometimes while still in the pod. They're sold fresh or frozen. We love the bright green color; sweet, nutty flavor; and firm, dense texture they provide salads, bowls, and rice dishes.

Lentilles du Puy | Black | Red | Brown

Eight Ways to Use a Chickpea

1 Smash
it for falafel
(page 126)

2 Mash
it for a deli-style
sandwich filling
(page 122)

3 Toss
it into salads
(page 163)

4 Stir
it into soups for
a hearty protein
(page 78)

5 Fry
it for a crispy
snack (page 246)

6 Puree
it for dips
(page 250)

7 Drain
it to use its
packing liquid as
an egg substitute
(page 34)

8 Bind
dishes with savory
chickpea flour
(page 40)

Protein Power

We've all heard it before: Tofu is bland and boring. And the same misconception applies to tempeh. But these soy-based proteins just need to be treated right: Season them well and apply flavor-building cooking techniques, and they're a delicious protein that can display a range of meaty textures. And nuts and seeds aren't just snacks; they're a key source of protein in everyday cooking. We've broken it all down.

THE WORLD OF TOFU

Tofu's clean, nutty, subtly sweet flavor is an ideal canvas for bold or aromatic sauces. It also takes to a wide variety of preparations, from stir-frying and sautéing to roasting and scrambling. Tofu is a great choice for vegans because in addition to being high in protein, it's also iron- and calcium-rich.

What is tofu, exactly? Tofu is the result of a process similar to making cheese: Curds, made from coagulating soy milk, are set in a mold and pressed to extract as much, or as little, of the liquid whey as desired. Depending on how long the tofu is pressed and how much coagulant is used, the amount of whey released will vary, creating a range of textures from soft to firm.

Buying Tofu

Tofu is available in extra-firm, firm, medium-firm, soft, and silken textures. In general, firmer varieties hold their shape during cooking, while softer varieties do not. Silken tofu has a soft, creamy texture, so you'll often see it used as the base of vegan smoothies or desserts or as an egg replacement; we don't like the rubbery texture it provides and the distinct flavor it lends these goods, so we don't call for it. These are the varieties we use.

Firm and Extra-Firm Tofu

We prefer firm or extra-firm tofu for stir-fries and noodle dishes, as they hold their shape in high-heat cooking applications and when tossed with noodles. Extra-firm is a bit more resilient than firm, though the two are often interchangeable. They're also both great marinated or tossed into salads or onto bowls.

Tasting Firm Tofu

Since we use firm tofu most often in our recipes, our tasting and testing team set out to find the best available product for the home cook. We tasted five tofus plain, coated in cornstarch and fried, and chopped and stir-fried in a filling for Thai-Style Tofu and Basil Lettuce Cups (page 213). Happily, tasters liked the flavor of every tofu in our lineup (just one had an unappealingly dense, eraser-like texture), so your supermarket options are many. However,

Nasoya Firm Tofu ($2.99 for 14 ounces) was our favorite. Its light, clean flavor earned praise in every tasting, and it struck just the right balance between firmness and tenderness.

Soft Tofu

Soft tofu boasts a creamy texture; we love to pan-fry this tofu, often coated with cornstarch, to achieve a crisp outside, which makes a nice textural contrast to the silky interior. Soft tofu is also great scrambled like eggs.

Storing Tofu

Tofu is highly perishable and has the best flavor and texture when it's fresh, so look for a package with the latest expiration date possible. To store an opened package, submerge the tofu in water in a covered container and refrigerate it, changing the water daily. Any hint of sourness means the tofu is past its prime.

Cutting and Drying Tofu

Draining and pressing tofu before cooking helps remove excess moisture and prevent watery dishes. Cutting the tofu before draining it exposes more surface area for draining.

To Cut Tofu into Slabs

Slice the block of tofu crosswise into ¾-inch slabs.

To Cut Tofu into Fingers

Cut the tofu crosswise into slabs and then slice each slab into fingers of the desired size.

To Cut Tofu into Cubes

Cut the tofu into fingers and then cut each finger into cubes of the desired size.

To Dry Tofu

Spread the tofu pieces evenly over a rimmed baking sheet lined with paper towels, and let it sit for 20 minutes to drain. Gently press the tofu dry with paper towels.

TEMPEH, THE FERMENTED ONE

Tempeh isn't quite as mainstream as tofu, but we love it just as much. It's made by fermenting cooked soybeans and then forming the mixture into a firm, dense cake. Most versions also contain beans, grains, and flavorings. (There are also soy-free tempehs made entirely from grains or other beans.) And because it's better than tofu at holding its shape when cooked, it's a good meat substitute and a versatile choice for many dishes from sandwiches to stir-fries. It has a strong nutty taste, but it also absorbs flavors easily. Tempeh is a healthful choice; it's high in protein, cholesterol-free, and low in fat, and it contains many essential vitamins and minerals.

Buying Tempeh

Tempeh is sold in most supermarkets and can be found with different grain and flavoring combinations. Any unflavored tempeh will work in our recipes.

Cutting Tempeh

If you cut tempeh into slabs, you can make delicious steaks. We also top breakfast dishes with seared cubes of tempeh, cook them in stir-fries, and grill skewers of them.

To Cut Tempeh into Slabs

Cut each piece crosswise into two 3½-inch-long pieces, then cut each piece horizontally into ⅜-inch-thick slabs.

A NOTE ON SEITAN . . .

Seitan, made from wheat gluten, is another common vegan protein source. While we love it in our Crispy Orange Seitan (page 209) because it has a chewy texture that mimics chicken when coated, fried, and draped in sauce, it's that same quality that typically make us turn away from it. For our Crispy Orange Seitan, we buy cubed seitan, which typically comes in large pieces. We cut the uneven cubes into uniform pieces ourselves so that they cook evenly and yield a better-textured dish.

 After draining and patting them dry, cut the seitan cubes into uniform 1-inch pieces to ensure even cooking.

SUSTAINING NUTS AND SEEDS

Sure, nuts make a great snack, but their use isn't limited to between meals. We use them to lend richness, substance, and crunch to recipes. With their abundant healthful fats, proteins, and other nutrients, nuts are an essential part of a vegan diet. But nuts in whole form are just half the story: Soaked or cooked and blended, they can transform into a rich dairy-free cream sauce and even can be made into vegan cheese (for more information on these, see pages 26 and 27). Ground, they give dishes like our Ultimate Vegan Chili (page 105) great flavor and body throughout. Seeds like sesame seeds and sunflower seeds in addition to chia, flax, and hemp, though more diminutive, are packed with flavor and protein and appear in recipes throughout the book.

Storing Nuts and Seeds

Nuts and seeds are high in oil and will become rancid rather quickly. In the test kitchen, we store all nuts and seeds in the freezer in zipper-lock freezer bags. Frozen nuts and seeds will keep for months, and there's no need to defrost them before toasting or chopping.

Nut Butters

Move over, peanut butter; people are increasingly adding other nut and seed butters to their pantries, from almond butter to sesame tahini. Not only do they add protein when spread on fruit, vegetables, or bread as a snack; they can also be used to make sauces or add a missing toasty, buttery flavor to baked goods like our Chocolate Chip Cookies (page 272). Making nut butters couldn't be easier, so we've provided recipes so you can whip them up at home.

SEEDS YOU MAY NOT KNOW
Flaxseeds

Flaxseeds aren't superfluous hippie food. They're a bit larger than sesame seeds and have a sweet, wheaty flavor. They're protein- and fiber-rich as well as one of the best sources for the omega-3 fatty acid called alpha-linolenic acid (ALA), which is found in only certain plant foods and oils and is essential for good health. They are sold both whole and ground, golden and brown. We prefer the milder flavor of golden flaxseeds, but you can use the two interchangeably. (For more information on using flaxseeds as an egg substitute, see page 34.) You should store flaxseeds in the freezer.

Chia Seeds

Chia seeds, from the flowering chia plant, look unassuming, like gray poppy seeds. But when they meet liquid, they swell into tapioca-like beads. Why do you want to eat them? They're full of protein, omega-3 fatty acids, and fiber, along with other nutrients. We particularly like our Chia Pudding with Fresh Fruit and Coconut (page 73) as a fun, filling, make-ahead breakfast option.

Hulled Hemp Hearts

They're a relative newcomer on the protein scene, but we love these hulled seeds of the hemp plant, which are soft and blend without a trace into smoothies. Like quinoa, they're a plant-based complete protein. They're also packed with healthful fats.

Hulled Hemp Hearts   Chia Seeds   Ground Golden Flaxseeds

ALMOND BUTTER
Makes 2 cups

4 cups (1¼ pounds) whole almonds
  Salt

1 Adjust oven rack to middle position and heat oven to 375 degrees. Spread almonds in single layer on rimmed baking sheet and toast until fragrant and darkened slightly, 5 to 10 minutes, rotating sheet halfway through cooking. Transfer almonds to food processor, add ½ teaspoon salt, and let cool completely, about 20 minutes.

2 Process almonds to smooth paste, 5 to 7 minutes, scraping down sides of bowl as needed. Season almond butter with salt to taste.

PEANUT BUTTER
Makes 2 cups

4 cups (1¼ pounds) dry-roasted,
  unsalted peanuts
  Salt

1 Adjust oven rack to middle position and heat oven to 375 degrees. Spread peanuts in single layer on rimmed baking sheet and toast until fragrant and darkened slightly, 5 to 10 minutes, rotating sheet halfway through cooking. Transfer peanuts to food processor, add ½ teaspoon salt, and let cool completely, about 20 minutes.

2a **FOR CREAMY PEANUT BUTTER** Process peanuts to smooth paste, 5 to 7 minutes, scraping down sides of bowl as needed.

2b **FOR CHUNKY PEANUT BUTTER** Pulse peanuts until coarsely chopped, 3 to 5 pulses. Reserve 1 cup chopped peanuts and continue processing remaining peanuts to smooth paste, 5 to 7 minutes, scraping down sides of bowl as needed. Add chopped peanuts and pulse until combined, 3 to 5 pulses.

3 Season peanut butter with salt to taste.

Flavor Boosters

Part of the joy of vegan cooking is allowing the varied flavors of vegetables, grains, beans, and other ingredients to shine, unobscured by heavy animal proteins. That said, vegan cooking sometimes gets a bad rap for being boring: We're here to tell you it doesn't have to be that way. Having a properly stocked vegan pantry will provide your cooking with all the dimension it needs. Utilizing the following ingredients is what sets our vegan cooking apart, for dishes that are bold-tasting and complex—and never boring.

Spices

Spices give meals warmth and make it easy to create interesting international dishes with authentic flavor. Spice blends like curry powder provide complexity in one fell swoop. We often reach for chili powder to add a bold, multilayered heat to spicy dishes, or our homemade Shichimi Togarashi (page 23) to liven up Asian dishes. We love the nut-based Egyptian spice blend Dukka (page 23) that's also a condiment.

Chiles

Nothing spices up a dish like adding some heat. But chiles—canned, fresh, and dried—don't just make foods hot; they add nuanced layers of flavor. Jalapeños are fresh and grassy-tasting, canned chipotle chiles in adobo are smoky, and New Mexican chiles are earthy, for example. Roasting fresh chiles adds smoky char; toasting dried ones brings out their fragrant qualities.

Vinegars

Beyond vinaigrettes, we use vinegar to perk up sauces, stews, soups, and grain dishes. Different types lend distinct flavors to dishes, and we reach for several varieties—red wine, white wine, balsamic, sherry, and even plain old distilled white vinegar—to lend nuanced flavor to recipes.

Citrus Juice

We frequently add lemon or lime juice (depending on the flavor profile of the dish) toward the end of cooking or just before serving to balance dishes with bright acidity. When purchasing lemons or limes at the supermarket, choose large ones that give to gentle pressure; hard ones have thicker skin and yield less juice. To get the most juice out of a lemon or lime, roll it vigorously on the counter before slicing it. This will bruise, break up, and soften the rind's tissues while it tears the membrane of the juice vesicles (tear-shaped juice sacs), thereby filling the fruit with juice even before it's squeezed. For juicing, we prefer either a wooden reamer with a sharp tip that can pierce the flesh or a manual citrus juicer. Always juice lemons and limes at the last minute, as their flavor mellows quickly.

Capers and Olives

These two refrigerator staples bring the same thing to the party: piquant brininess. In Kale Caesar Salad (page 142), capers mimic the flavor that anchovies classically provide. Kalamata olives make our Whole-Wheat Spaghetti with Greens, Beans, and Tomatoes (page 194) taste bright and pleasantly salty without cheese or cured meats.

Soy Sauce

Soy sauce is an essential ingredient in vegan cooking; this salty liquid is made from fermented soybeans and wheat, barley, or rice, and it's rich in glutamates, taste bud stimulators that give food the meaty, savory flavor known as umami. Although it is traditionally an Asian ingredient, we use it in all types of dishes to add depth.
(continued)

Kalamata Olives

Tomato Paste

Dried Shiitake Mushrooms

Distilled White Vinegar

Curry Powder

Chipotle Chile in
Adobo Sauce

Capers

Dukka

Dried New
Mexico Chiles

Nutritional Yeast

White Miso

Jalapeño

Chili Powder

Dried Mushrooms

Dried mushrooms offer the same umami flavor as fresh mushrooms in a concentrated package, giving recipes a major dose of meatiness. When buying dried mushrooms, always inspect them closely. They should be either tan or brown, not black. Avoid dried mushrooms with small holes, or those with excess dust and grit. Nicely flavored dried mushrooms will have an earthy, not musty or stale, aroma.

We also sometimes call for adding dried mushroom powder, most often from porcini mushrooms, to recipes that need a savory flavor boost. We grind the dried mushrooms to a fine powder in a spice grinder.

Tomato Paste

Tomato paste is tomato puree that's been cooked to remove almost all its moisture. It's often used to boost the tomato flavor in soups, stews, and sauces or to add a vegetal sweetness. Because it's so concentrated, it's also naturally full of glutamates. We find that when we add it to dishes it brings out subtle depths and savory notes.

Thai Curry Paste

Store-bought curry paste provides a wallop of authentic Thai flavor—rich herbal notes, complexity, and heat—in one little jar. Green curry paste is made from fresh green Thai chiles, lemon grass, galangal (Thai ginger), garlic, and other spices. Red curry paste combines a number of hard-to-find authentic Thai aromatics—including galangal, red bird's eye chiles, lemon grass, and kaffir lime leaves.

Miso

Miso paste is made by fermenting soybeans and sometimes grains (such as rice, barley, or rye) with a mold called *koji*. Although countless variations of the salty, deep-flavored ingredient are available, we use sweeter white miso (*shiromiso*) and more pungent red miso (*akamiso*). Flavor profiles are altered by changing the type of grain in the mix, adjusting the ratio of grain to soybeans, tweaking the amounts of salt and mold, and extending or decreasing the fermentation time, which can range from a few weeks to a few years. In addition to adding sweet-savory, pleasantly funky flavor, miso can give broths body and even sometimes a glossy sheen. Miso will easily keep for up to a year in the refrigerator (and some sources say it keeps indefinitely).

Nutritional Yeast

Affectionately referred to as "nooch" by many, this savory flaky substance is a vegan cook's best friend. Simply yeast that's grown on a mixture of beet molasses and sugarcane and heated to deactivate its leavening properties, it's often used to mimic the flavor of cheese for good reason—it has a funky, nutty, almost salty (although there's no salt in it) depth that matches cheese in its complexity. Why? Nutritional yeast is high in glutamates. We add it to dishes that are traditionally cheesy, like Creamy Cashew Mac and Cheese (page 184), Nacho Dip (page 258), and our homemade Vegan Parmesan Substitute (page 27); but it also helps build depth in less expected places like in our Chickpea Noodle Soup (page 78), where it provides the soul-satisfying savoriness that you find in a long-simmered chicken stock.

BUY IT OR DIY IT

You can purchase the following flavor boosters at the supermarket, but we often like to make our own—packing a punch and free from stabilizers or preservatives—when we have the chance. Whether you buy it or DIY it, these ingredients deserve a prime spot in your pantry.

Bragg Liquid Aminos

Liquid aminos is a product that is made from 16 amino acids derived from soybeans. It makes a great vegan stand-in for fish sauce, giving our Asian recipes the same meaty, savory, fermented flavor of traditional fish sauce.

VEGAN FISH SAUCE SUBSTITUTE
Makes about 1¼ cups

Use this for any recipe in this book that calls for vegan fish sauce substitute or anywhere you would traditionally use fish sauce. It's a homemade alternative to liquid aminos.

3 cups water
3 tablespoons salt
2 tablespoons soy sauce
¼ ounce dried sliced shiitake mushrooms

Simmer all ingredients in large saucepan over medium heat until mixture is reduced by half, 20 to 30 minutes. Strain liquid through fine-mesh strainer and let cool completely. (Fish sauce substitute can be refrigerated for up to 2 months.)

Vegetable Broth

A good vegetable broth is one of the most essential ingredients in the vegan kitchen. It provides a flavorful backbone to a wide range of dishes, from soups and stews to risotto and pasta. But it's important to be a savvy shopper—we've found that many commercial vegetable broths are terrible, with overly sweet, tinny flavors. We love our recipe for Vegetable Broth Base (recipe follows) in which we grind a selection of fresh vegetables, salt, and savory ingredients to a paste that we can store in the freezer and reconstitute as needed. For a store-bought option, we like to use superconcentrated **Orrington Farms Vegan Chicken Flavored Broth Base & Seasoning** in our vegan recipes. Vegetable broths found in the carton can't stand up to its meaty flavor and make recipes taste wan in comparison; we cannot recommend them in vegan cooking.

VEGETABLE BROTH BASE
Makes about 1¾ cups base; enough for 7 quarts broth

For the best balance of flavors, measure the prepped vegetables by weight. Kosher salt aids in grinding the vegetables. The broth base contains enough salt to keep it from freezing solid, making it easy to remove 1 tablespoon at a time. To make 1 cup of broth, stir 1 tablespoon of fresh or frozen broth base into 1 cup of boiling water. If particle-free broth is desired, let the broth steep for 5 minutes and then strain it through a fine-mesh strainer.
(continued)

2 leeks, white and light green parts only,
   chopped and washed thoroughly
   (2½ cups or 5 ounces)
2 carrots, peeled and cut into ½-inch pieces
   (⅔ cup or 3 ounces)
½ small celery root, peeled and cut into
   ½-inch pieces (¾ cup or 3 ounces)
½ cup (½ ounce) fresh parsley leaves and
   thin stems
3 tablespoons dried minced onions
2 tablespoons kosher salt
1½ tablespoons tomato paste
3 tablespoons soy sauce

1 Process leeks, carrots, celery root, parsley, minced onions, and salt in food processor, scraping down sides of bowl frequently, until paste is as fine as possible, 3 to 4 minutes. Add tomato paste and process for 1 minute, scraping down sides of bowl every 20 seconds. Add soy sauce and continue to process 1 minute longer.

2 Transfer mixture to airtight container and tap firmly on counter to remove air bubbles. Press small piece of parchment paper flush against surface of mixture and cover. Freeze for up to 6 months.

Vegan Mayonnaise and Other Sauces

We like to keep flavorful sauces in our fridge to liven up just about anything, from a bowl of rice to a composed dish. Our recipes for multipurpose sauces from Cilantro Sauce (page 166) to Miso-Ginger Sauce (page 167) often use vegan mayonnaise as the base; it adds richness and body. Our favorite store-bought vegan mayonnaise is **Just Mayo**—it's a good substitute for the real thing and tastes significantly better than any of the other store-bought mayos we tasted, which ranged from rancid and off-tasting to too acidic in flavor and from slimy to foamy in texture. When we made our own delicious Vegan Mayonnaise (recipe follows), we couldn't believe how much it tasted like the real, egg yolk–based thing.

VEGAN MAYONNAISE
Makes about 1 cup

Aquafaba, the liquid found in a can of chickpeas (for more information on aquafaba, see page 34), gives our mayo volume and emulsified body. It's devoid of off-flavors or off-textures, which was not the case when we tried creating mayo with soy milk, tofu, cashews, or miso.

⅓ cup aquafaba (see page 34)
1½ teaspoons lemon juice
½ teaspoon salt
½ teaspoon organic sugar (see page 31)
½ teaspoon Dijon mustard
1¼ cups vegetable oil
3 tablespoons extra-virgin olive oil

1 Process aquafaba, lemon juice, salt, sugar, and mustard in food processor for 10 seconds. With processor running, gradually add vegetable oil in slow steady stream until mixture is thick and creamy, scraping down sides of bowl as needed, about 3 minutes.

2 Transfer mixture to bowl. Whisking constantly, slowly add olive oil until emulsified. If pools of oil form on surface, stop addition of oil and whisk mixture until well combined, then resume adding oil. Mayonnaise should be thick and glossy with no oil pools on surface. (Mayonnaise can be refrigerated for up to 1 week.)

Spices contribute warmth, heat, or floral notes when added at different stages of your cooking. But there are some spice blends—mixtures of spices, and sometimes nuts, seeds, or legumes—that when simply sprinkled over a finished dish, contribute a final, bright layer of flavor. Here are two we love to have on hand to give meals a quick boost.

Shichimi Togarashi (Sesame-Orange Spice Blend)
MAKES ¼ CUP

We like to serve this seasoning with our Shiitake Ramen (page 233), but this Japanese table condiment is great sprinkled on rice and noodle dishes of all kinds.

- ¾ teaspoon grated orange zest
- 2 teaspoons sesame seeds
- 1½ teaspoons paprika
- 1 teaspoon pepper
- ¼ teaspoon garlic powder
- ¼ teaspoon ground ginger
- ⅛ teaspoon cayenne pepper

Place orange zest in small bowl and microwave, stirring every 20 seconds, until zest is dry and no longer clumping together, 1 minute 30 seconds to 2 minutes 30 seconds. Stir in sesame seeds, paprika, pepper, garlic powder, ginger,

and cayenne. (Spice blend can be stored in airtight container at room temperature for up to 1 week.)

Dukka
MAKES 2 CUPS

Part spice mixture, part condiment, this Egyptian mixture includes herbs, spices, and nuts and can be sprinkled on roasted vegetables, dips, rice dishes, proteins, or eaten with bread and olive oil.

- 1 (15-ounce) can chickpeas, rinsed
- 1 teaspoon extra-virgin olive oil
- ½ cup shelled pistachios, toasted
- ⅓ cup black sesame seeds, toasted
- 2½ tablespoons coriander seeds, toasted
- 1 tablespoon cumin seeds, toasted
- 2 teaspoons fennel seeds, toasted
- 1½ teaspoons pepper
- 1¼ teaspoons salt

1 Adjust oven rack to middle position and heat oven to 400 degrees. Pat chickpeas dry with paper towels and toss with oil. Spread chickpeas into single layer in rimmed baking sheet and roast until browned and crisp, 40 to 45 minutes, stirring every 5 to 10 minutes; let cool completely.

2 Process chickpeas in food processor until coarsely ground, about 10 seconds; transfer to bowl. Pulse pistachios and sesame seeds in now-empty food processor until coarsely ground, about 15 pulses; transfer to bowl with chickpeas. Process coriander, cumin, and fennel seeds in again-empty food processor until finely ground, 2 to 3 minutes; transfer to bowl with chickpeas. Add pepper and salt and whisk until mixture is well combined. (Dukka can be refrigerated for up to 1 month.)

Milk without the Moo: Vegan Dairy Substitutes

There are a lot of dairy alternatives on the market that slide easily into vegan versions of your favorite dishes. You may already have a go-to dairy-free milk or yogurt, but we've found that specific products work better in certain dishes, so it's worth branching out. We love oat milk in many of our baked goods (for more information on baking with dairy-free milks, see page 32), but its sweet flavor is out of place in many savory dishes. Soy milk is a good neutral base, but it can give mild dishes a soy taste. Almond milk, which you can easily make at home (recipe follows), is also neutral and a favorite in savory cooking, but it can make sweet dishes taste a little salty. Coconut milk can straddle sweet and savory recipes, but it tends to be a bit bland. We don't use rice milk; we found it starchy and watery.

Dairy-Free Yogurt

As with dairy-free milks, dairy-free yogurts are not interchangeable; each has a distinct flavor and consistency. Depending on the recipe, we turn to either almond milk yogurt or coconut milk yogurt. We had good luck with Kite Hill Artisan Almond Milk Yogurt and So Delicious Unsweetened Dairy Free Coconut Milk Yogurt Alternative. Dairy-free yogurt, when paired with fruit or granola, is also a good quick breakfast or snack option. That's why we also like to make our own wholesome almond milk yogurt (recipe follows).

ALMOND MILK
Makes about 4 cups

Almond milk is a refreshing dairy-free alternative to milk. Since many store varieties include thickeners, stabilizers, and gums, we often like to make our own. This recipe can be easily doubled.

1¼ cups whole blanched almonds
⅛ teaspoon salt
2 teaspoons sugar (optional)

1 Place almonds in bowl and add cold water to cover by 1 inch. Soak almonds at room temperature for at least 8 hours or up to 24 hours. Drain and rinse well.

2 Line fine-mesh strainer with triple layer of cheesecloth that overhangs edges and set over large bowl. Process soaked almonds and 4 cups water in blender until almonds are finely ground, about 2 minutes. Transfer mixture to prepared strainer and press to extract as much liquid as possible. Gather sides of cheesecloth around almond pulp and gently squeeze remaining milk into bowl; discard spent pulp. Stir in salt and sugar, if using, until dissolved. (Almond milk can be refrigerated for up to 2 weeks.)

ALMOND MILK YOGURT

Makes about 3 cups

To promote the fermentation required in making yogurt, we elected to use probiotic capsules, since typical yogurt starters are often sourced from dairy products. You can find agar-agar and probiotic capsules at your local natural food store. The flavor of the yogurt may vary depending on the brand of probiotic used; we developed this recipe using Renew Life Ultimate Flora Critical Care 50 Billion probiotic capsules. Do not substitute agar-agar flakes for the agar-agar powder.

1¾ teaspoons agar-agar powder
¼ cup water
3 cups Almond Milk
1 50-billion probiotic capsule

1 Adjust oven rack to middle position. Sprinkle agar-agar over water in small bowl and let sit until softened, about 10 minutes.

2 Heat milk in large saucepan over medium-low heat until just simmering. Add softened agar-agar and cook, whisking constantly, until fully dissolved. Transfer mixture to bowl and let cool, stirring occasionally, until mixture registers 110 degrees, about 20 minutes.

3 Twist open probiotic capsule and whisk contents into cooled milk mixture; discard capsule's casing. Cover bowl tightly with plastic wrap, place in oven, and turn on oven light. Let yogurt sit undisturbed for at least 12 hours or up to 24 hours. (Yogurt will not thicken while sitting.)

4 Refrigerate yogurt until completely chilled and set, about 4 hours. Process yogurt in blender until smooth, about 30 seconds. (Yogurt can be refrigerated for up to 1 week.)

All About Coconut Milk Products

Coconut products, with their silky texture, richness, and pleasant flavor, have many uses in vegan cooking. But with multiple liquid coconut items on the market—coconut milk, canned coconut milk, canned coconut cream, and cream of coconut—parsing these products can be puzzling.

Coconut milk is sold in a carton near the soy and almond milk and is labeled "coconut milk beverage." This is what we're talking about when we call for "coconut milk" in an ingredient list. It's made by blending canned coconut milk with water and additives, which make it creamy, despite the water that it contains. Coconut milk has about an eighth of the fat content of canned coconut milk and does not taste strongly of coconut.

Canned coconut milk is made by steeping shredded coconut in water and then pressing it to yield a creamy, coconut-flavored liquid. We use it in savory cooking, often in Thai dishes, as well as in sweet recipes like our Creamy Chocolate Frosting (page 285). When you open a can of coconut milk, you may find that it's separated—there will be a more solid mass above the watery liquid—but not always. Some recipes require using just the solid part, while others call for the whole thing. If your recipe calls for just the solid part, to make the separation distinct, you must refrigerate the cans of coconut milk for 24 hours. Then, you can skim away the thick cream more easily. Do not confuse canned coconut milk with canned coconut cream (the ratio of coconut meat to liquid is higher) or cream of coconut (which is sweetened and contains thickeners and emulsifiers).

Better than Cheddar: Cheese Flavor—without Cheese

Hands down—and we know we aren't alone in thinking this—the hardest savory ingredient to give up when we were diving into vegan cooking was cheese. At least it was hard at first. The many vegan cheese substitutes available in the supermarket didn't help. Some are soy-based and others nut-based—and all of them vary wildly across brands in terms of flavor, texture, and meltability. We found it difficult to compensate for this lack of consistency in our recipes and, frankly, we didn't like the flavor, waxy texture, or long ingredient lists of any of these products.

We might not like store-bought vegan cheeses, but we weren't willing to give up comforting, traditionally "cheesy" recipes—enchiladas, lasagna, even mac and cheese have their place in a vegan diet. After many, many tests, we got results that, if not replicating cheese exactly, produced many of the qualities we like about cheese, and often turned out less oily and heavy than the originals. How? As it turns out, several common ingredients, from vegetables to pantry staples, when manipulated and combined properly, mimic the flavor and texture of cheese.

FAKING THE FUNK

Cheese, depending on the variety, typically has saltiness, nuttiness, savoriness, and tang. Add nutritional yeast to your food and you're on the fast track to these flavors. (For more information on nutritional yeast, see page 20.) But there are some less obvious products that provide cheesiness. Plain old distilled white vinegar turned out to be a powerful secret ingredient for us. In both our Creamy Cashew Mac and Cheese (page 184) and our Nacho Dip (page 258), its clean acidity adds the tang that other "cheesy" vegan ingredients can't mimic. Mustard powder performs similarly but has a nuanced bite that nails the rounder flavors of cheese. Miso paste captures cheese's savory side in Fettuccine Alfredo (page 189) and Almost Hands-Free Mushroom Risotto (page 196).

NUTS OVER CREAM SAUCE

Some of the comfort foods we wanted to veganize don't call just for a sprinkling of grated cheese, but for a rich cream sauce, forcing us to approximate both the cheese and the cream. A common base in vegan cooking is cashew cream. Soaked cashews, blended to a creamy, grit-free consistency, enrich full-bodied soups and casseroles. We took advantage of mild-flavored cashew cream sauces like the one in our Fettuccine Alfredo (page 189). However, we found that cashew cream, on its own, could weigh down dishes, making them overly rich or nutty-tasting. That's where another secret weapon came in: cauliflower. Yes, the healthful vegetable helps make a decadent cream sauce. When you boil cauliflower and puree it with the cashews, it lightens the cashew cream and goes unnoticed. And this doesn't require an extra step: You can throw the cashews in the pot with the cauliflower and blend everything together.

HOT POTATO

It seemed miraculous: We developed a gooey Nacho Dip (page 258) that had us plowing through bags of tortilla chips. The secret was the humble potato. We boiled some potato and then broke the most fundamental of mashed potato rules: We whirred it in the blender until it was sticky and gluey. What makes for really bad mashed potatoes turns out a creamy sauce with the viscosity of real cheese.

TOP IT OFF

Sometimes cheese is used simply, sprinkled on pastas or dolloped on pizzas and casseroles. Since we've found the store-bought stuff to be subpar, we've created our own alternatives. Cashew Ricotta is creamy and dreamy. It's made from pureed soaked cashews and is flavored with olive oil, lemon juice, and salt and pepper. To satisfy our craving for the salty, nutty, savory punch that grated Parmesan adds to dishes, we also developed a Vegan Parmesan Substitute. We grind a toasted mixture of cashews for sweetness and pine nuts for savory depth with nutritional yeast, salt, and briny olives. It even has a texture similar to that of the crystalline bits in high-quality aged Parmesan.

CASHEW RICOTTA
Makes about 1 cup

1 cup raw cashews
2 tablespoons extra-virgin olive oil
2 teaspoons lemon juice, plus extra for
  seasoning
  Salt and pepper

1 Place cashews in bowl and add water to cover by 1 inch. Soak cashews at room temperature for at least 8 hours or up to 24 hours. Drain and rinse well.

2 Process cashews, ¼ cup water, oil, lemon juice, and ¼ teaspoon salt in food processor until smooth, about 2 minutes, scraping down sides of bowl as needed. Adjust consistency with additional water as needed. Season with salt, pepper, and extra lemon juice to taste. (Ricotta can be refrigerated for up to 1 week.)

VEGAN PARMESAN SUBSTITUTE
Makes about 1½ cups

¾ cup raw cashews
3 tablespoons nutritional yeast
2 tablespoons raw pine nuts
1 tablespoon chopped green olives, patted dry
¾ teaspoon salt

1 Adjust oven rack to middle position and heat oven to 275 degrees. Process cashews, nutritional yeast, pine nuts, olives, and salt in food processor until finely ground, about 1 minute, scraping down sides of bowl as needed.

2 Spread mixture on rimmed baking sheet in even layer. Bake until mixture is light golden and dry to the touch, about 20 minutes, stirring mixture and rotating pan halfway through baking.

3 Let mixture cool completely, about 15 minutes. Break apart any large clumps before serving. (Parmesan substitute can be refrigerated for up to 1 month.)

Anatomy of a Meal: Vegan Bowls

When you're eliminating some foods, you want the ones you are eating to be as interesting as possible—not just compartmentalized elements on a plate. In fact, our new favorite way to eat isn't on a plate at all, but in a bowl. Vegan bowls are a hearty meal, containing the right balance of protein, fat, and carbohydrates to nourish you. And they're a vessel for experimentation, with various flavors, textures, and even temperatures of foods. On top of a generous bed of warm grains or noodles, we layer vegetables, a protein source, a sauce to bring the components together, and a fresh or crunchy flourish to top it off. Here's a deconstructed look at how we build our Farro Bowl with Tofu, Mushrooms, and Spinach (page 172). Use our recipes, but also follow these rules to build your own bowls for endless delicious flavor combinations.

Step 1: Lay the Base

Our bowls start with a warm hearty grain. Here, farro provides both fiber and protein, and its chewy, nutty grains are satisfying and substantial. Other good choices are quinoa, brown rice, barley, or even rice noodles.

Step 2: Bulk It Up

Grains are filling and sustaining, but sometimes we want a little extra for textural contrast and heft. Here, fried crisp-crusted, creamy-centered slabs of tofu make our bowl a hearty meal. Beans, tempeh, and nuts are other protein-packed options.

Steps 3 and 4: Pick Your Produce

Unlike a leafy salad, the vegetables in a bowl aren't the base but are instead toppings that enliven the grains. We rarely pick just one vegetable and like to use a couple that have different textures when cooked. We cook the vegetables in batches in the same pan to ensure the perfect texture—and to keep the dishes minimal. Silky sautéed spinach and meaty mushrooms amped with soy sauce work well here.

Step 5: Drizzle It

We've developed flavor-packed sauces to add richness to bowls and other dishes. Drizzle the sauce on top, mix up the ingredients, and enjoy your artfully composed bowl. This recipe is topped with our bold Miso-Ginger Sauce (page 167) that's a little spicy and a little sweet, and it jazzes up everything below.

Step 6: Top It Off

If you've gotten this far, you have a balanced, filling bowl. The rest is fun: Add slices of raw vegetables, pickles, seeds, or herbs for final hits of texture and flavor that make your meal special. Our farro bowl has so many interesting flavors and textures that all it requires is the fresh bite of sliced scallions.

A New World of Baking

We predicted that vegan baking would be a challenge—and we were right. After all, the ingredients that make cakes fluffy and tall, that give cookies structure, that produce delicate flakes in pie dough, and that keep brownies moist—eggs, butter, and milk—are all off the table. And obvious one-for-one swaps—vegan egg replacers for eggs, butter-flavored baking sticks for butter, and dairy-free milks for traditional milk—do not a good vegan baked good make: These products can produce off-flavored, lackluster results. No, vegan baking isn't just about making ingredient substitutions; it requires abandoning some of the rules we long followed and learning a new way to bake. But, despite this, with our guidelines, turning out vegan treats of all kinds is not difficult. The baked goods in this book aren't great vegan baked goods—they're just plain great, with the texture and flavor you'd expect from your favorite desserts.

THE VEGAN BAKING PANTRY

These are the ingredients we found ourselves reaching for over and over again in our vegan baking. You'll want some of these ingredients on hand at all times as they're also used in savory cooking.

Coconut Oil

Made by extracting oil from the meat of coconuts, coconut oil is sold in two forms, both of which are solid at room temperature: refined, which has virtually no taste or aroma, and unrefined (also called virgin), which retains a strong coconut flavor. We always want a neutral-tasting fat, so we use refined coconut oil in our baking recipes, though both perform the same way. Note that when our recipes call for coconut oil, we mean room temperature, solid oil; we specify melted when necessary. If your kitchen is warmer than room temperature (around 75 degrees and warmer), the coconut oil will liquefy. Don't store coconut oil in the refrigerator as it becomes very hard, breaking off in shards and becoming difficult to manipulate in doughs and batters. Coconut oil keeps at room temperature for up to one year.

Coconut oil makes a good substitute for butter because, like butter, it's a saturated fat and it can be used both solid and melted, so it has various applications. Melted coconut oil, for example, makes our Savory Drop Biscuits (page 55) ultratender. When the melted oil hits the cold coconut milk in the recipe, it forms clumps that disperse evenly through the batter. For Currant Scones (page 56) and pie dough (page 292), we pinch off pieces of solid coconut oil and pulse the pieces into the flour in the food processor. Unlike butter, which is about 16 to 18 percent water, coconut oil is 100 percent fat; it lubricates the flour granules with fat, limiting gluten development, which occurs when flour meets liquid and which makes baked goods chewy. That means fluffy, not bready, biscuits and tender pie crust.

Vegetable Oil

Just as it's a staple in traditional baking, vegetable oil can also make ultramoist vegan baked goods. It gives our vegan Banana Bread (page 67) the right moist, dense texture. As a mostly unsaturated fat, it gives our Fudgy Brownies (page 278) chew rather than the cakey, tender texture that saturated fats, which are solid at room temperature, tend to provide baked goods. Note: Vegetable oil and coconut oil are not interchangeable.

Organic Sugar

Conventional cane sugar is often not vegan; some manufacturers process it through animal bone char. (For more information on sugar, see page 5.) Organic sugar is never processed this way, so it's a safe choice. Organic sugar comes in granulated, light brown, dark brown, and powdered forms (confectioners' sugar). Note that organic sugars have a coarser grind than conventional sugars and do not dissolve as readily. However, this did not impact the results of our baked goods except for Aquafaba Meringues (page 276), and we found an easy workaround. If you're not a strict vegan, you can use regular granulated, brown, and confectioners' sugar in our vegan recipes with success.

Vegan Chocolate

Many chocolates are not vegan. Even bittersweet or dark chocolates can contain milk fat. Also, chocolate contains sugar that may or may not be processed with bone char.

We used dairy-free chocolates for our recipe development in the test kitchen. We cannot guarantee that these chocolates use vegan sugar, however, so if you're a strict vegan, you may choose to purchase only chocolates that are labeled "vegan."

Unsweetened chocolate is the purest form of chocolate. With no sugar, it's almost always vegan. Our favorite, Hershey's Unsweetened Baking Bar, containing only chocolate and cocoa, is vegan. The test kitchen's winning bittersweet chocolate, Ghirardelli 60% Cacao Bittersweet Chocolate Premium Baking Bar, contains milk fat, so we used Lindt Excellence 70%, which does not contain milk fat, in our testing. Finally, chocolate chips come in many different styles. Curiously, our favorite chocolate chip, Ghirardelli 60% Cacao Bittersweet Chocolate Chips, contains milk fat while the Semi-Sweet Chocolate Baking Chips do not, and we used them for our testing.

BAKING WITH DAIRY SUBSTITUTES

Each dairy-free milk, creamer, and yogurt variety has its loyalists (for more information on dairy-free milks, see page 24); however, we've found that they each perform differently in baked goods, not just in terms of flavor (flavor differences usually didn't make or break baked goods) but in terms of texture, too. That's why you'll see dairy-free testing notes throughout the chapters. In these sections, we outline what milk, creamer, or yogurt we had the best luck using in a specific recipe, and we make note of the characteristics of the baked good when we swapped in another. Sometimes you can use the dairy substitute of your choice, but sometimes baked goods suffer. This makes sense. As you can see in the chart below, the nutritional makeup of dairy-free milks varies depending on what they're made from. We recommend keeping different dairy-free items on hand for the best results.

Nutritional Makeup of Dairy-Free Milks

MILK PER 1 CUP, UNSWEETENED	ALMOND	COCONUT	OAT	SOY
Fat	2.5g	4.5g	2.5g	4g
Saturated Fat	0g	4g	0g	0.5g
Protein	1g	0g	4g	7g
Sugar	0g	<1g	19g	1g

Milkless Buttermilk

Buttermilk gives baked goods like pancakes or biscuits tang. But it also has textural effects. The acidic buttermilk, when combined with baking soda, lightens baked goods because it increases the effect of the leavener. Its acidity also tenderizes baked goods. So how do you mimic buttermilk's abilities in vegan baked goods? Add acid. Adding an acid with your dairy-free milk manually makes it, well, acidic, so its properties are similar. Many vegan cookbooks call for using apple cider vinegar, but we saw better results with lemon juice. Why? Lemon juice has a lower pH than vinegars—about one pH unit lower, meaning it's about 10 times more acidic than vinegar, so the baking soda can act even more effectively.

pH lemon juice = 2.0–2.6
pH distilled vinegar = 2.4–3.4
pH apple cider vinegar = 3.10

Oat Milk Takes the Cake

We found ourselves turning to oat milk again and again for cakes. One thing that immediately stands out in the chart is its natural sugar content. It's much higher than that of the other milks, so it not only works for baked goods that are sweet (after all, dairy milk has a sweetness to it), but it also helps baked goods brown. This is a particular boon in vegan baking. Without the milk proteins from dairy, vegan baked goods, even when baked to the upper time range, can be pale—even white. Coconut milk tended to make pale, bland-tasting cakes. The difference in browning between yellow cake layers made with these milks is clear in the photo below. The top cake layers were made with oat milk, and the bottom cake layers were made with coconut milk.

No Yolks: A Guide to Vegan Egg Substitutes

Most vegan cookbook authors have a preferred substitute for eggs. But they all act differently in different baked goods. That's thanks to the many powers of the egg. An egg is composed of watery, protein-rich whites and fatty, emulsifying yolks. It whips, it leavens, it builds structure, and it binds—no wonder it's called "incredible." Since eggs have many talents, different baked goods tend to showcase those talents differently. Take a fluffy yellow cake and a pancake. A yellow cake often calls for folding in egg whites to give it lift and more bounce to the ounce. In the pancake, by contrast, the egg just provides moisture and holds the cakes together. Each egg substitute has a strength that mimics one or more of the qualities of eggs—but never all of them.

Fabulous Aquafaba

You've likely been throwing away what we've found is one of the most valuable ingredients in the vegan baking larder—and it's free: aquafaba. When we refer to aquafaba, we're talking about the liquid in a can of chickpeas, not other beans, as it works the best. The starchy stuff is a great binder straight from the can. But what really makes it magic is that it whips and creates a foam, which means it's able to trap air, giving items structure at the same time it delivers a fluffy crumb and lift.

More than a (Flax)seed

Ground flaxseed, when combined with liquid, forms a mixture that has a gluey texture similar to that of an egg white, so it's a good binder. Plus, it can be hydrated with the liquid ingredients in a recipe so you don't need to adjust for extra liquid. While we use flaxseeds as an egg substitute in our Classic Pancakes (page 61) for these reasons, we found we liked aquafaba better than flax in cakes because it can both bind and trap air. Plus, flax's flavor can muddy mild-mannered baked goods.

Leave It to Leavener

We found in many of our baked goods that by increasing the amount of baking powder and/or baking soda in the recipe, and sometimes adding extra acid to activate that leavener, we were able to get the lift and structure we needed—without any egg substitutes. Lush, fudgy brownies, for example, don't traditionally require baking powder or soda. Eggs give them moisture and bind them; they don't need lift. But in the absence of eggs, adding some leavener gives brownies just enough rise to have structure. And the perfect pairing of leavener and lemon juice is the secret to the success of our Banana Bread (page 67). The test kitchen's conventional banana bread contains ¾ teaspoon of baking soda that acts in conjunction with the acidic yogurt in the recipe. For our vegan loaf, we added 1 tablespoon of lemon juice on top of the almond milk yogurt. With this superconcentrated shot of acidity, the cake got the lift it needed. The effects are clear from looking at one loaf made with the lemon juice addition (left) and one without (right). The one with lemon juice not only has more height, but its rise is more even. This translates to a moist, sturdy crumb, whereas the bread baked without lemon juice is crumbly and dissolves to paste upon eating.

If you were to survey the field of vegan recipes, you'd find a lot of other egg substitutes. Why do we talk only about three, aquafaba, flaxseeds, and leavener/acid? We tried what's out there in our initial tests of vegan baked goods and yet we always found ourselves turning to the same three. Here are some other common egg substitutes we tried—and they failed.

Powdered Egg Replacer
(Ener-G is a common brand)
Baked goods have an off-flavor and color; package equivalents don't work.

Tofu
Baked goods are dense, sticky, heavy, and taste distinctively of soy.

Applesauce
Baked goods are pasty, wet, and heavy.

ALL ABOUT AQUAFABA

Because we turned to aquafaba again and again in our recipe development, we learned a lot about how to work with it. These are our helpful hints for incorporating this magical ingredient into your cooking and baking.

Bean for Egg: Measuring Aquafaba

Through our thorough testing, we've determined just the right amount of aquafaba that works for each recipe. To measure out the amount of aquafaba called for in a recipe, start by shaking the unopened can of chickpeas well. Drain the chickpeas through a fine-mesh strainer over a bowl and reserve the beans for another use. Whisk the aquafaba liquid and then measure. While it may not be visible, the starches in the chickpea liquid settle in the can. In order to take advantage of them, you'll want to make sure they're evenly distributed throughout the liquid.

Storing Aquafaba

For ease, we like to freeze the aquafaba in 1-tablespoon portions in ice cube trays. Once the bean liquid cubes are frozen solid, you can pop them into a freezer bag for future use. Frozen-then-thawed aquafaba whips just as successfully as fresh aquafaba. To speed things along, you can also defrost the aquafaba in the microwave (do not cook). Chickpea liquid stored in the refrigerator will last for 1 week.

Miracle Whip

We think aquafaba's most magical property is its ability to whip to a stiff, fluffy foam. We fold this foam into Blueberry Muffins (page 58) to lighten them. We even whip aquafaba with sugar and vanilla to make egg-free Aquafaba Meringues (page 276). We had luck with chickpea liquid from every can of chickpeas we tried (organic brands and those with preservatives, salted and no-salt-added brands) except for Progresso brand, which did not consistently reach a foam; we don't recommend it. We also couldn't create a decent foam with the liquid from chickpeas cooked at home.

Whipping Aquafaba

1 Underwhipped aquafaba.

2 Properly whipped aquafaba.

As it does with egg whites, adding a stabilizing ingredient improved the structure of whipped aquafaba. In sweet recipes, that's usually sugar. But there's another ingredient that we often whip with egg whites for stability: cream of tartar. Why? Cream of tartar is acidic; when added to egg whites, it prevents the egg proteins from bonding too tightly to each other and denatures them so they can create a foam that traps air bubbles and water more quickly and holds them in place for less weeping. *(continued)*

Stabilizing Whipped Aquafaba

To determine how to work with whipped aquafaba in our baked goods, we tried stabilizing the foam with both sugar and cream of tartar, as we do with egg whites in baked goods. Aquafaba whipped with cream of tartar maintained a stiff foam and weeped very little liquid, even when left to sit for an hour. This translated to baked goods with better structure.

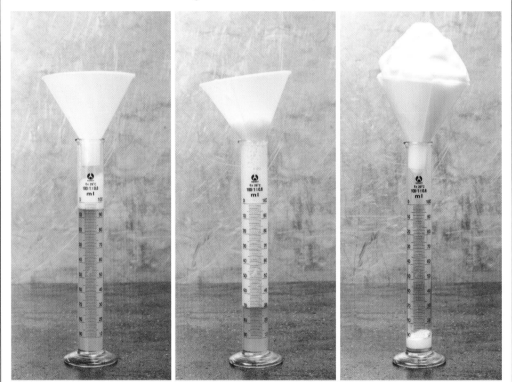

1 Aquafaba whipped alone after 1 hour.

2 Aquafaba whipped with sugar after 1 hour.

3 Aquafaba whipped with cream of tartar after 1 hour.

While aquafaba isn't protein-rich like egg whites, we wanted to know if cream of tartar could benefit our vegan baked goods as well. To find out, we conducted an experiment. We whipped 4 ounces of aquafaba to a stiff foam three ways: aquafaba alone, aquafaba with ¼ cup of sugar, and aquafaba with ¼ teaspoon of cream of tartar. We transferred each foam to a funnel set over a graduated cylinder. We took note of how long it took to whip the aquafaba to a stiff foam on high speed in a stand mixer as well as how much liquid weeped out when the foam was left to sit for 1 hour.

After 1 hour, it was clear that cream of tartar stabilizes aquafaba foams as it does egg foams. The aquafaba whipped alone took 10 minutes to reach stiff foam, and it had completely deflated after just 20 minutes, filling the cylinder almost completely, with about 95 mL of liquid. The aquafaba whipped with sugar fared better; it still took 10 minutes to reach stiff peaks (like egg whites, aquafaba whipped with sugar gets to stiff, sticky peaks rather than just a foam). The mixture filled the cylinder in 1 hour, but it had weeped only about 30 mL of liquid. The aquafaba whipped with cream of tartar was the star, however: It took only 4½ minutes to reach a stiff foam. And after 1 hour, only about 2 mL of liquid collected in the graduated cylinder, and only the slightest amount of foam slid through the funnel.

This fun experiment translated to better baked goods, like Blueberry Muffins (page 58). The muffin made with cream of tartar has more height and better doming. As a bonus, cream of tartar boosts the potential of the leavener in a recipe, contributing to a fluffier crumb.

Whipping Small Amounts of Aquafaba

Some recipes call for as little as 3 tablespoons of aquafaba. If you have a very large stand mixer, the whisk may not be able to engage with the small amount of liquid to properly whip it. In this case, aquafaba can also be whipped with an electric handheld mixer.

Best Bean

We wanted to see if the liquid in cans of other kinds of beans worked in baked goods. We made meringues using chickpea liquid and inky-dark black bean liquid. Chickpea liquid was by far the winner. We had to whip the black bean liquid for much longer to see any action, and at that, it didn't reach stiff peaks. As shown below, without stable stiff peaks, black bean liquid made pancake-flat meringues, while chickpea meringues held their peaks and had solid, consistent interiors after baking.

Fabulous Blueberry Muffins

left Muffin made with cream of tartar–enhanced aquafaba foam

right Muffin made with plain aquafaba foam

Faba Failure

left Meringues made with black bean liquid

right Meringues made with chickpea liquid

Tofu Frittata with Mushrooms

serves 6 to 8

28 ounces firm tofu, drained and patted dry

3 tablespoons extra-virgin olive oil
Salt

½ teaspoon turmeric

½ teaspoon garlic powder

⅛ teaspoon pepper

¼ cup chickpea flour

8 ounces cremini mushrooms, trimmed and sliced thin

2 shallots, minced

1 garlic clove, minced

1 teaspoon minced fresh thyme

1 tablespoon minced fresh parsley

Why This Recipe Works Tofu is a wonder ingredient. Not only is it good for you (packed with protein), it has a mild taste and comes in a variety of textures, so it can take on many flavors and yield dishes of many forms. Case in point: our vegan frittata. More substantial than an omelet and less fussy than a quiche, frittatas are a test kitchen favorite, and we found we could make a truly extraordinary version with tofu just as easily as we do with a carton of eggs and a mess of dairy. Silken tofu seemed like an obvious starting point; it has a creamy texture that would blend into a scrambled egg–like base in the food processor. We like a sliceable frittata, however, and the silken tofu proved too wet. Could firm tofu work? Happily, we found that firm tofu became perfectly smooth when we processed it. For additional structure to balance the frittata's eggy softness, we added some chickpea flour; unlike wheat flour or cornstarch, chickpea flour added heft and structure without making the frittata pasty; plus, it heightened the frittata's savory profile. Turmeric gave the fritatta an eggy color, and garlic powder provided umami depth. After sautéing mushrooms and aromatics until deeply caramelized, we stirred the tofu puree into the vegetables and baked the frittata until it was set throughout and lightly golden. After a 5-minute rest in the pan, the frittata slid right out and sliced into neat wedges. Finished with a sprinkling of parsley, our tofu frittata is sure to please any group of brunch guests. Do not use silken, soft, or extra-firm tofu in this recipe.

1 Adjust oven rack to middle position and heat oven to 350 degrees. Process tofu, 1 tablespoon oil, 1 teaspoon salt, turmeric, garlic powder, and pepper in food processor until smooth, about 30 seconds, scraping down sides of bowl as needed. Add chickpea flour and process until well combined, about 15 seconds.

2 Heat remaining 2 tablespoons oil in 12-inch ovensafe nonstick skillet over medium-high heat until shimmering. Add mushrooms and ¼ teaspoon salt and cook until mushrooms have released their liquid and are beginning to brown, 5 to 7 minutes. Stir in shallots and cook until mushrooms are well browned, 5 to 7 minutes. Stir in garlic and thyme and cook until fragrant, about 30 seconds.

3 Off heat, stir in tofu mixture and spread into even layer. Transfer skillet to oven and bake until center is set and surface is slightly puffed, dry, and lightly golden, 30 to 35 minutes, rotating skillet halfway through baking.

4 Carefully remove skillet from oven (skillet handle will be hot) and let frittata sit for 5 minutes. Using spatula, loosen frittata from skillet and slide onto cutting board. Sprinkle with parsley, cut into wedges, and serve hot or at room temperature.

Tofu Scramble with Bell Pepper, Shallot, and Herbs

serves 4

14 ounces soft tofu, drained and patted dry

1½ teaspoons vegetable oil

1 small red bell pepper, stemmed, seeded, and chopped fine

1 shallot, minced

¾ teaspoon salt

⅛ teaspoon turmeric

⅛ teaspoon pepper

2 tablespoons finely chopped fresh basil, parsley, tarragon, or marjoram

Why This Recipe Works Some of the best breakfasts are not only satisfying but also quick and easy enough to make on a weekday before you've had your morning coffee, and a scramble fits this bill. Scrambles made from tofu can be rich and creamy and great alongside toast and jam or tucked into a portable breakfast burrito or taco. But while recipes for tofu scrambles are numerous, some seem like bland or boring imitations of their eggy counterparts. We wanted a recipe that offered a creamy, egg-like texture and a subtle but satisfying flavor, made more interesting with the addition of some fresh vegetables. We tried silken, soft, medium, and firm tofu, and the soft tofu proved to have a texture closest to eggs, yielding pieces that, when crumbled, were smooth and creamy. (Silken tofu produced a looser scramble, and firmer tofu varieties developed into hard curds.) A small amount of turmeric was key, contributing depth of flavor and a nice touch of color without overwhelming the dish with actual curry flavor. We also found that the tofu could be crumbled into smaller or larger pieces to resemble egg curds of different sizes. If you cannot find soft tofu, you can use silken tofu but your scramble will be significantly wetter. Do not use firm tofu in this recipe.

1 Crumble tofu into ¼- to ½-inch pieces. Spread tofu on paper towel–lined baking sheet and let drain for 20 minutes, then gently press dry with paper towels. Heat oil in 10-inch nonstick skillet over medium heat until shimmering. Add bell pepper and shallot and cook until softened, about 5 minutes.

2 Stir in crumbled tofu, salt, curry powder, and pepper and cook until tofu is hot, about 2 minutes. Off heat, stir in basil and serve.

VARIATION

Tofu Scramble with Tomato and Scallions
Omit red bell pepper. Add 1 seeded and finely chopped tomato and 1 minced garlic clove to pan with shallot in step 1; cook until tomato is no longer wet, 3 to 5 minutes. Substitute 2 tablespoons minced scallions for basil.

Tofu Ranchero

serves 4

2 (28-ounce) cans diced tomatoes
1 tablespoon packed organic brown sugar (see page 31)
1 tablespoon lime juice
1 onion, chopped
½ cup canned chopped green chiles
3 tablespoons extra-virgin olive oil
3 tablespoons plus ½ teaspoon chili powder
4 garlic cloves, sliced thin
Salt and pepper
14 ounces firm tofu, halved lengthwise, then cut crosswise into ¾-inch-thick slabs
1 avocado, halved, pitted, and diced
¼ cup minced fresh cilantro
2 scallions, sliced thin
8 (6-inch) corn tortillas, warmed

Why This Recipe Works Huevos rancheros, with its fine-tuned combination of spicy sauce and rich toppings, makes for an eye-opening breakfast option, and we found that we could easily replace the eggs (the *"huevos"*) in this dish with supple squares of firm tofu. Like a poached egg, the tofu achieved a creamy, silky interior texture while still holding its shape during cooking. The backbone of our tofu ranchero is the sauce, so nailing it was key: For maximum flavor with little effort, we roasted diced tomatoes with brown sugar, lime juice, green chiles, chili powder, and garlic. Roasting on a sheet pan allowed moisture to quickly evaporate and a nice char to form on the vegetables. We seared seasoned tofu while the sauce cooked to give it a beautiful golden brown color. Finishing the sauce and tofu together on the stovetop allowed the flavors to meld and gave the tofu perfect texture. Topped with avocado, cilantro, and scallions and served with warm corn tortillas, tofu ranchero is a spicy, hearty way to start the day. Use a heavyweight rimmed baking sheet for this recipe, as flimsy sheets will warp in the oven.

1 Adjust oven rack to middle position and heat oven to 500 degrees. Line rimmed baking sheet with parchment paper. Drain tomatoes in fine-mesh strainer set over bowl, pressing to extract as much juice as possible. Reserve 1¾ cups tomato juice and discard remainder. Whisk sugar and lime juice into tomato juice.

2 Combine onion, chiles, 2 tablespoons oil, 3 tablespoons chili powder, garlic, ½ teaspoon salt, and drained tomatoes in second bowl. Transfer tomato mixture to prepared baking sheet and spread in even layer to edges of sheet. Roast until charred in spots, 35 to 40 minutes, stirring and redistributing into even layer halfway through baking.

3 Meanwhile, spread tofu on paper towel–lined baking sheet and let drain for 20 minutes. Gently press dry with paper towels, season with salt and pepper, and sprinkle both sides with remaining ½ teaspoon chili powder.

4 Heat remaining 1 tablespoon oil in 12-inch nonstick skillet over medium-high heat until just smoking. Add tofu and cook until golden and crisp on both sides, 5 to 7 minutes; transfer to paper towel–lined plate.

5 Transfer roasted tomato mixture to now-empty skillet and stir in reserved tomato juice mixture. Season with salt and pepper to taste, then spread into even layer. Nestle tofu in sauce. Bring to simmer over medium heat, cover, and cook until tofu is warmed through and sauce thickens slightly, about 2 minutes. Off heat, sprinkle with avocado, cilantro, and scallions. Serve with warm tortillas.

Sweet Potato Red Flannel Hash with Tempeh

serves 4

Why This Recipe Works Red flannel hash gets its name from the deep red beets scattered throughout like the check on a flannel plaid. Our vegan version features tempeh instead of the eggs and sweet potato in addition to the classic combination of beets and russet potatoes for a dish that feels like real weekend comfort food. The tempeh was a particularly satisfying and delicious addition; the seasoned and browned cubes provided a hearty bite and a savory flavor that made tasters go back for seconds and thirds. To make the process speedy, we parcooked the vegetables in the microwave until tender and then moved them to the skillet to brown and crisp. We rounded out the flavors with onion, garlic, and thyme and then stirred in some coconut creamer for richness and binding. As for the tempeh, we first tried cooking it along with the vegetables, but it kept the hash from cohering. Instead, we seared the tempeh separately, built the hash, and then scattered satisfying cubes over the top along with a handful of scallions. The hash stayed together, and the salty richness of the tempeh perfectly balanced the sweet vegetables underneath for a hearty, colorful breakfast. Any dairy-free creamer will work in this recipe.

1 russet potato (8 ounces), peeled and cut into ½-inch pieces

1 small sweet potato (8 ounces), peeled and cut into ½-inch pieces

8 ounces beets, peeled and cut into ½-inch pieces

¼ cup vegetable oil
Salt and pepper

8 ounces tempeh, cut into ½-inch pieces

1 tablespoon soy sauce

1 onion, chopped fine

2 garlic cloves, minced

½ teaspoon minced fresh thyme or ¼ teaspoon dried

⅓ cup unsweetened coconut creamer

2 scallions, sliced thin

1 Combine russet potato, sweet potato, beets, 1 tablespoon oil, ½ teaspoon salt, and ½ teaspoon pepper in bowl. Microwave, covered, stirring occasionally, until russet potato is translucent around edges and sweet potato and beets are fork-tender, 8 to 10 minutes.

2 Meanwhile, heat 1 tablespoon oil in 12-inch nonstick skillet over medium-high heat until just smoking. Add tempeh, soy sauce, ¼ teaspoon salt, and ¼ teaspoon pepper and cook, stirring occasionally, until well browned, 4 to 6 minutes. Transfer to bowl and tent with foil.

3 Heat remaining 2 tablespoons oil in now-empty skillet over medium-high heat until shimmering. Add onion and cook until softened, about 5 minutes. Stir in garlic and thyme and cook until fragrant, about 30 seconds.

4 Stir in microwaved vegetables and any accumulated juices and coconut creamer. Using back of spatula, firmly pack vegetables into skillet and cook undisturbed for 2 minutes. Flip hash, 1 portion at a time, and repack into pan. Repeat flipping process every few minutes until vegetables are nicely browned, 6 to 8 minutes. Top with reserved tempeh, sprinkle with scallions, and serve.

Black Beans on Toast with Avocado and Tomato

serves 4

Why This Recipe Works Avocado toast is one of our favorite snacks and a great way to start the day. But we wanted a topped toast that was a bit more substantial and could stand alone as breakfast. We chose a bold Southwestern flavor profile to liven up our morning; the simple rusticity of mashed black beans on toast elevated with a bit of spice, fresh tomato, some creamy avocado, and a good squeeze of lime is hard to argue with. But we weren't in the mood to dirty a pan to cook beans en route to a quick breakfast. By simply mashing our beans with a little hot water, oil, and lime zest and juice, we were able to get a flavorsome and well-textured base. For a splash of color, heat, and acidity, we really liked the addition of spicy quick-pickled onions, which can be made up to a week ahead. (If you don't have them on hand, a pinch of red pepper flakes will give you back that heat.) A liberal garnish of cilantro leaves freshened all the flavors. With just 10 minutes of work, we had a fantastic upgrade to breakfast toast. For an accurate measure of boiling water, bring a full kettle of water to boil and then measure out the desired amount.

4 ounces cherry tomatoes, quartered

4 teaspoons extra-virgin olive oil
Salt and pepper

1 (15-ounce) can black beans, rinsed

¼ cup boiling water

½ teaspoon grated lime zest plus 1 tablespoon juice

4 (½-inch-thick) slices crusty bread

1 ripe avocado, halved, pitted, and sliced thin

¼ cup Quick Sweet-and-Spicy Pickled Red Onions (page 121) (optional)

¼ cup fresh cilantro leaves

1 Combine tomatoes, 1 teaspoon oil, pinch salt, and pinch pepper in bowl. Mash beans, boiling water, lime zest and juice, ½ teaspoon salt, pinch pepper, and remaining 1 tablespoon oil with potato masher to coarse puree in second bowl, leaving some whole beans intact.

2 Adjust oven rack 4 inches from broiler element and heat broiler. Place bread on aluminum foil–lined baking sheet and broil until golden, 1 to 2 minutes per side.

3 Spread mashed bean mixture evenly on toasts, then top with avocado and season with salt to taste. Top with pickled onions, if using; tomatoes; and cilantro leaves and serve.

Overnight Three-Grain Breakfast Porridge
serves 4

4 cups water
½ cup millet, rinsed
½ cup prewashed white quinoa
¼ cup amaranth, rinsed
½ teaspoon salt
2 cups unsweetened oat milk, plus extra as needed
½ teaspoon ground cinnamon
⅛ teaspoon ground nutmeg
1½ cups (7½ ounces) blueberries
3 tablespoons maple syrup

Why This Recipe Works A warm, creamy breakfast bowl of porridge is a great way to pack healthful ingredients into breakfast. For this hearty three-grain porridge, we chose a blend of quinoa, millet, and amaranth and mixed in a generous amount of blueberries for sweet, fruity bursts in every bite. We found that equal parts quinoa and millet (½ cup each), along with ¼ cup of amaranth, gave us a harmonious balance of textures and flavors. Millet, with its mellow corn flavor and fine, starchy texture was balanced by the nutty, earthy flavors of quinoa, while the amaranth added bold anise flavor and an intriguing caviar-like texture. Since each of these grains absorbs liquid differently, our challenge was to figure out how to cook them together perfectly. After testing numerous ratios of liquid to grains and various simmering times, we pinpointed the perfect compromise of 30 minutes of cooking and 6 cups of liquid to 1¼ cups of grains. The high amount of liquid encouraged the grains to swell and some to burst and release their starches, creating a creamy porridge. However, the lengthy 30-minute simmering time was off-putting for what was meant to be a quick breakfast. The solution was stirring the grains into boiling water the night before so the grains hydrated and softened overnight. In the morning, all we had to do was add oat milk and simmer the mixture for about 10 minutes. If you buy unwashed quinoa (or if you are unsure whether it's washed), be sure to rinse it before cooking to remove its bitter protective coating (called saponin).

1 Bring water to boil in large saucepan over high heat. Remove pan from heat and stir in millet, quinoa, amaranth, and salt. Cover saucepan and let sit at room temperature overnight.

2 Stir in oat milk, cinnamon, and nutmeg and bring to simmer over medium-high heat. Reduce heat to medium-low and simmer, stirring occasionally, until grains are fully tender and mixture is thickened, 8 to 10 minutes.

3 Stir in blueberries and maple syrup. Adjust consistency with extra oat milk as needed (porridge will thicken as it sits). Serve.

TESTING NOTES **Dairy-Free Milks**
OUR FAVORITE **Oat Milk**
OTHERS TESTED Almond milk gives the porridge savory notes. Coconut milk makes the porridge less sweet. Soy milk lends the porridge a distinct soy flavor.

Creamy Breakfast Grits with Chives

serves 4 to 6

3 tablespoons extra-virgin olive oil
½ onion, chopped fine
1 cup old-fashioned grits
4¼ cups unsweetened almond milk
Salt and pepper
1 tablespoon minced fresh chives

Why This Recipe Works A Southern specialty, warm grits have tons of appeal, whether served alone or alongside other breakfast fare. We love the creamy kind that's thick and luxurious, with savory flavor to boot. But while creamy grits are simple fare, making them vegan wasn't such a simple affair, since it's usually butter and cream that make them so good. First, to give the grits a savory backbone, we experimented with cooking them in vegetable stock and adding a go-to flavor booster, nutritional yeast, but we ultimately decided that nothing beat a base of simple sautéed onion. To achieve creaminess without dairy, we were optimistic about a mainstay vegan ingredient, cashew cream (cashews that have been soaked in water and pureed). While tasters liked the milkiness of the cashew mixture, we found that the liquid it added watered down our grits and produced a pasty, oatmeal-like texture. Ultimately, we found that almond milk was a suitable cooking liquid for the grits, providing richness without any unexpected flavors or textures. The result is classic grits, creamy and savory, great as the main attraction or as a canvas for toppings like sautéed veggies or browned tempeh.

1 Heat 1 tablespoon oil in medium saucepan over medium heat. Add onion and cook until softened and starting to brown, 5 to 7 minutes. Stir in grits and cook, stirring often, until fragrant, about 3 minutes.

2 Whisk in almond milk and ½ teaspoon salt. Increase heat to medium-high and bring to boil. Reduce heat to low, cover, and simmer, whisking often, until thick and creamy, about 15 minutes.

3 Off heat, stir in remaining 2 tablespoons oil. Season with salt and pepper to taste, sprinkle with chives, and serve.

TESTING NOTES **Dairy-Free Milks**
OUR FAVORITE **Almond Milk**
OTHERS TESTED Coconut milk makes the grits taste a bit less savory. Oat milk makes the grits taste sweet. Soy milk gives the grits a brown hue and a slightly pasty texture.

Savory Drop Biscuits

makes 8 biscuits

2 cups (10 ounces) all-purpose flour
2 teaspoons baking powder
1 teaspoon organic sugar
  (see page 31)
¾ teaspoon salt
½ teaspoon baking soda
1 cup unsweetened coconut milk,
  chilled
8 tablespoons coconut oil,
  melted and cooled (see page 30)
1 tablespoon lemon juice

Why This Recipe Works As far as baking goes, drop biscuits are about as easy as it gets—and they're delicious, whether eaten out of hand for breakfast, served alongside a scramble, or even paired with a warm bowl of soup. These rich, tender biscuits get their name from their signature method of simply stirring the liquid ingredients (usually melted fat and buttermilk) into the dry ingredients. You "drop" this clumpy, wet batter onto the baking sheet and pop it into the oven. The method seems fail-safe and yet sometimes it turns out squat, gummy, and disappointing biscuits. We found the same challenge to be true in developing our vegan drop biscuits, but it was easy to overcome: We melted and slightly cooled coconut oil before adding it to cold coconut milk, and the coconut oil instantly solidified into tiny little clumps. These lumps of coconut oil worked to our advantage when stirred throughout the biscuit batter; they added rich and flavorful fat pockets, making for consistently tender biscuits. Adding lemon juice to the batter gave our biscuits a welcome buttermilk-like tang, and it boosted the leavener's power to create light and fluffy biscuits that are a breeze to whip up for any occasion. Be sure to bake the biscuits on two stacked baking sheets so the bottoms don't scorch.

1 Adjust oven rack to middle position and heat oven to 475 degrees. Set rimmed baking sheet in second baking sheet and line with parchment paper.

2 Whisk flour, baking powder, sugar, salt, and baking soda together in large bowl. Whisk coconut milk, melted oil, and lemon juice together in second bowl (oil will clump). Stir milk mixture into flour mixture until just incorporated.

3 Using greased ⅓-cup dry measuring cup, drop level scoops of batter 1½ inches apart on prepared sheet. Bake until tops are golden, 12 to 14 minutes, rotating sheet halfway through baking.

4 Transfer biscuits to wire rack and let cool for at least 5 minutes. Serve warm or at room temperature.

TESTING NOTES **Dairy-Free Milks**
OUR FAVORITE Coconut Milk
OTHERS TESTED Almond milk makes the biscuits a bit tougher and a little salty-tasting. Oat milk produces noticeably sweeter biscuits. Soy milk imparts a distinct soy flavor and a slightly wetter crumb.

breakfast and brunch

Currant Scones
makes 8 scones

2 cups (10 ounces) all-purpose flour
3 tablespoons organic sugar
  (see page 31)
1 tablespoon baking powder
½ teaspoon salt
5 tablespoons coconut oil
  (see page 30)
½ cup dried currants
¾ cup unsweetened soy creamer

Why This Recipe Works Light, fluffy, barely sweet British-style cream scones are made by cutting cubes of chilled butter into the dry ingredients. We liked coconut oil for the fat in our vegan version. Like butter, the oil is solid at room temperature, and it delivered a rich flavor. But coconut oil doesn't have the water in it that butter does, so it behaves slightly differently. We found we didn't need to chill the coconut oil like butter; instead, we pinched room-temperature coconut oil into pieces and pulsed them into the dry ingredients in the food processor. This way ensured even distribution of the oil, and it coated some of the flour granules with fat, which limited gluten development for a tender, cakey crumb. The dough will be quite soft and wet; dust the counter and your hands with flour. Make sure not to overwork the dough. Be sure to bake the scones on two stacked baking sheets so the bottoms don't scorch.

1 Adjust oven rack to middle position and heat oven to 450 degrees. Set rimmed baking sheet in second rimmed baking sheet and line with parchment paper.

2 Pulse flour, sugar, baking powder, and salt in food processor until combined, about 3 pulses. Pinch off ¼-inch pieces of oil into flour mixture and pulse until mixture resembles coarse cornmeal with some pea-size pieces of oil remaining, about 10 pulses. Transfer mixture to large bowl and stir in currants. Stir in soy creamer until dough begins to form, about 30 seconds.

3 Turn dough and any floury bits out onto floured counter and knead until rough, slightly sticky ball forms, 5 to 10 seconds. Pat dough into 8-inch round and cut into 8 wedges. Space wedges about 2 inches apart on prepared sheet. Bake until tops are light golden brown, 12 to 15 minutes, rotating sheet halfway through baking. Transfer scones to wire rack and let cool for at least 10 minutes. Serve warm or at room temperature.

VARIATIONS
Lemon-Glazed Ginger Scones
Substitute ½ cup chopped crystallized ginger for currants and add ginger to food processor with oil. Whisk 1¾ cups organic confectioners' sugar, 1 teaspoon grated lemon zest, and 3 tablespoons lemon juice in bowl until smooth. Pour glaze over cooled scones and let sit for 10 minutes before serving.

Maple-Glazed Pecan Scones
Substitute ½ cup pecans, toasted and chopped, for currants. Whisk 1¾ cups organic confectioners' sugar, 6 tablespoons maple syrup, and 1 tablespoon water in bowl until smooth. Pour glaze over cooled scones and let sit for 10 minutes before serving.

TESTING NOTES **Dairy-Free Creamer**

OUR FAVORITE Soy Creamer

OTHERS TESTED Almond creamer adds a slightly salty flavor and produces slightly chewier scones. Coconut creamer makes drier, denser scones.

Blueberry Muffins

makes 12 muffins

2⅔ cups (13⅓ ounces) all-purpose
    flour
1 cup (7 ounces) organic
    granulated sugar (see page 31)
1 tablespoon baking powder
½ teaspoon baking soda
¾ teaspoon salt
5 ounces (1 cup) blueberries
1 cup plain almond milk
    yogurt
⅔ cup unsweetened oat milk
7 tablespoons vegetable oil
3 tablespoons aquafaba
    (see page 34)
½ teaspoon cream of tartar
2 tablespoons turbinado sugar

Why This Recipe Works The blueberry muffin never goes out of style. For a light vegan muffin with a tender, delicate crumb, we turned to a simple combination of almond yogurt, oat milk, and vegetable oil to replace the dairy-based ingredients in our classic recipe. These swaps were easy; replacing the eggs in our recipe was not. Eggs provide muffins with the lift and structure to support an open crumb, and most of the common substitutes we tried left us with heavy, tight-crumbed muffins. After making and tasting more than 100 batches, we learned that aquafaba, the liquid found in canned chickpeas, whipped to stiff peaks like egg whites and folded into the muffin batter, acted as the perfect stand-in for eggs in our muffin. The whipped aquafaba can trap tiny air bubbles, translating to a fluffy crumb identical to that of our classic muffin. (For more information on aquafaba, see page 34.) A sprinkling of turbinado sugar over the tops sealed the deal, creating golden brown, crisp, and shimmering muffin tops. You can substitute frozen (unthawed) blueberries for fresh in this recipe.

1 Adjust oven rack to upper-middle position and heat oven to 425 degrees. Thoroughly grease 12-cup muffin tin.

2 Whisk flour, sugar, baking powder, baking soda, and salt together in large bowl. Add blueberries and gently toss to combine. Whisk almond milk yogurt, oat milk, and oil in second bowl until smooth; set aside.

3 Using stand mixer fitted with whisk, whip aquafaba and cream of tartar on high speed until stiff foam that clings to whisk forms, 3 to 9 minutes. Using rubber spatula, fold yogurt mixture into flour mixture until no dry flour remains; do not overmix (batter will be thick). Stir one-third of whipped aquafaba into batter to lighten, then add remaining aquafaba and gently fold batter with rubber spatula until no white streaks remain.

4 Divide batter evenly among prepared muffin cups. Sprinkle turbinado sugar over top. Bake until golden and toothpick inserted in center comes out clean, 18 to 22 minutes, rotating muffin tin halfway through baking. Let muffins cool in muffin tin for 20 minutes, then transfer to wire rack and let cool for at least 10 minutes. Serve warm or at room temperature.

TESTING NOTES
Dairy-Free Yogurts
OUR FAVORITE **Almond Milk Yogurt**
OTHERS TESTED Coconut milk yogurt produces muffins with a slightly denser crumb and a slightly thicker crust. Soy milk yogurt gives the muffins a slightly pasty crumb and a distinct soy flavor.

Dairy-Free Milks

OUR FAVORITE **Oat Milk**

OTHERS TESTED Almond milk produces paler muffins that are slightly less sweet. Coconut milk muffins are slightly paler and drier. Soy milk makes the muffins overly moist and imparts a distinct soy flavor.

Classic Pancakes

serves 4 to 6

2 cups (10 ounces) all-purpose flour

2 tablespoons organic sugar (see page 31)

1 tablespoon baking powder

½ teaspoon baking soda

1 teaspoon ground golden flaxseeds (see page 16)

¾ teaspoon salt

2 cups unsweetened oat milk, room temperature

3 tablespoons coconut oil, melted and cooled, plus 2 teaspoons coconut oil (see page 30)

2 tablespoons lemon juice

Why This Recipe Works We set out to create a buttermilk-style vegan pancake that was fluffy, tender, and full of toasty rise-and-shine flavor. We needed to find successful substitutes for the buttermilk and eggs—and we didn't want to compromise on flavor or texture. Acidic buttermilk, when combined with alkaline baking soda, yields a fluffy crumb and a rich, complex flavor in pancakes. We were able to achieve this effect using a combination of oat milk and lemon juice, plus baking soda, and to our surprise, the pancakes boasted a nutty, butter-like flavor. When we simply omitted eggs from the recipe, our pancakes were pasty and mushy. We tested our way through substitutes, and we liked the way ground flaxseeds provided structure and just the right amount of chew. We simply added the flax to the dry ingredients; the oat milk hydrated it and unleash its binding properties. We prefer ground golden flaxseeds for their mild flavor and more golden color, and the marginally fluffier texture they give our pancakes, but ground brown flaxseed can be used. The pancakes can be cooked on an electric griddle. Set the griddle temperature to 350 degrees and cook as directed.

1 Adjust oven rack to middle position and heat oven to 200 degrees. Set wire rack in rimmed baking sheet and place in oven.

2 Whisk flour, sugar, baking powder, baking soda, ground flaxseeds, and salt together in large bowl. Whisk oat milk, 3 tablespoons melted oil, and lemon juice together in second bowl. Make well in center of flour mixture, add milk mixture to well, and gently whisk until just incorporated with few lumps remaining (do not overmix).

3 Heat 1 teaspoon oil in 12-inch nonstick skillet over medium heat until shimmering. Using paper towels, carefully wipe out oil, leaving thin film of oil on bottom and sides of pan. Using ¼-cup measure, portion batter into pan in 3 places. Cook until edges are set, first side is golden, and bubbles on surface are just beginning to break, 2 to 3 minutes.

4 Flip pancakes and continue to cook until second side is golden, 1 to 2 minutes. Serve immediately or transfer to wire rack in oven and tent loosely with aluminum foil. Repeat with remaining batter, using remaining oil as necessary.

TESTING NOTES **Dairy-Free Milks**

OUR FAVORITE Oat Milk

OTHERS TESTED Coconut milk yields pancakes that are paler, milder in flavor, and slightly more moist. Almond milk makes the pancakes taste slightly savory. Soy milk produces slightly denser pancakes with a distinct soy flavor.

100-Percent Whole-Wheat Pancakes

serves 4 to 6

2 cups (11 ounces) whole-wheat
flour

2 tablespoons packed organic
brown sugar (see page 31)

2 teaspoons baking powder

½ teaspoon baking soda

¾ teaspoon salt

2½ cups unsweetened oat milk,
room temperature

¼ cup coconut oil, melted and
cooled, plus 2 teaspoons
coconut oil (see page 30)

2 tablespoons lemon juice

2 teaspoons vanilla extract

Why This Recipe Works Think a delicious and superlatively light and fluffy whole-wheat pancake—that's also vegan—is impossible? Think again; we developed a recipe for just that. Many whole-wheat pancakes call for a mix of whole-wheat and all-purpose flours, but we found that we got an even better (and more nutritious) result using only whole-wheat flour. That's because whole-wheat flour doesn't contribute to gluten development to the degree that white flour does, so our pancakes were ultratender. To replace the usual egg, we tried multiple substitutes, but all they did was weigh down our pancakes. In fact, we found that, unlike with our Classic Pancakes (page 61), which became pasty and mushy without any substitutes, we liked the whole-wheat pancakes best with no egg replacers. The whole-wheat flour is high in protein, so it's hefty enough to support a crumb that's made fluffy by just the right combination of baking soda and lemon juice. For the best flavor, we recommend starting with a freshly opened bag of whole-wheat flour or one that you've stored in the freezer. The pancakes can be cooked on an electric griddle. Set the griddle temperature to 350 degrees and cook as directed.

1 Adjust oven rack to middle position and heat oven to 200 degrees. Set wire rack in rimmed baking sheet and place in oven.

2 Whisk flour, sugar, baking powder, baking soda, and salt together in large bowl. Whisk oat milk, ¼ cup melted oil, lemon juice, and vanilla together in second bowl. Make well in center of flour mixture, add milk mixture to well, and whisk until smooth.

3 Heat 1 teaspoon oil in 12-inch nonstick skillet over medium heat until shimmering. Using paper towels, carefully wipe out oil, leaving thin film of oil on bottom and sides of pan. Using ¼-cup measure, portion batter into pan in 3 places. Cook until edges are set, first side is golden, and bubbles on surface are just beginning to break, 2 to 3 minutes.

4 Flip pancakes and continue to cook until second side is golden, 1 to 2 minutes. Serve immediately or transfer to wire rack in oven and tent loosely with aluminum foil. Repeat with remaining batter, using remaining oil as necessary.

TESTING NOTES **Dairy-Free Milks**
OUR FAVORITE **Oat Milk**
OTHERS TESTED Coconut milk produces slightly heavier, less sweet pancakes. Almond milk makes slightly pasty pancakes. Soy milk creates pancakes with a distinct soy flavor and a tougher texture.

Belgian Waffles

makes four 7-inch waffles

2 cups (10 ounces) all-purpose flour

3 tablespoons cornstarch

2 tablespoons organic sugar (see page 31)

1 tablespoon baking powder

¼ teaspoon baking soda

½ teaspoon salt

2 cups unsweetened soy milk, room temperature

¼ cup coconut oil, melted and cooled (see page 30)

1 tablespoon lemon juice

1 teaspoon vanilla extract

Why This Recipe Works There are different styles of waffles, but our ideal version is the Belgian waffle—nice and thick, with deep pockets, plus a crispy, browned crust and a rich, custardy interior that soaks up liberal pours of maple syrup without becoming soggy. We were able to create a vegan waffle that not only met this ideal but surpassed other nonvegan waffles we've had. Ours owe their custardy interior in large part to a key ingredient: cornstarch. Without cornstarch, the waffles had an airy, hollow interior, while too much cornstarch yielded a dense and doughy interior. A moderate amount, however, produced a delicate yet pleasantly chewy, nearly soufflé-like texture—without eggs. To achieve a crisp, golden, slightly lacy exterior, we opted for coconut oil over vegetable oil, which yielded a tougher, chewier crust. We also found that a small amount of baking soda helped our butter- and dairy-free waffles brown like conventional versions. The final step in getting a golden, crisp crust was nailing the cooking time; we needed to cook our waffles for 5 to 6 minutes, significantly longer than for many other waffle recipes. We developed this recipe using our winning waffle maker, the Waring Pro Double Belgian Waffle Maker. While this waffle maker has an indicator light and an audible alert to tell you your waffle is done, we always suggest following the visual cues to determine doneness.

1 Heat waffle iron according to manufacturer's instructions. Adjust oven rack to middle position and heat oven to 200 degrees. Set wire rack in rimmed baking sheet and place in oven.

2 Whisk flour, cornstarch, sugar, baking powder, baking soda, and salt together in large bowl. Whisk soy milk, melted oil, lemon juice, and vanilla together in second bowl. Make well in center of flour mixture, add milk mixture to well, and gently whisk until just incorporated with few lumps remaining (do not overmix).

3 Spray preheated waffle iron with vegetable oil spray. Add scant 1 cup batter to waffle iron and cook according to manufacturer's instructions until crisp, firm, and golden, 5 to 6 minutes. Serve immediately or transfer to wire rack in oven. Repeat with remaining batter.

TESTING NOTES **Dairy-Free Milks**

OUR FAVORITE **Soy Milk**

OTHERS TESTED Coconut milk produces a paler waffle that is less sweet with a less custardy center. Oat milk makes sweeter waffles. Almond milk creates a chewier, more savory waffle.

Banana Bread
makes 1 loaf

2 cups (10 ounces) all-purpose flour

¾ cup (5¼ ounces) organic sugar (see page 31)

¾ teaspoon baking soda

½ teaspoon salt

½ cup walnuts, toasted and chopped coarse (optional)

3 ripe but firm large bananas (1¼ pounds), peeled

6 tablespoons vegetable oil

⅓ cup plain almond milk yogurt

1 tablespoon lemon juice

2 teaspoons vanilla extract

Why This Recipe Works Classic banana bread is cherished for its moist texture and deep banana flavor. Baking banana bread is often the project of thrifty cooks; recipes call for those overripe, darkly speckled bananas you forgot in the fruit bowl because of their moisture and high sugar content. (When left to sit, most of the starches in bananas convert to sugars.) But while developing a vegan version of this beloved treat, we found ourselves turning out loaf after loaf of dense, wet, and sticky banana breads—not the kind of moisture we had in mind. That's how we discovered something surprising: Ripe but firm bananas—those that look good enough to eat—are the best for vegan banana bread. Because just-ripe bananas are starchier, they contributed to a banana bread with a more open crumb and a structure so sturdy on its own that it didn't even require the addition of an egg substitute. And the just-ripe fruit still lent the requisite banana flavor in spades. The best part: You don't need to plan ahead by letting bananas sit on the counter for days before baking in order to prepare this stellar vegan quick bread. The test kitchen's preferred loaf pan measures 8½ by 4½ inches; if you use a 9 by 5-inch loaf pan, start checking for doneness 5 minutes earlier than advised in the recipe.

1 Adjust oven rack to lower-middle position and heat oven to 350 degrees. Grease 8½ by 4½-inch loaf pan. Whisk flour, sugar, baking soda, and salt together in large bowl. Stir in walnuts, if using; set aside.

2 Pulse bananas in food processor until mostly smooth, with some ½-inch lumps remaining, about 10 pulses. Add oil, almond milk yogurt, lemon juice, and vanilla and continue to pulse until well combined and only pea-size lumps of banana remain, about 4 pulses.

3 Gently fold milk mixture into flour mixture until just combined. Transfer batter to prepared pan and smooth top. Bake until top is firm and deep golden, about 1 hour, rotating pan halfway through baking.

4 Let bread cool in pan for 10 minutes. Remove bread from pan and let cool completely on wire rack, about 3 hours, before serving.

TESTING NOTES **Dairy-Free Yogurts**
OUR FAVORITE **Almond Milk Yogurt**
OTHERS TESTED Coconut milk yogurt yields moister banana bread with a slightly tighter crumb. Soy milk yogurt makes chewier, slightly wet banana bread with a distinct soy flavor.

Coffee Cake

serves 8 to 10

Why This Recipe Works With its rich flavor and warm spices, coffee cake is the most comforting of breakfast treats. A perfect one consists of two simple elements: a rich cake and a lightly spiced crumb topping. But most vegan coffee cakes we encountered were either dry and cottony or dense and sticky. We set out to make the ultimate vegan coffee cake—flavorful and tender yet with enough structure to support a nutty spiced topping. For simplicity and less cleanup, we used our food processor from start to finish to make both the nutty topping and the cake batter. Substituting vegan products for the dairy elements of the cake was easy, and after testing our way through a roster of vegan egg substitutes, we found that the best substitute was none at all! Our eggless coffee cake was tender, but it needed more lift. So to ensure a fluffy crumb and a cake that rose properly without eggs, we increased the leavener and liquid in our working recipe by a small amount. We also found that using both all-purpose flour and a hefty amount of whole-wheat flour gave our cake great structure and a rich, hearty flavor. A final trick: Letting the cake batter rest in the pan for just 15 minutes before sprinkling the streusel topping ensured that the cake rose properly under its weight (don't skip this step). A bit of melted coconut oil and water were the perfect binder for a nutty topping that crumbed perfectly into sturdy nuggets on top of our cake.

STREUSEL

½ cup pecans, toasted

¼ cup packed (1¾ ounces) organic brown sugar (see page 31)

⅓ cup (1⅔ ounces) all-purpose flour

½ teaspoon ground cinnamon

⅛ teaspoon salt

2 tablespoons coconut oil, melted and cooled (see page 30)

2 teaspoons water

CAKE

1¼ cups (6¼ ounces) all-purpose flour

1¼ cups (8¾ ounces) organic granulated sugar (see page 31)

¾ cup (4⅛ ounces) whole-wheat flour

1¼ teaspoons ground cinnamon

1¼ teaspoons baking powder

½ teaspoon baking soda

¾ teaspoon salt

6 tablespoons coconut oil, cut into 6 pieces (see page 30)

1¼ cups unsweetened almond milk

4 teaspoons lemon juice

1¼ teaspoons vanilla extract

1 FOR THE STREUSEL Adjust oven rack to lower-middle position and heat oven to 350 degrees. Grease 9-inch springform pan. Place pan on rimmed baking sheet. Process pecans and sugar in food processor until finely ground, about 10 seconds. Add flour, cinnamon, and salt and pulse to combine, about 5 pulses. Add melted oil and water and pulse until oil is fully incorporated and mixture begins to form clumps, 8 to 10 pulses. Transfer streusel to bowl. Using your fingers, break apart any large clumps (streusel should have fine, sandy texture); set aside.

2 FOR THE CAKE Process all-purpose flour, sugar, whole-wheat flour, cinnamon, baking powder, baking soda, and salt in clean, dry food processor until combined, about 10 seconds. Add oil and pulse until mixture resembles fine meal, five to eight 5-second pulses. Add almond milk, lemon juice, and vanilla; pulse until dry ingredients are moistened, 4 to 5 pulses. Scrape down sides of bowl. Continue to pulse until mixture is well combined, 4 to 5 pulses. Transfer batter to prepared pan and smooth top. Let batter rest for 15 minutes.

3 Starting at edges of pan, sprinkle streusel in even layer over batter, breaking apart any large clumps that may have formed. Bake on baking sheet until center is firm and skewer inserted into center comes out clean, 55 minutes to 1 hour. Transfer cake to wire rack and let cool in pan for 20 minutes. Remove sides of pan and let cake cool completely, about 3 hours. Slide offset spatula between cake and pan bottom and carefully slide cake onto platter. Cut into wedges with serrated knife and serve.

All-Morning Energy Bars

makes 10 bars

½ cup whole raw almonds

½ cup raw cashews

⅓ cup raw pepitas

¼ cup raw sunflower seeds

3 tablespoons whole golden flaxseeds (see page 16)

1 tablespoon sesame seeds

4½ ounces pitted dates, chopped (¾ cup)

¼ cup warm tap water

2 tablespoons maple syrup

½ teaspoon grated orange zest

½ teaspoon salt

Why This Recipe Works We wanted a tasty, nutritious breakfast bar that was easy to make and packed with protein—and without the list of processed ingredients found in store-bought options. A collection of toasted nuts and seeds gave our bars a roasted flavor, and a blitzed mix of dates and maple syrup helped hold them together. However, the bars still lacked cohesion. Grinding some of our flaxseeds in the recipe and adding water did the trick. We stirred chopped dates into the mixture for bursts of sweetness and added orange zest for aromatic depth. After baking the mixture in a pan, we cut it into bars, spread them on a baking sheet, and finished baking them. The result: evenly toasted bars with crunch and a slight chew. We prefer golden flaxseeds for their milder flavor, but brown flaxseeds can be used. Be sure not to overcook the nuts and seeds in step 2; they will continue to toast during baking.

1 Adjust oven rack to middle position and heat oven to 300 degrees. Make foil sling for 8-inch square baking pan by folding 2 long sheets of aluminum foil so each is 8 inches wide. Lay sheets of foil in pan perpendicular to each other, with extra foil hanging over edges of pan. Push foil into corners and up sides of pan, smoothing foil flush to pan. Grease foil.

2 Spread almonds, cashews, pepitas, sunflower seeds, 2 tablespoons flaxseeds, and sesame seeds on foil-lined rimmed baking sheet. Bake, stirring occasionally, until pale golden and fragrant, 15 to 20 minutes.

3 Meanwhile, grind remaining 1 tablespoon flaxseeds in spice grinder until finely ground, about 15 seconds. Transfer nut mixture to food processor, let cool slightly, then pulse until coarsely chopped, about 5 pulses; transfer to large bowl. Process ¼ cup dates, water, maple syrup, orange zest, salt, and ground flaxseeds in now-empty processor until smooth, scraping down sides of bowl as needed, about 30 seconds. Stir processed date mixture and remaining ½ cup chopped dates into nut mixture until well combined.

4 Transfer mixture to prepared pan and press firmly into even layer with greased metal spatula. Bake bars until light golden, about 20 minutes, rotating pan halfway through baking. Do not turn off oven.

5 Let bars cool in pan for 15 minutes. Using foil sling, remove bars from pan, transfer to cutting board, and cut into 10 bars. Space bars evenly on parchment paper–lined baking sheet and bake until golden brown, 15 to 20 minutes. Let bars cool completely on wire rack, about 1 hour. Serve. (Bars can be stored at room temperature for up to 1 week.)

Chia Pudding with Fresh Fruit and Coconut

serves 4

2 cups unsweetened soy milk, plus extra for serving

½ cup chia seeds

2 tablespoons maple syrup, plus extra for serving

1½ teaspoons vanilla extract

¼ teaspoon salt

2 cups (10 ounces) blueberries, raspberries, blackberries, or sliced strawberries, and/or sliced bananas

¼ cup flaked coconut, toasted

Why This Recipe Works Chia pudding comes together by what seems like Jack and the Beanstalk–level magic. When chia seeds are combined with liquid and left to soak overnight they create a gel, which thickens and produces a no-cook tapioca-like pudding—a spectacular alternative to the usual yogurt for breakfast. Pudding alchemy aside, chia is great because it's a nutritional powerhouse, packed with fiber, protein, and omega-3 fatty acids; plus, it has a neutral flavor that's the perfect canvas for fruity toppings. This recipe takes little effort, just time. We tried to cut back on that by scalding the milk to speed up the thickening process. And indeed we could: After just 15 minutes the pudding had thickened as much as it had after a cold overnight soak. But that speed came with downsides: a decidedly grassier, "seedier" flavor and the loss of the fresh, milky notes we enjoyed in the soaked pudding. So we stuck with the hands-off overnight method. Before we put it to bed for the night, we gave the pudding a quick second whisk 15 minutes after its initial mixing to make sure all the chia hydrated and to prevent clumping. To flavor the pudding, we kept things simple with vanilla extract and maple syrup, which pair nicely with almost any toppings you have at your breakfast table.

1 Whisk soy milk, chia seeds, maple syrup, vanilla, and salt together in bowl. Let mixture sit for 15 minutes, then whisk again to break up any clumps. Cover bowl with plastic wrap and refrigerate for at least 8 hours or up to 1 week.

2 Adjust consistency of pudding with additional soy milk as needed. Top individual portions of pudding with ½ cup fruit, 1 tablespoon coconut, and drizzle with maple syrup to taste before serving.

TESTING NOTES **Dairy-Free Milks**
OUR FAVORITE **Soy Milk**
OTHERS TESTED Almond milk makes the pudding taste slightly savory. Coconut milk makes a slightly bland pudding. Oat milk gives the pudding a brown color and a chalky texture.

Smoothies

serves 2

Why This Recipe Works Making a smoothie is easy, but we didn't want our vegan smoothies to just taste great—they had to be filling enough to call them breakfast, too. Our task would be determining how to add protein to fresh, bright-tasting shakes to keep us going. We chose three flavor profiles so we could regularly add smoothies to our weekday breakfast rotation. The sweet-tart mix of berries and bananas made a classic smoothie that pleased everyone. A feel-good "green" smoothie with kale and pineapple tasted great while also making us feel virtuous. And a smoothie with mango, pineapple, and banana transported us to a tropical island—a welcome destination first thing in the morning. For a creamy texture in our two fruit smoothies, we blended them with mild-flavored coconut milk yogurt. And for our green smoothie, rich, nutritious, and subtly sweet avocado fit the bill. We tried every protein add-in imaginable, from commonly used almond butter to the new and novel, like cannellini beans. We wanted something that packed a nutritional punch but wouldn't overwhelm the flavor of our smoothies. Unsurprisingly, the beans made our smoothies taste bland and starchy. Almond butter and wheat germ were good, but we ultimately came away with a favorite that worked with any flavor combination we threw at it, and it was a surprise: hemp seed hearts. The hulled center of the hemp seed, a soft, almost waxy nugget, blended beautifully into our drink, leaving just a trace of pleasantly grassy, sweet flavor. We like the neutral flavor and color of hemp seed hearts, but you can use 2 tablespoons almond butter or ¼ cup wheat germ in its place.

Mixed Berry Smoothie

10 ounces (2 cups) frozen blackberries, blueberries, and raspberries
 1 cup unsweetened plain coconut milk yogurt
 1 cup water
 1 ripe banana, peeled and halved lengthwise
 2 tablespoons maple syrup
 2 tablespoons hemp seed hearts
 ⅛ teaspoon salt

Combine all ingredients in blender. Process on low speed until mixture is combined but still coarse in texture, about 10 seconds. Increase speed to high and puree until completely smooth, about 1 minute.

Green Smoothie

Do not use frozen chopped kale for this recipe.

1 ounce (1 cup) baby kale
1 cup frozen pineapple chunks
1 cup water
1 ripe banana, peeled and halved lengthwise
½ cup pineapple juice
½ ripe avocado, pitted and cut into quarters
2 tablespoons hemp seed hearts
⅛ teaspoon salt

Combine all ingredients in blender. Process on low speed until mixture is combined but still coarse in texture, about 10 seconds. Increase speed to high and puree until completely smooth, about 1 minute.

Tropical Fruit Smoothie

2 ripe bananas, peeled and halved lengthwise
1 cup frozen mango chunks
1 cup frozen pineapple chunks
1 cup water
1 cup unsweetened coconut milk yogurt
2 tablespoons maple syrup
2 tablespoons hemp seed hearts
⅛ teaspoon salt

Combine all ingredients in blender. Process on low speed until mixture is combined but still coarse in texture, about 10 seconds. Increase speed to high and puree until completely smooth, about 1 minute.

TESTING NOTES **Dairy-Free Yogurts**
OUR FAVORITE **Coconut Milk Yogurt**
OTHERS TESTED Soy milk yogurt yields slightly bland-tasting smoothies. Almond milk yogurt yields tarter and thinner smoothies.

soups
stews
and
chilis

Chickpea Noodle Soup

serves 6

2 tablespoons vegetable oil
1 onion, chopped fine
3 carrots, peeled and sliced ¼ inch thick
2 celery ribs, sliced ¼ inch thick
Salt and pepper
3 tablespoons nutritional yeast
2 teaspoons minced fresh thyme or ¾ teaspoon dried
2 bay leaves
6 cups vegetable broth
2 (15-ounce) cans chickpeas, rinsed
2 ounces (½ cup) ditalini pasta
2 tablespoons minced fresh parsley

Why This Recipe Works We wanted a robust vegan spin on the ultimate comfort food: chicken noodle soup—one that anyone would be excited to make. Veganizing this classic sounded like a fruitless task—the best chicken soups have a deeply savory broth—but we actually found this one-pot dish flavorful and fast to make with a pantry-friendly combination of broth and noodles. To replace the chicken, we chose chickpeas; we liked the creamy texture, neutral flavor, and heartiness they added to the soup—and the fun phonetic similarity between the two ingredients certainly wasn't lost on us. To start, we sautéed onion, carrots, and celery to infuse our soup with flavor, but this broth still lacked the soul-satisfying comfort of chicken noodle. In efforts to capture the missed "meatiness," we tested various go-to vegan-friendly flavor enhancers ranging from miso paste to porcini powder before settling on a unanimous favorite, umami-packed nutritional yeast, a naturally occurring yeast that's heated to deactivate the leavening power that baker's yeast has. This seasoning is like savory magic dust: It has a deep nutty and almost tangy flavor that turned our soup from ordinary to one that reminded us of Grandma's soup. Simmering the chickpeas, sautéed aromatics, and broth together before adding the noodles fully developed the soup's flavor while also creating a creamy texture in the chickpeas. Lastly, in place of traditional egg noodles, we opted for ditalini pasta, a great choice for its spoon-friendly slurp-ability. We strongly prefer our favorite vegetable broths, Orrington Farms Vegan Chicken Broth or our homemade Vegetable Broth Base (page 21). (For more information on vegetable broth, see page 21.)

1 Heat oil in Dutch oven over medium heat until shimmering. Add onion, carrots, celery, and ¼ teaspoon pepper and cook, stirring occasionally, until softened, 5 to 7 minutes. Stir in nutritional yeast, thyme, and bay leaves and cook until fragrant, about 30 seconds.

2 Stir in broth and chickpeas and bring to boil. Reduce heat to medium-low and simmer, partially covered, until flavors meld, about 10 minutes.

3 Stir in pasta, increase heat to medium-high, and boil until just tender, about 10 minutes. Off heat, discard bay leaves and stir in parsley. Season with salt and pepper to taste, and serve.

Creamless Creamy Tomato Soup

serves 6 to 8

¼ cup extra-virgin olive oil,
plus extra for serving
1 onion, chopped fine
3 garlic cloves, minced
1 bay leaf
Pinch red pepper flakes
(optional)
2 (28-ounce) cans whole peeled
tomatoes
3 slices hearty white sandwich
bread, crusts removed, torn into
1-inch pieces
1 tablespoon packed organic
brown sugar (see page 31)
2 cups vegetable broth
2 tablespoons brandy (optional)
Salt and pepper
¼ cup minced fresh chives

Why This Recipe Works Creamy tomato soup is a rainy-day favorite, so we wondered if we could develop a comforting recipe with velvety smoothness and a bright tomato taste—without cream. Most recipes for tomato soup pack in so much of the stuff that they're more pink than red, which is fitting because missing too is rich, tangy tomato flavor. For our creamless vegan soup, we started with canned tomatoes for their convenience and year-round availability and added a touch of brown sugar to balance their acidity. The soup tasted good, but it seemed thin without the swirl of cream. Looking to give our soup luxurious body, we turned to a surprise ingredient: slices of white bread. Torn into pieces and added to the pot, the bread disintegrated and blended into the soup like magic, thickening it without muting the vibrant tomato flavor. Finally, a touch of fruity extra-virgin olive oil added some welcome richness. Make sure to purchase canned whole tomatoes in juice, not in puree. We strongly prefer our favorite vegetable broths, Orrington Farms Vegan Chicken Broth or our homemade Vegetable Broth Base (page 21). (For more information on vegetable broth, see page 21.) If half of the soup fills your blender by more than two-thirds, process the soup in three batches. For an even smoother soup, pass the pureed mixture through a fine-mesh strainer after blending it. Serve with Classic Croutons (page 82), if desired.

1 Heat 2 tablespoons oil in Dutch oven over medium-high heat until shimmering. Add onion, garlic, bay leaf, and pepper flakes, if using, and cook until onion is softened, about 5 minutes. Stir in tomatoes and their juice. Using potato masher, mash tomatoes until no pieces bigger than 2 inches remain. Stir in bread and sugar and bring to boil. Reduce heat to medium and cook, stirring occasionally, until bread is completely saturated and starts to break down, about 5 minutes. Discard bay leaf.

2 Transfer half of soup to blender. Add 1 tablespoon oil and process until soup is smooth and creamy, 2 to 3 minutes. Transfer to large bowl and repeat with remaining soup and remaining 1 tablespoon oil. Return pureed soup to clean pot.

3 Stir in broth and brandy, if using. Return soup to boil and season with salt and pepper to taste. Serve, sprinkling individual bowls with chives and drizzling with extra oil.

soups, stews, and chilis

Farmhouse Vegetable and Barley Soup

serves 6 to 8

Why This Recipe Works Vegetable and barley soup should be hearty and satisfying, with lots of vegetables accented by nutty, chewy grains of barley. We started by simmering leeks, carrots, and celery in a combination of wine and soy sauce until we had a potent aromatic backbone for our soup. Then we added the barley along with broth and water, dried porcini mushrooms for supersavory flavor, and herbs for freshness. As the barley softened, the mushrooms and herbs infused the broth with their respective flavors and the grain's starch contributed body. Next, we added more vegetables—chunks of Yukon Gold potatoes, turnip, and some cabbage provided substance. Once all the vegetables were tender, we stirred in some frozen peas, lemon juice, and parsley for a pop of bright flavor. We prefer an acidic, unoaked white wine such as Sauvignon Blanc for this recipe. We strongly prefer our favorite vegetable broths, Orrington Farms Vegan Chicken Broth or our homemade Vegetable Broth Base (page 21). (For more information on vegetable broth, see page 21.) Serve with Classic Croutons (recipe follows), if desired.

8 sprigs fresh parsley plus
   3 tablespoons chopped
4 sprigs fresh thyme
1 bay leaf
⅛ ounce dried porcini mushrooms
2 tablespoons vegetable oil
1½ pounds leeks, white and
   light green parts only, halved
   lengthwise, sliced ½ inch thick,
   and washed thoroughly
2 carrots, peeled and cut into
   ½-inch pieces
2 celery ribs, cut into ¼-inch pieces
⅓ cup dry white wine
2 teaspoons soy sauce
   Salt and pepper
6 cups water
4 cups vegetable broth
½ cup pearl barley
1 garlic clove, peeled and smashed
1½ pounds Yukon Gold potatoes,
   peeled and cut into ½-inch pieces
8 ounces turnip, peeled and cut
   into ¾-inch pieces
1½ cups chopped green cabbage
1 cup frozen peas
1 teaspoon lemon juice

1 Using kitchen twine, tie parsley sprigs, thyme sprigs, and bay leaf together. Grind porcini in spice grinder until finely ground.

2 Heat oil in Dutch oven over medium heat until shimmering. Add leeks, carrots, celery, wine, soy sauce, and 2 teaspoons salt. Cook, stirring occasionally, until liquid has evaporated and celery is softened, about 10 minutes. Stir in water, broth, barley, garlic, herb bundle, and ground porcini. Increase heat to high and bring to boil. Reduce heat to medium-low and simmer gently, partially covered, for 25 minutes.

3 Stir in potatoes, turnip, and cabbage and simmer until barley and vegetables are tender, 18 to 20 minutes. Off heat, discard herb bundle. Stir in peas, lemon juice, and chopped parsley. Season with salt and pepper to taste, and serve.

Classic Croutons makes about 5 cups
Either fresh or stale bread can be used in this recipe.

6 slices hearty white sandwich bread, cut into ½-inch cubes (6 cups)
3 tablespoons extra-virgin olive oil
   Salt and pepper

Adjust oven rack to middle position and heat oven to 350 degrees. Toss bread with oil, season with salt and pepper, and spread on rimmed baking sheet. Bake, stirring occasionally, until golden brown and crisp, 20 to 25 minutes. Let cool completely before serving. (Croutons can be stored at room temperature for up to 3 days.)

Super Greens Soup with Lemon-Tarragon Cream

serves 4 to 6

3 cups plus 1 tablespoon water

6 tablespoons dairy-free sour cream

2 tablespoons plus ½ teaspoon extra-virgin olive oil

½ teaspoon minced fresh tarragon

¼ teaspoon finely grated lemon zest plus ½ teaspoon juice
  Salt and pepper

1 onion, halved and sliced thin

¾ teaspoon organic brown sugar (page 31)

3 ounces white mushrooms, trimmed and sliced thin

2 garlic cloves, minced
  Pinch cayenne pepper

3 cups vegetable broth

⅓ cup Arborio rice

12 ounces Swiss chard, stemmed and chopped coarse

9 ounces kale, stemmed and chopped coarse

¼ cup fresh parsley leaves

2 ounces (2 cups) baby arugula

Why This Recipe Works We wanted a deceptively delicious, silky-smooth soup with deep, complex flavor that delivered a big dose of nutrient-packed greens. First, we built a flavorful foundation of sweet caramelized onions and earthy sautéed mushrooms. We added broth, water, and lots of greens (we liked a mix of chard, kale, arugula, and parsley for balance) and simmered them until tender before blending them. The flavor was great, but the soup was thin. Many recipes we found used potatoes as a thickener, but they lent an overwhelming earthy flavor. Instead, we tried Arborio rice with great success. The rice's high starch content thickened the soup to a velvety, lush consistency without clouding its vegetal flavors. For a vibrant finish, we whisked vegan sour cream with a little water, lemon zest, lemon juice, and tarragon and drizzled it over each serving. We prefer the flavor and consistency of Tofutti Better Than Sour Cream. Other dairy-free sour creams will add their distinctive flavor to the cream and you may need to adjust the consistency with additional water. We strongly prefer our favorite vegetable broths, Orrington Farms Vegan Chicken Broth or our homemade Vegetable Broth Base (page 21). (For more information on vegetable broth, see page 21.) Serve with Classic Croutons (page 82), if desired.

1 Combine 1 tablespoon water, dairy-free sour cream, ½ teaspoon oil, tarragon, and lemon zest and juice in bowl. Season with salt to taste, cover, and refrigerate until ready to serve.

2 Heat remaining 2 tablespoons oil in Dutch oven over medium-high heat until shimmering. Stir in onion, sugar, and 1 teaspoon salt and cook until onion releases some moisture, about 5 minutes. Reduce heat to low and cook, stirring often and scraping up any browned bits, until onion is deeply browned and slightly sticky, about 30 minutes. (If onion is sizzling or scorching, reduce heat. If onion is not browning after 20 minutes, increase heat.)

3 Stir in mushrooms and cook until they have released their moisture, about 5 minutes. Stir in garlic and cayenne and cook until fragrant, about 30 seconds. Stir in remaining 3 cups water, broth, and rice, scraping up any browned bits. Increase heat to high and bring to boil. Reduce heat to low, cover, and simmer for 15 minutes.

4 Stir in chard, kale, and parsley, 1 handful at a time, until wilted and submerged in liquid. Return to simmer, cover, and cook until greens are tender, about 10 minutes. Off heat, stir in arugula until wilted. Working in batches, process soup in blender until smooth, about 1 minute. Return pureed soup to clean pot and season with salt and pepper to taste. Serve, drizzling individual bowls with lemon-tarragon cream.

Creamy Curried Cauliflower Soup

serves 4 to 6

1 head cauliflower (2 pounds)
¼ cup extra-virgin olive oil, plus extra for serving
1 leek, white and light green parts only, halved lengthwise, sliced thin, and washed thoroughly
1 small onion, halved and sliced thin
    Salt
1½ tablespoons grated fresh ginger
1 tablespoon curry powder
4½ cups water
½ cup canned coconut milk
1 tablespoon lime juice
2 scallions, sliced thin on bias

Why This Recipe Works If you judged cauliflower by the typical soups it makes, you'd think it was a characterless white vegetable. That's because classic cauliflower soups are loaded with cream and thickened with flour. These soups are neither vegan nor very appealing. We wanted a vegan cauliflower soup with a creamy texture without the addition of ingredients that would dull the vegetable's flavor, which is delicate, nutty, and sweet on its own. We found that cauliflower easily blends into a velvety puree because it's extremely low in insoluble fiber, the type of fiber in vegetables that doesn't readily break down. Great—no cream needed. We added the cauliflower to simmering water in two stages to bring out the grassy flavor of just-cooked cauliflower and the sweeter, nuttier flavor of longer-cooked cauliflower in our soup. A modest amount of curry powder, sautéed onion, and leek gave our soup a delicious flavor profile. To complement the curry, we stirred in ½ cup of canned coconut milk—just enough to add some flair—and a touch of lime juice. Finally, we browned cauliflower florets to use as a flavorful garnish. Be sure to thoroughly trim the cauliflower's core of green leaves and leaf stems, which can be fibrous and can contribute to a grainy texture in the soup.

1 Pull off outer leaves of cauliflower and trim stem. Using paring knife, cut around core to remove; slice core thin and reserve. Cut heaping 1 cup of ½-inch florets from head of cauliflower; set aside. Cut remaining cauliflower crosswise into ½-inch-thick slices.

2 Heat 3 tablespoons oil in large saucepan over medium-low heat until shimmering. Add leek, onion, and 1½ teaspoons salt and cook, stirring often, until leek and onion are softened but not browned, about 7 minutes. Stir in ginger and curry powder and cook until fragrant, about 30 seconds. Stir in water, sliced core, and half of sliced cauliflower. Increase heat to medium-high and bring to simmer. Reduce heat to medium-low and simmer gently for 15 minutes. Add remaining sliced cauliflower and simmer until cauliflower is tender and crumbles easily, 15 to 20 minutes.

3 Meanwhile, heat remaining 1 tablespoon oil in 8-inch skillet over medium heat until shimmering. Add reserved florets and cook, stirring often, until golden brown, 6 to 8 minutes; transfer to bowl and season with salt to taste.

4 Working in batches, process soup in blender until smooth, about 45 seconds. Return pureed soup to clean pot and bring to brief simmer over medium heat. Off heat, stir in coconut milk and lime juice and season with salt to taste. Serve, sprinkling individual bowls with browned florets and scallions and drizzling with extra oil.

Roasted Eggplant and Tomato Soup

serves 4 to 6

2 pounds eggplant, cut into
½-inch pieces

6 tablespoons extra-virgin olive oil,
plus extra for serving

1 onion, chopped
Salt and pepper

2 garlic cloves, minced

1½ teaspoons ras el hanout

½ teaspoon ground cumin

4 cups vegetable broth, plus extra
as needed

1 (14.5-ounce) can diced
tomatoes, drained

¼ cup raisins

1 bay leaf

2 teaspoons lemon juice

2 tablespoons slivered almonds,
toasted

2 tablespoons minced fresh
cilantro

Why This Recipe Works Eggplant is rich, meaty, and hearty—perfect for a vegan soup. Taking inspiration from the many eastern Mediterranean dishes that pair eggplant with tomato, we developed a supersatisfying soup in which we puree the eggplant and tomato for a wonderfully creamy and hefty base. We found we could skip the common prep task of salting, rinsing, and drying the eggplant before cooking since we would be pureeing it. We left the skin on for deeper eggplant flavor, diced the eggplant, and broiled it to develop some smoky char. To build our soup, we started with the usual aromatics—onion and garlic—and added the flavorful North African warm spice blend *ras el hanout* (plus some extra cumin), which gave the soup a complexly spiced base. Looking to obtain a subtle sweetness without the cloying addition of sugar, we added ¼ cup of earthy raisins, which, once pureed, also gave our soup body. And we reserved some eggplant to add to the pureed soup for a pleasantly chunky texture. Lemon juice provided brightness, a sprinkling of almonds contributed a pleasant crunch, and cilantro added freshness. We strongly prefer our favorite vegetable broths, Orrington Farms Vegan Chicken Broth or our homemade Vegetable Broth Base (page 21). (For more information on vegetable broth, see page 21.)

1 Adjust oven rack 4 inches from broiler element and heat broiler. Toss eggplant with 5 tablespoons oil, then spread on aluminum foil–lined rimmed baking sheet. Broil eggplant for 10 minutes. Stir eggplant and continue to broil until mahogany brown, 5 to 7 minutes; let cool on baking sheet. Set aside 2 cups eggplant.

2 Heat remaining 1 tablespoon oil in large saucepan over medium heat until shimmering. Add onion, ¾ teaspoon salt, and ¼ teaspoon pepper and cook until onion is softened and lightly browned, 5 to 7 minutes. Stir in garlic, ras el hanout, and cumin and cook until fragrant, about 30 seconds. Stir in broth, tomatoes, raisins, bay leaf, and remaining eggplant and bring to simmer. Reduce heat to low, cover, and simmer gently until eggplant is softened, about 20 minutes.

3 Discard bay leaf. Working in batches, process soup in blender until smooth, about 2 minutes. Return soup to clean saucepan and stir in reserved 2 cups eggplant. Heat soup gently over low heat until hot and adjust consistency with extra hot broth as needed. Stir in lemon juice and season with salt and pepper to taste. Serve, sprinkling individual bowls with almonds and cilantro and drizzling with extra oil.

soups, stews, and chilis

Classic Gazpacho

serves 8 to 10

1½ pounds tomatoes, cored and cut into ¼-inch pieces

2 red bell peppers, stemmed, seeded, and cut into ¼-inch pieces

2 small cucumbers, 1 cucumber peeled, both sliced lengthwise, seeded, and cut into ¼-inch pieces

½ small sweet onion, chopped fine, or 2 large shallots, minced

⅓ cup sherry vinegar

2 garlic cloves, minced
Salt and pepper

5 cups tomato juice

8 ice cubes

1 teaspoon hot sauce (optional)
Extra-virgin olive oil

Why This Recipe Works A good gazpacho is perfect summer weather fare that should showcase the brightness of fresh vegetables, yet many recipes turn out bland, thin soups that aren't worth eating, no matter how hot the kitchen is. We wanted to develop a foolproof recipe with distinct vegetables in a bright tomato broth. We started by chopping the vegetables by hand, which ensured they retained their color and firm texture. Letting them sit briefly in a sherry vinegar marinade guaranteed well-seasoned vegetables, while a combination of tomato juice and ice cubes (which helped chill the soup) provided the right amount of liquid. Chilling our soup for a minimum of 4 hours was critical to allow the flavors to develop and meld. Use a Vidalia, Maui, or Walla Walla onion here. This recipe makes a large quantity because the leftovers are so good, but it can be halved if you prefer. Traditionally, diners garnish their gazpacho with more of the same diced vegetables that are in the soup, so cut some extra vegetables when you prepare those called for in the recipe. You can also serve the soup with Classic Croutons (page 82), chopped pitted black olives, and finely diced avocados, if desired. Serve in chilled bowls.

1 Combine tomatoes, bell peppers, cucumbers, onion, vinegar, garlic, and 2 teaspoons salt in large (at least 4-quart) bowl and season with pepper to taste. Let stand until vegetables just begin to release their juices, about 5 minutes.

2 Stir in tomato juice, ice cubes, and hot sauce, if using. Cover and refrigerate to let flavors blend, at least 4 hours or up to 2 days.

3 Discard any unmelted ice cubes and season with salt and pepper to taste. Serve cold, drizzling individual bowls with oil.

VARIATION
Spicy Gazpacho with Chipotle Chile and Lime
For a less spicy soup, reduce the amount of chipotles. We recommend garnishing bowls of this spicy soup with finely diced avocado.

Omit hot sauce. Add 2 tablespoons minced fresh cilantro, 1 tablespoon minced canned chipotle chile in adobo sauce, and 2 teaspoons grated lime zest plus 6 tablespoons juice (3 limes) with tomato juice and ice cubes.

Tortilla Soup

serves 6 to 8

8 (6-inch) corn tortillas, cut into
½-inch-wide strips

3 tablespoons vegetable oil
Salt and pepper

2 tomatoes, cored and quartered

1 large white onion, quartered

½ jalapeño chile, stemmed,
seeded, and quartered

4 garlic cloves, peeled

1 tablespoon minced canned
chipotle chile in adobe sauce

8 cups vegetable broth

2 (15-ounce) cans black beans,
rinsed

8 sprigs fresh cilantro

1 sprig fresh oregano

Why This Recipe Works Chicken may seem integral to the classic tortilla soup (known in Mexico as *sopa Azteca*), but when we consider what makes this soup so special, we think of its light and clean-tasting yet deeply flavorful broth. By breaking down tortilla soup into its three main components—the flavor base (tomatoes, garlic, onion, and chiles), the stock, and the garnishes (including fried tortilla strips)—we found that we could devise techniques and substitute ingredients to make a compelling vegan version. Typically, the vegetables are charred on a *comal* (griddle) and then pureed and fried. To simplify this, we made a puree from smoky chipotles in adobe sauce, tomatoes, onion, garlic, and jalapeño and then fried the puree in a small amount of oil in the pot. We then added vegetable broth along with cilantro and oregano sprigs (a substitute for the Mexican herb epazote). Instead of the traditional chicken, we used black beans, which added heartiness without taking away from the shining star of this soup—our robust broth. Finally, for the garnish, we oven-toasted lightly oiled tortilla strips instead of frying them. For a spicier soup, reserve, mince, and add the ribs and seeds from the jalapeño. We strongly prefer our favorite vegetable broths, Orrington Farms Vegan Chicken Broth or our homemade Vegetable Broth Base (page 21). (For more information on vegetable broth, see page 21.) Serve with diced avocado, chopped fresh cilantro, and lime wedges, if desired.

1 Adjust oven rack to middle position and heat oven to 425 degrees. Toss tortilla strips with 1 tablespoon oil, spread on rimmed baking sheet, and bake, stirring occasionally, until deep golden brown and crisp, 8 to 12 minutes. Season lightly with salt and transfer to paper towel–lined plate.

2 Meanwhile, process tomatoes, onion, jalapeño, garlic, and chipotle in food processor until smooth, about 30 seconds, scraping down sides of bowl as needed. Heat remaining 2 tablespoons oil in Dutch oven over medium heat until shimmering. Add pureed tomato mixture and ⅛ teaspoon salt and cook, stirring frequently, until mixture has darkened in color and liquid has evaporated, about 10 minutes.

3 Stir in broth, beans, cilantro sprigs, and oregano sprig, scraping up any browned bits, and bring to simmer. Cook until flavors meld, about 20 minutes.

4 Off heat, remove herb sprigs and season with salt and pepper to taste. Place some tortilla strips in bottom of individual bowls and ladle soup over top. Serve, passing remaining tortilla strips separately.

soups, stews, and chilis

93

Turkish Tomato, Bulgur, and Red Pepper Soup

serves 6 to 8

2 tablespoons extra-virgin olive oil

2 red bell peppers, stemmed, seeded, and chopped

1 onion, chopped
Salt and pepper

3 garlic cloves, minced

1 teaspoon dried mint, crumbled

½ teaspoon smoked paprika

⅛ teaspoon red pepper flakes

1 tablespoon tomato paste

½ cup dry white wine

1 (28-ounce) can diced fire-roasted tomatoes

4 cups vegetable broth

2 cups water

¾ cup medium-grind bulgur, rinsed

⅓ cup chopped fresh mint

Why This Recipe Works In addition to being deeply flavorful, many soups hailing from the Mediterranean and Middle East are particularly intriguing because they are enriched with filling, good-for-you grains—perfect for a vegan dinner. We're particularly fond of this Turkish tomato and red pepper soup that incorporates bulgur. We started by softening the red peppers and onion before creating a solid flavor backbone with garlic, tomato paste, white wine, dried mint, smoked paprika, and red pepper flakes. For additional smokiness, canned fire-roasted tomatoes did the trick. When stirred into the soup, the bulgur absorbed the surrounding flavors and gave off starch that created a silky texture. Since bulgur is so quick-cooking, we stirred it in toward the end, giving it just enough time to become tender. A sprinkle of fresh mint gave the soup a final punch of flavor. When shopping, don't confuse bulgur with cracked wheat, which has a much longer cooking time and will not work in this recipe. We strongly prefer our favorite vegetable broths, Orrington Farms Vegan Chicken Broth or our homemade Vegetable Broth Base (page 21). (For more information on vegetable broth, see page 21.)

1 Heat oil in Dutch oven over medium heat until shimmering. Add bell peppers, onion, ¾ teaspoon salt, and ¼ teaspoon pepper and cook until vegetables are softened and lightly browned, 6 to 8 minutes. Stir in garlic, dried mint, paprika, and pepper flakes and cook until fragrant, about 30 seconds. Stir in tomato paste and cook for 1 minute.

2 Stir in wine, scraping up any browned bits, and simmer until reduced by half, about 1 minute. Add tomatoes and their juice and cook, stirring occasionally, until tomatoes soften and begin to break apart, about 10 minutes.

3 Stir in broth, water, and bulgur and bring to simmer. Reduce heat to low, cover, and simmer gently until bulgur is tender, about 20 minutes. Season with salt and pepper to taste. Serve, sprinkling individual bowls with mint.

soups, stews, and chilis

Red Lentil Soup with North African Spices

serves 4 to 6

¼ cup extra-virgin olive oil
1 large onion, chopped fine
   Salt and pepper
¾ teaspoon ground coriander
½ teaspoon ground cumin
¼ teaspoon ground ginger
⅛ teaspoon ground cinnamon
   Pinch cayenne pepper
1 tablespoon tomato paste
1 garlic clove, minced
4 cups vegetable broth, plus extra
   as needed
2 cups water
10½ ounces (1½ cups) red lentils,
   picked over and rinsed
2 tablespoons lemon juice,
   plus extra for seasoning
1½ teaspoons dried mint, crumbled
1 teaspoon paprika
¼ cup chopped fresh cilantro

Why This Recipe Works While every lentil variety has unique characteristics, small red lentils are in a league of their own. Unlike firmer brown and green lentils, red lentils don't hold their shape when cooked, and they break down quickly into a creamy thick puree in hearty, satisfying soups. Their mild flavor is pleasant but does require a bit of embellishment, so we created a soup with a North African flavor profile, sautéing onion in olive oil and using the warm mixture to bloom fragrant coriander, cumin, ginger, cinnamon, and cayenne pepper. Tomato paste and garlic completed the base before the addition of the lentils, and a mix of broth and water gave the soup a full, rounded character. After only 15 minutes of cooking, the lentils were soft enough to be pureed—and with just a whisk. A generous dose of lemon juice brought the flavors into focus, and a drizzle of spice-infused oil and a sprinkle of fresh cilantro completed the transformation of commonplace ingredients into a lively yet comforting soup. We strongly prefer our favorite vegetable broths, Orrington Farms Vegan Chicken Broth or our homemade Vegetable Broth Base (page 21). (For more information on vegetable broth, see page 21.)

1 Heat 2 tablespoons oil in large saucepan over medium heat until shimmering. Add onion and ½ teaspoon salt and cook, stirring occasionally, until softened, about 5 minutes. Stir in coriander, cumin, ginger, cinnamon, ¼ teaspoon pepper, and cayenne and cook until fragrant, about 2 minutes. Stir in tomato paste and garlic and cook for 1 minute.

2 Stir in broth, water, and lentils and bring to vigorous simmer. Cook, stirring occasionally, until lentils are soft and about half are broken down, about 15 minutes.

3 Whisk soup vigorously until broken down to coarse puree, about 30 seconds. Adjust consistency with extra hot broth as needed. Stir in lemon juice and season with salt and extra lemon juice to taste. Cover and keep warm.

4 Heat remaining 2 tablespoons oil in small skillet over medium heat until shimmering. Off heat, stir in mint and paprika. Serve, drizzling individual bowls with 1 teaspoon spiced oil and sprinkling with cilantro.

Thai Coconut Soup with Tofu

serves 8

1 tablespoon vegetable oil

4 ounces shiitake mushrooms, stemmed and cut into ½-inch pieces

1–2 stalks lemon grass, trimmed to bottom 6 inches and minced (3 tablespoons)

2 tablespoons minced fresh ginger

1 garlic clove, minced

4 teaspoons Thai red curry paste

6 cups vegetable broth

3 tablespoons fish sauce substitute (see page 21)

1 tablespoon organic sugar (see page 31)

2 (14-ounce) cans coconut milk

14 ounces extra-firm tofu, cut into ½-inch pieces

6 ounces snow peas, strings removed, cut into ½-inch pieces

3 tablespoons lime juice (2 limes)
Salt and pepper

½ cup fresh cilantro leaves

3 scallions, green parts only, sliced thin on bias
Lime wedges

Why This Recipe Works Thai coconut soup is velvety and rich with a coconut flavor that's balanced by aromatic heat and fresh-tasting add-ins. As in many Southeast Asian dishes, a lively contrast of ingredients and flavors is essential: Fragrant lemon grass, pungent fish sauce (in this case, fish sauce substitute), fiery chiles, tart citrus juice, peppery ginger, sharp garlic, and aromatic herbs combine to create a tantalizing dish. While chicken is traditionally used to bulk up this soup, we opted for tofu along with meaty shiitake mushrooms and crunchy snow peas. Thai curry paste, which packs a spicy (and convenient) punch along with floral, fruity flavors, was a good stand-in for hard-to-locate tiny Thai chiles. We sautéed the shiitake mushrooms at the start along with the aromatics to deeply infuse the soup with their flavor, and we waited until the last 5 minutes of cooking to heat the tofu and snow peas through and maintain their delicate texture. With a final garnish of cilantro leaves, sliced scallion greens, and lime wedges, this soup was ready to serve. Not all brands of red curry paste are vegan, so read labels carefully. We strongly prefer our favorite vegetable broths, Orrington Farms Vegan Chicken Broth or our home-made Vegetable Broth Base (page 21). (For more information on vegetable broth, see page 21.)

1 Heat oil in Dutch oven over medium heat until shimmering. Add mushrooms, lemon grass, ginger, and garlic and cook, stirring constantly, until fragrant, about 30 seconds. Add curry paste and cook, stirring constantly, until fragrant, about 30 seconds. Whisk ½ cup broth into pot, scraping up any browned bits and smoothing out any lumps.

2 Stir in remaining 5½ cups broth, fish sauce substitute, and sugar and bring to boil. Reduce heat to low and simmer, partially covered, for 20 minutes.

3 Stir in coconut milk, tofu, snow peas, and lime juice and bring to simmer. Cook until tofu is warmed through and snow peas are just tender, about 5 minutes. Season with salt and pepper to taste, and serve with cilantro, scallions, and lime wedges.

Quinoa and Vegetable Stew

serves 6 to 8

2 tablespoons vegetable oil

1 onion, chopped

1 red bell pepper, stemmed, seeded, and cut into ½-inch pieces

5 garlic cloves, minced

1 tablespoon paprika

2 teaspoons ground coriander

1½ teaspoons ground cumin

6 cups vegetable broth

1 pound red potatoes, unpeeled and cut into ½-inch pieces

1 cup prewashed white quinoa

1 cup fresh or frozen corn

2 tomatoes, cored and chopped coarse

1 cup frozen peas
  Salt and pepper

1 avocado, halved, pitted, and diced

½ cup minced fresh cilantro

Why This Recipe Works Quinoa stews are common in many South American regions, and we loved the idea of making protein-packed quinoa the star of a hearty stew. But authentic recipes for this stew call for obscure ingredients, such as annatto powder or Peruvian varieties of potatoes and corn. We set out to make a traditional quinoa stew with an easy-to-navigate ingredient list. We found that paprika has a similar flavor profile to annatto powder; we rounded it out with cumin and coriander. Red bell pepper, tomatoes, red potatoes, sweet corn, and frozen peas were a nice mix of vegetables. We added the quinoa after the potatoes had softened and cooked it until it released starch to help give body to the stew. Finally, we added some traditional garnishes: avocado and cilantro. We like the convenience of prewashed quinoa. If you buy unwashed quinoa (or if you are unsure whether it's washed), be sure to rinse it before cooking to remove its bitter protective coating (called saponin). We strongly prefer our favorite vegetable broths, Orrington Farms Vegan Chicken Broth or our homemade Vegetable Broth Base (page 21). (For more information on vegetable broth, see page 21.) This stew tends to thicken as it sits; add additional warm vegetable broth as needed before serving to loosen. Do not omit the garnishes; they are important to the flavor of the stew.

1 Heat oil in Dutch oven over medium heat until shimmering. Add onion and bell pepper and cook until softened, 5 to 7 minutes. Stir in garlic, paprika, coriander, and cumin and cook until fragrant, about 30 seconds. Stir in broth and potatoes and bring to boil over high heat. Reduce heat to medium-low and simmer gently for 10 minutes.

2 Stir in quinoa and simmer for 8 minutes. Stir in corn and simmer until potatoes and quinoa are just tender, 5 to 7 minutes. Stir in tomatoes and peas and simmer until heated through, about 2 minutes.

3 Off heat, season with salt and pepper to taste. Serve, sprinkling individual bowls with avocado and cilantro.

Mushroom and Farro Stew

serves 4

3½ cups vegetable broth
1½ cups farro
   Salt and pepper
1 pound portobello mushroom caps, halved and sliced ½ inch wide
18 ounces assorted mushrooms, trimmed and halved if small or quartered if large
2 tablespoons extra-virgin olive oil
1 onion, chopped fine
½ ounce dried porcini mushrooms, rinsed and minced
3 garlic cloves, minced
1 teaspoon minced fresh thyme or ¼ teaspoon dried
¼ cup dry Madeira
1 (14.5-ounce) can diced tomatoes, drained and chopped
2 tablespoons minced fresh parsley

Why This Recipe Works A mushroom ragout is a rich, intensely flavorful stew made with a variety of exotic wild mushrooms. We wanted a recipe for a simple ragout with great savory flavor. Meaty, substantial portobellos plus a mix of assorted mushrooms gave the dish balanced mushroom flavor. A small amount of dried porcini added even more complexity. To make our ragout hearty enough to be dinner, we wanted to include a grain in addition to the meaty mushrooms. Delicate quinoa disappeared next to the big bites of mushrooms, and wheat berries took too long to cook, but farro was a hit: Its nutty flavor and chewy texture complemented the mushrooms nicely. Tomatoes and a splash of dry Madeira wine cut through the richness. For the best flavor, we prefer to use a combination of white, shiitake, and oyster mushrooms; however, you can choose just one or two varieties if you like. The woody stems of shiitakes are unpleasant to eat so be sure to remove them. Drizzle individual portions with good balsamic vinegar before serving, if desired. We strongly prefer our favorite vegetable broths, Orrington Farms Vegan Chicken Broth or our homemade Vegetable Broth Base (page 21). (For more information on vegetable broth, see page 21.)

1 Bring broth and farro to simmer in large saucepan and cook until farro is tender and creamy, 20 to 25 minutes. Season with salt and pepper to taste; cover and keep warm.

2 Meanwhile, combine portobellos and assorted mushrooms in covered bowl and microwave until tender, 6 to 8 minutes. Drain, reserving mushroom juices.

3 Heat oil in Dutch oven over medium-high heat until shimmering. Add onion and dried porcini mushrooms and cook until softened and lightly browned, 5 to 7 minutes. Stir in drained mushrooms and cook, stirring often, until mushrooms are lightly browned, about 5 minutes.

4 Stir in garlic and thyme and cook until fragrant, about 30 seconds. Stir in Madeira and reserved mushroom juices, scraping up any browned bits. Stir in tomatoes and simmer gently until sauce is thickened slightly, about 8 minutes.

5 Off heat, stir in parsley and season with salt and pepper to taste. Serve, topping individual bowls of farro with mushroom mixture.

Ultimate Vegan Chili

serves 6 to 8

Salt

1 pound (2½ cups) assorted dried beans, picked over and rinsed

2 dried ancho chiles

2 dried New Mexican chiles

½ ounce dried shiitake mushrooms, chopped coarse

4 teaspoons dried oregano

½ cup walnuts, toasted

1 (28-ounce) can diced tomatoes, drained with juice reserved

3 tablespoons tomato paste

1–2 jalapeño chiles, stemmed and chopped coarse

3 tablespoons soy sauce

6 garlic cloves, minced

¼ cup vegetable oil

2 pounds onions, chopped fine

1 tablespoon ground cumin

⅔ cup medium-grind bulgur

¼ cup minced fresh cilantro

Why This Recipe Works We wanted to develop a vegan version of classic chili so satisfying that meat lovers would enjoy it. We'd need to find replacements for the different ways that meat adds depth. Along with two kinds of beans, bulgur bulked up the chili. A combination of umami-rich ingredients—soy sauce, dried shiitake mushrooms, and tomatoes—added deep, savory flavor. Walnuts are also high in flavor-boosting glutamates; when we ground some and stirred them in, they contributed richness and body. For the chiles, we chose a combination of dried ancho and New Mexican chiles, toasted them in the oven until fragrant, and then ground them and added them in. To substitute chili powder for the dried chiles, grind the shiitakes and oregano and add them to the pot with ¼ cup of chili powder in step 4. We recommend a mix of at least two types of beans, one creamy (such as cannellini or navy) and one earthy (such as pinto, black, or red kidney). When shopping, don't confuse bulgur with cracked wheat, which has a much longer cooking time and will not work in this recipe. For a spicier chili, use both jalapeños. Serve the chili with lime wedges, dairy-free sour cream, diced avocado, and chopped red onion, if desired.

1 Dissolve 3 tablespoons salt in 4 quarts cold water in large container. Add beans and soak at room temperature for at least 8 hours or up to 24 hours. Drain and rinse well.

2 Adjust oven rack to middle position and heat oven to 300 degrees. Spread anchos and New Mexican chiles on rimmed baking sheet and toast until fragrant and puffed, about 8 minutes. Transfer to plate, let cool for 5 minutes, then remove stems and seeds. Working in batches, grind toasted chiles, mushrooms, and oregano in spice grinder until finely ground.

3 Process walnuts in food processor until finely ground, about 30 seconds; transfer to bowl. Process tomatoes, tomato paste, jalapeño(s), soy sauce, and garlic in food processor until tomatoes are finely chopped, about 45 seconds.

4 Heat oil in Dutch oven over medium-high heat until shimmering. Add onions and 1¼ teaspoons salt and cook, stirring occasionally, until onions begin to brown, 8 to 10 minutes. Reduce heat to medium, stir in ground chile mixture and cumin, and cook, stirring constantly, until fragrant, about 1 minute. Stir in beans and 7 cups water and bring to boil. Cover pot, transfer to oven, and cook for 45 minutes.

5 Stir in bulgur, walnuts, tomato mixture, and reserved tomato juice. Continue to cook, covered, until beans are fully tender, about 2 hours. Remove pot from oven, stir well, and let stand, uncovered, for 20 minutes. Stir in cilantro before serving.

Roasted Poblano and White Bean Chili

serves 4 to 6

5 poblano chiles, halved lengthwise, stemmed, and seeded
3 Anaheim chiles, halved lengthwise, stemmed, and seeded
3 tablespoons vegetable oil
3 ears corn, kernels cut from cobs and cobs reserved
2 onions, cut into large pieces
2 jalapeño chiles, stemmed, seeded, and chopped
2 (15-ounce) cans cannellini beans, rinsed
4 cups vegetable broth
6 garlic cloves, minced
1 tablespoon tomato paste
1 tablespoon ground cumin
1½ teaspoons ground coriander
Salt and pepper
1 (15-ounce) can pinto beans, rinsed
4 scallions, green parts only, sliced thin
¼ cup minced fresh cilantro
1 tablespoon lime juice

Why This Recipe Works Fresh chiles take center stage in white bean chili. A trio of poblanos, Anaheims, and jalapeños provided the complexity we were looking for. We broiled the poblanos and Anaheims to develop depth and smokiness and kept the jalapeño flavor bright by simply sautéeing them. Processing some of the roasted peppers with a portion of the beans and broth thickened the chili. For a spicier chili, reserve, mince, and add the ribs and seeds from the chiles. If you can't find Anaheim chiles, add two extra poblanos and one extra jalapeño. We strongly prefer our favorite vegetable broths, Orrington Farms Vegan Chicken Broth or our homemade Vegetable Broth Base (page 21). (For more information on vegetable broth, see page 21.) Serve with dairy-free sour cream, tortilla chips, and lime wedges, if desired.

1 Adjust oven rack 6 inches from broiler element and heat broiler. Toss poblanos and Anaheims with 1 tablespoon oil and spread, skin side up, on aluminum foil–lined rimmed baking sheet. Broil until chiles begin to blacken and soften, about 10 minutes, rotating pan halfway through broiling. Transfer broiled chiles to bowl, cover with plastic wrap, and let steam until skins peel off easily, 10 to 15 minutes. Peel poblanos and Anaheims, then cut into ½-inch pieces, reserving any accumulated juice.

2 Meanwhile, toss corn kernels with 1 tablespoon oil, spread evenly on foil-lined baking sheet, and broil, stirring occasionally, until beginning to brown, 5 to 10 minutes; let cool on baking sheet.

3 Pulse onions and jalapeños in food processor to consistency of chunky salsa, 6 to 8 pulses; transfer to bowl. In now-empty food processor, process 1 cup cannellini beans, 1 cup broth, and ½ cup chopped roasted chiles and any accumulated juice until smooth, about 45 seconds.

4 Heat remaining 1 tablespoon oil in Dutch oven over medium heat until shimmering. Add onion-jalapeño mixture and cook until softened, 5 to 7 minutes. Stir in garlic, tomato paste, cumin, coriander, and ½ teaspoon salt and cook until tomato paste begins to darken, about 2 minutes. Stir in remaining 3 cups broth, scraping up any browned bits. Stir in pureed chile-bean mixture, remaining roasted chiles, remaining cannellini beans, pinto beans, and corn cobs. Bring to simmer, then reduce heat to low and simmer gently until thickened and flavorful, about 40 minutes.

5 Discard corn cobs. Stir in broiled corn kernels and let heat through, about 1 minute. Off heat, stir in scallions, cilantro, and lime juice and season with salt and pepper to taste. Serve.

Butternut Squash Chili with Quinoa and Peanuts

serves 6

Why This Recipe Works This stick-to-your-ribs African-style butternut squash chili features bold spices, a hefty amount of garlic and ginger, and aromatic coconut milk. It gets its silky body from a combination of blended peanuts and squash, which we roasted with chopped onions until both the squash and the onions started to char around the edges, giving the soup incredible flavor. We pureed a portion of the roasted vegetables with the dry-roasted peanuts for a rich, smooth base to our soup. We sautéed sweet bell pepper and spicy jalapeño and briefly bloomed the warm spices before adding in the liquid. A combination of diced tomatoes and coconut milk made a creamy but bright broth, and nutty quinoa added heartiness and a subtle pop of texture. If you buy unwashed quinoa (or if you are unsure whether it's washed), be sure to rinse it before cooking to remove its bitter protective coating (called saponin). For more spice, include the ribs and seeds from the jalapeño. Serve with hot sauce.

3 pounds butternut squash, peeled, seeded, and cut into ½-inch pieces (9 cups)

2 onions, cut into ½-inch pieces

6 tablespoons vegetable oil
Salt and pepper

5 cups water, plus extra as needed

¾ cup dry-roasted salted peanuts, chopped

1 large red bell pepper, stemmed, seeded, and cut into ½-inch pieces

1 jalapeño chile, stemmed, seeded, and minced

2 tablespoons grated fresh ginger

3 garlic cloves, minced

¾ teaspoon ground cinnamon

¾ teaspoon ground coriander

½ teaspoon cayenne pepper

1 (14.5-ounce) can diced tomatoes

1 (14-ounce) can coconut milk

1 cup prewashed white quinoa

¼ cup minced fresh cilantro or parsley

1 Adjust oven racks to upper-middle and lower-middle positions and heat oven to 450 degrees. Toss squash, onions, ¼ cup oil, 1 teaspoon salt, and ½ teaspoon pepper together in bowl. Spread vegetables in even layer over 2 rimmed baking sheets. Roast vegetables, stirring occasionally, until tender, 45 to 50 minutes, switching and rotating sheets halfway through roasting.

2 Process ½ cup roasted vegetables, 2 cups water, and ¼ cup peanuts in food processor until smooth, about 1 minute.

3 Heat remaining 2 tablespoons oil in Dutch oven over medium-high heat until shimmering. Add bell pepper, jalapeño, and 2 teaspoons salt and cook until peppers start to soften, about 5 minutes. Stir in ginger, garlic, cinnamon, coriander, cayenne, and ¾ teaspoon pepper and cook until fragrant, about 30 seconds.

4 Stir in tomatoes and their juice, coconut milk, quinoa, and remaining 3 cups water and bring to boil. Reduce heat to low and simmer, stirring occasionally, until quinoa is tender, about 15 minutes.

5 Stir in pureed vegetable mixture and remaining roasted vegetables and let heat through, about 3 minutes. Season with salt and pepper to taste. Adjust consistency with additional hot water as needed. Serve, sprinkling individual bowls with cilantro and remaining ½ cup peanuts.

soups, stews, and chilis

bu

sandw

rgers,
iches,
and
pizzas

Lentil and Mushroom Burgers

serves 12

¾ cup brown lentils, picked over and rinsed

Salt

½ cup vegetable oil, plus extra as needed

1 pound cremini mushrooms, trimmed and sliced thin

2 onions, chopped fine

1 celery rib, minced

1 small leek, white and light green parts only, chopped fine and washed thoroughly (½ cup)

2 garlic cloves, minced

¾ cup medium-grind bulgur, rinsed

1 cup raw cashews

⅓ cup aquafaba (see page 34)

2 cups panko bread crumbs

12 burger buns

Why This Recipe Works Store-bought frozen veggie burgers—both vegan and not—are convenient but so often bland, stodgy, mushy, and just not worth it. We wanted to create a homemade vegan veggie burger that was worth the effort. Lentils gave our burgers earthy flavor, and bulgur further bulked them and absorbed any excess moisture that the lentils retained after cooking. Some well-browned mushrooms added meatiness, but tasters still craved an umami boost. We knew from previous testing that ground nuts could provide this, so we incorporated mild cashews. They added savory richness without disturbing the flavors. Our final obstacle was binding the ingredients; many veggie burgers call for an egg. Ground flaxseed imparted a muddy flavor; using a decent amount—⅓ cup—of aquafaba, plus panko bread crumbs, gave us excellent cohesion. Don't confuse bulgur with cracked wheat, which has a much longer cooking time and will not work in this recipe. For burger sauce and topping options, see page 120.

1 Bring 3 cups water, lentils, and 1 teaspoon salt to boil in medium saucepan over high heat. Reduce heat to medium-low and simmer until lentils just begin to fall apart, about 25 minutes. Drain lentils, transfer to paper towel–lined baking sheet, and pat dry.

2 Meanwhile, heat 2 tablespoons oil in 12-inch nonstick skillet over medium heat until shimmering. Add mushrooms and cook until golden, about 12 minutes. Stir in onions, celery, leek, and garlic and cook until browned, 10 to 15 minutes. Transfer to sheet with lentils and let cool completely, about 30 minutes.

3 Combine 2 cups water, bulgur, and ¼ teaspoon salt in large bowl and microwave, covered, until softened, about 5 minutes. Drain bulgur in fine-mesh strainer and press with rubber spatula to remove excess moisture; let cool slightly. Pulse cashews in food processor until finely ground, about 25 pulses.

4 Combine lentil mixture, bulgur, ground cashews, and aquafaba in bowl. Pulse half of bulgur mixture in now-empty food processor until coarsely ground but cohesive, about 15 pulses. Transfer mixture to large bowl. Repeat with remaining bulgur mixture and transfer to bowl. Stir in panko and 1 teaspoon salt.

5 Adjust oven rack to middle position and heat oven to 200 degrees. Divide mixture into 12 equal portions and pack into 4-inch-wide patties.

6 Heat 2 tablespoons oil in now-empty skillet over medium heat until shimmering. Gently lay 4 patties in skillet and cook until crisp and well browned on first side, about 4 minutes. Gently flip patties and cook until crisp and well browned on second side, about 4 minutes, adding extra oil if skillet looks dry.

7 Transfer burgers to wire rack set in rimmed baking sheet and place in oven to keep warm. Wipe out skillet with paper towels and repeat in 2 batches with remaining oil and remaining patties. Transfer to buns and serve.

Black Bean Burgers
serves 6

2 (15-ounce) cans black beans, rinsed, with 6 tablespoons bean liquid reserved
2 tablespoons all-purpose flour
4 scallions, minced
3 tablespoons minced fresh cilantro
2 garlic cloves, minced
1 teaspoon ground cumin
1 teaspoon hot sauce (optional)
½ teaspoon ground coriander
¼ teaspoon salt
¼ teaspoon pepper
1 ounce tortilla chips, crushed (½ cup)
¼ cup vegetable oil
6 burger buns

Why This Recipe Works Satisfying black beans seem like a natural base for a hearty vegan burger, but most black bean burgers are mushy or fall apart when flipped. We managed to harness the sticking power of the beans' natural starches and, with just a few additions, create a great burger. For a dry binder, we used tortilla chips that we ground in the food processor; their corn flavor added a pleasing Southwestern flair to our burgers, which we enhanced with scallions, fresh cilantro, garlic, ground cumin and coriander, and hot sauce. We pulsed the beans with the chips near the end of processing the chips so the beans maintained some texture. When looking for something other than an egg to pull everything together, we didn't have to go far. Instead of opening a can of chickpeas for the aquafaba, we found that the liquid from the can of black beans we were using provided the necessary cohesion, and the beans were sticky enough to hold together without an additional ingredient. The black bean liquid also boosted the overall flavor of the burgers. We dried the rinsed beans well to ensure we had control over the moisture content of our burgers. When forming the patties, it's important to pack them together firmly. For sauce and topping options, see page 120.

1 Line rimmed baking sheet with triple layer of paper towels, spread beans over towels, and let sit for 15 minutes.

2 Whisk reserved bean liquid and flour in large bowl until well combined and smooth. Stir in scallions; cilantro; garlic; cumin; hot sauce, if using; coriander; salt; and pepper until well combined. Process tortilla chips in food processor until finely ground, about 30 seconds. Add black beans and pulse until beans are coarsely ground, about 5 pulses. Transfer bean mixture to bowl with flour mixture and mix until well combined.

3 Adjust oven rack to middle position and heat oven to 200 degrees. Divide mixture into 6 equal portions and pack firmly into 3½-inch-wide patties.

4 Heat 1 tablespoon oil in 10-inch nonstick skillet over medium heat until shimmering. Gently lay 3 patties in skillet and cook until crisp and well browned on first side, about 5 minutes. Gently flip patties, add 1 tablespoon oil, and cook until crisp and well browned on second side, 3 to 5 minutes.

5 Transfer burgers to wire rack set in rimmed baking sheet and place in oven to keep warm. Wipe out skillet with paper towels and repeat with remaining 2 tablespoons oil and remaining patties. Transfer to buns and serve.

Pinto Bean–Beet Burgers
serves 8

Salt and pepper
⅔ cup medium-grind bulgur, rinsed
1 large beet (9 ounces), peeled and shredded
¾ cup walnuts
½ cup fresh basil leaves
2 garlic cloves, minced
1 (15-ounce) can pinto beans, rinsed
1 (4-ounce) jar carrot baby food
1 tablespoon whole-grain mustard
1½ cups panko bread crumbs
6 tablespoons vegetable oil, plus extra as needed
8 burger buns

Why This Recipe Works Vegan burgers are often bean-based; starchy, protein-packed beans taste great, hold together well, and are satisfying. Looking for a modern twist on the typical bean burger, we combined pinto beans with vibrant shredded beets, and we also packed in a generous amount of basil leaves. The result was a substantial but fresh-tasting burger with some sweetness from the beets and the bright, complementary aroma of basil. Learning from our Lentil and Mushroom Burgers (page 112), we incorporated bulgur for heft and ground nuts for meaty richness. Garlic and mustard deepened the savory flavors. While the bulgur cooked, we pulsed the other ingredients in the food processor to just the right consistency. To bind the burgers, we turned to a surprising ingredient: carrot baby food. The carrot added tackiness, and its subtle sweetness heightened that of the shredded beets; plus, it was already conveniently pureed. Panko bread crumbs further bound the mixture and helped the patties sear up with a crisp crust. When shopping, don't confuse bulgur with cracked wheat, which has a much longer cooking time and will not work in this recipe. Use a coarse grater or the shredding disk of a food processor to shred the beets. For sauce and topping options, see page 120.

1 Bring 1½ cups water and ½ teaspoon salt to boil in small saucepan. Off heat, stir in bulgur, cover, and let stand until tender, 15 to 20 minutes. Drain bulgur, spread onto rimmed baking sheet, and let cool slightly.

2 Meanwhile, pulse beet, walnuts, basil, and garlic in food processor until finely chopped, about 12 pulses, scraping down sides of bowl as needed. Add beans, carrot baby food, 2 tablespoons water, mustard, 1½ teaspoons salt, and ½ teaspoon pepper and pulse until well combined, about 8 pulses. Transfer mixture to large bowl and stir in panko and cooled bulgur.

3 Adjust oven rack to middle position and heat oven to 200 degrees. Divide mixture into 8 equal portions and pack into 3½-inch-wide patties.

4 Heat 3 tablespoons oil in 12-inch nonstick skillet over medium-high heat until shimmering. Gently lay 4 patties in skillet and cook until crisp and well browned on first side, about 4 minutes. Gently flip patties and cook until crisp and well browned on second side, about 4 minutes, adding extra oil if skillet looks dry.

5 Transfer burgers to wire rack set in rimmed baking sheet and place in oven to keep warm. Wipe out skillet with paper towels and repeat with remaining 3 tablespoons oil and remaining patties. Transfer to buns and serve.

burgers, sandwiches, and pizzas

Grilled Portobello Burgers

serves 4

4 portobello mushrooms caps
  (4 to 5 inches in diameter), gills
  removed
½ cup extra-virgin olive oil
3 tablespoons red wine vinegar
1 garlic clove, minced
  Salt and pepper
½ cup jarred roasted red peppers,
  patted dry and chopped
½ cup oil-packed sun-dried
  tomatoes, patted dry and
  chopped
¼ cup vegan mayonnaise
¼ cup chopped fresh basil
4 (½-inch-thick) slices red onion
4 burger buns
1 ounce (1 cup) baby arugula

Why This Recipe Works Too often the "vegan option" is a limp portobello that's carelessly thrown on a bun. Our version, layered with a sun-dried tomato and roasted red pepper topping and spread with basil mayo, would make the vegan option the one everybody reaches for. We started by marinating the portobellos in a simple vinaigrette, which boosted their complexity considerably. Cutting a shallow crosshatch pattern into the caps not only allowed the mushrooms to soak up more marinade, but also prevented the skin from turning chewy while it cooked—a common pitfall. We grilled the mushrooms alongside sliced red onions, which we brushed with the remaining marinade to unify the flavors. Once the mushrooms had taken on rich char, we topped them with our mixture of roasted red peppers and sun-dried tomatoes; the briny topping brightened the rich, meaty star. Then we stacked the stuffed mushrooms on buns along with the onions, peppery arugula, and a smear of aromatic basil mayonnaise. These burgers were thick, rich, and juicy, an outstanding dinner option—vegan or not. We strongly prefer our favorite vegan mayonnaise, Just Mayo, or our homemade Vegan Mayonnaise (page 22). (For more information on vegan mayonnaise, see page 22.)

1 Cut $1/16$-inch-deep slits on top side of mushroom caps, spaced ½ inch apart, in crosshatch pattern. Combine oil, vinegar, garlic, 1 teaspoon salt, and ½ teaspoon pepper in 1-gallon zipper-lock bag. Add mushroom caps, press out air, seal, turn to coat, and let sit for at least 30 minutes or up to 1 hour.

2 Combine red peppers and sun-dried tomatoes in bowl. Combine mayonnaise and basil in second bowl. Push 1 toothpick horizontally through each onion slice to keep rings intact. Remove mushroom caps from bag, then brush onions all over with any remaining marinade in bag.

3a FOR A CHARCOAL GRILL Open bottom vent completely. Light large chimney starter filled with charcoal briquettes (6 quarts). When top coals are partially covered with ash, pour evenly over grill. Set cooking grate in place, cover, and open lid vent completely. Heat grill until hot, about 5 minutes.

3b FOR A GAS GRILL Turn all burners to high, cover, and heat grill until hot, about 15 minutes. Turn all burners to medium-high.

4 Clean and oil cooking grate. Place mushrooms, gill side up, and onions on grill. Cook (covered if using gas) until mushrooms have released their liquid and are charred on first side, 4 to 6 minutes. Flip mushrooms and onions and continue to cook (covered if using gas) until mushrooms are charred on second side, 3 to 5 minutes.

5 Transfer onions to platter and discard toothpicks. Transfer mushrooms to platter, gill side up, and divide pepper-tomato mixture evenly among caps, packing down mixture.

6 Grill buns cut sides down until lightly charred, about 1 minute. Spread basil mayonnaise evenly over bun bottoms. Assemble 4 burgers by layering mushrooms, onions, then arugula on bun bottoms. Top with bun tops and serve.

Sandwich Sauces and Toppings

LEVEL UP YOUR LUNCH
We've developed recipes for fresh and filling vegan burgers (made from beans, grains, and vegetables of all kinds) and sandwiches. While delicious on their own, these sauces, pickles, and condiments give anything between bread extra pizzazz. Try them also on salads and grain bowls.

Creamy Chipotle Sauce   makes about ½ cup

We prefer the flavor and consistency of Tofutti Better Than Sour Cream. Other dairy-free sour creams will add their distinctive flavor and you may need to adjust the consistency with water. We strongly prefer our favorite vegan mayonnaise, Just Mayo, or our homemade Vegan Mayonnaise (page 22). (For more information on vegan mayonnaise, see page 22.)

¼ cup vegan mayonnaise
¼ cup dairy-free sour cream
1 tablespoon lime juice
1 tablespoon minced canned chipotle chile in adobo sauce
1 garlic clove, minced

Combine all ingredients in small bowl. (Sauce can be refrigerated for up to 4 days.)

Pub-Style Burger Sauce   makes about 1 cup

We strongly prefer our favorite vegan mayonnaise, Just Mayo, or our homemade Vegan Mayonnaise (page 22). (For more information on vegan mayonnaise, see page 22.)

¾ cup vegan mayonnaise
2 tablespoons soy sauce
1 tablespoon packed dark brown sugar
1 tablespoon vegan Worcestershire sauce
1 tablespoon minced fresh chives
1 garlic clove, minced
¾ teaspoon ground black pepper

Whisk all ingredients together in bowl. (Sauce can be refrigerated for up to 4 days.)

Tahini Sauce   makes about 1¼ cups

½ cup tahini
½ cup water
¼ cup lemon juice
2 garlic cloves, minced
  Salt

Whisk tahini, water, lemon juice, and garlic in bowl until smooth. Season with salt to taste. (Sauce can be refrigerated for up to 4 days. Bring to room temperature and stir to combine before serving.)

Quick Pickled Radishes   makes about 1 cup

 6 large radishes, trimmed and sliced thin
 1 shallot, sliced thin
¼ cup lime juice (2 limes)
 1 teaspoon organic sugar (seepage 31)
½ teaspoon salt

Combine all ingredients in bowl, cover, and let sit at room temperature for 15 minutes. Drain vegetables in colander and serve. (Pickled radishes can be refrigerated for up to 1 hour; radishes will begin to turn limp, gray, and bitter after 1 hour.)

Quick Sweet-and-Spicy Pickled Red Onions   makes about 1 cup

 1 red onion, halved and sliced thin through root end
 1 cup red wine vinegar
⅓ cup organic sugar (see page 31)
 2 jalapeño chiles, stemmed, seeded, and sliced into thin rings
¼ teaspoon salt

Place onion in bowl. Bring vinegar, sugar, jalapeños, and salt to simmer over medium-high heat in small saucepan, stirring occasionally, until sugar dissolves. Pour vinegar mixture over onion, cover, and let cool completely, about 1 hour. Drain cooled vegetables in colander. (Pickled onions can be refrigerated for up to 1 week; onions will turn harsh after 1 week.)

Crispy Onions   makes about 3 cups

 1 onion, sliced into thin rings
½ cup white vinegar
½ cup all-purpose flour
   Salt and pepper
¼ teaspoon cream of tartar
 2 cups vegetable oil

1 Separate onion rings and combine with vinegar in bowl. Combine flour, ½ teaspoon salt, ¼ teaspoon pepper, and cream of tartar in large bowl.

2 Heat oil in 12-inch nonstick skillet over medium-high heat to 350 degrees. Drain onion rings; toss with flour mixture until evenly coated. Working in batches, fry onions, stirring occasionally, until golden brown and crisp, about 5 minutes. Transfer to paper towel–lined plate, season with salt and pepper to taste.

Chickpea Salad Sandwiches

serves 6

2 (15-ounce) cans chickpeas, rinsed
½ cup vegan mayonnaise
¼ cup water
1 tablespoon lemon juice
  Salt and pepper
2 celery ribs, finely chopped
⅓ cup dill pickles, finely chopped
2 scallions, sliced thin
2 tablespoons minced fresh
  parsley, dill, or tarragon
12 slices hearty multigrain bread,
  toasted

Why This Recipe Works A creamy deli-style salad makes for a satisfying sandwich that's hard to beat when lunchtime rolls around. Chicken, egg, and tuna salads are classics, but we wanted to put a vegan spin on this category by using protein-packed chickpeas as our base. When we simply mashed our chickpeas and stirred our ingredients together, however, our salads turned out dry, crumbly, and pasty. We wanted the richness and almost saucy texture of a traditional deli salad. Vegan mayonnaise helped the cause, lending a rich smoothness, but too much of it masked the savory chickpea flavor. Since we were already opening cans of chickpeas, why not make a hummus-style puree for creaminess? We buzzed a portion of the chickpeas with vegan mayo, water, and lemon juice in the food processor for the perfect creamy binder. Then we added the remaining chickpeas to the mixture and briefly pulsed them to give us just the right textural contrast. To round things out, we turned to classic flavors: Chopped celery provided crunch, dill pickle brought a salty brininess, and scallions and herbs finished the salad with bright, fresh flavor. Served on toasted bread, this salad makes a creamy, luscious sandwich sure to satisfy any lunchtime craving. We strongly prefer our favorite vegan mayonnaise, Just Mayo, or our homemade Vegan Mayonnaise (page 22). (For more information on vegan mayonnaise, see page 22.) Serve with lettuce, tomato, sliced avocado, and/or sprouts, if desired. This salad is also delicious served in lettuce wraps.

1 Process ¾ cup chickpeas, mayonnaise, water, lemon juice, and ½ teaspoon salt in food processor until smooth, about 30 seconds, scraping down sides of bowl as needed.

2 Add remaining chickpeas to food processor and pulse until coarsely chopped with some larger pieces remaining, about 4 pulses.

3 Combine chickpea mixture, celery, pickles, scallions, and parsley in large bowl and season with salt and pepper to taste. Spread chickpea salad evenly over 6 bread slices. Top with remaining bread slices and serve.

VARIATION
Curried Chickpea Salad Sandwiches
Add 1 tablespoon curry powder to chickpea mixture in food processor in step 1 and substitute ½ cup golden raisins for pickles.

Tofu Banh Mi

serves 4

14 ounces firm tofu, sliced crosswise into ½-inch-thick slabs
  Salt and pepper
2 carrots, peeled and shredded
½ cucumber, peeled, halved lengthwise, seeded, and sliced thin
1 teaspoon grated lime zest plus 1 tablespoon juice
1 tablespoon fish sauce substitute (see page 21)
¼ cup vegan mayonnaise
1 tablespoon Sriracha sauce
⅓ cup cornstarch
3 tablespoons vegetable oil
4 (8-inch) Italian sub rolls, split and toasted
⅓ cup fresh cilantro leaves

Why This Recipe Works Vietnamese street food is some of the best in the world, and the *banh mi* is one stellar dish that's been embraced with open arms in the United States. In Vietnam, banh mi is simply a term for all kinds of bread, but Americans recognize it as a terrific sandwich featuring chicken, pork, or tofu on a mayo-slathered roll, with crunchy pickled vegetables and fresh herbs to offset the protein and mayo's richness. For our vegan version, we obviously chose tofu. Of course, simply stuffing a sandwich with slabs of tofu wouldn't do the dish justice. Instead, we sliced the tofu and drained the slices on paper towels to sop up the excess water, which can inhibit browning and crisping during cooking. Then we dredged the slabs in cornstarch and seared them in a hot skillet until they were nicely browned. The cornstarch coating created a pleasingly delicate crispy-fried crust without relying on an abundance of oil. For the vegetables, we quick-pickled cucumber slices and shredded carrot in lime juice and fish sauce substitute. The cucumber was cooling and the carrots added sweet crunch. The mayo-based sauce brings the components of a banh mi together. We spiked vegan mayonnaise with Sriracha sauce for a spicy kick, and we sprinkled on fresh cilantro, an authentic garnish. We strongly prefer our favorite vegan mayonnaise, Just Mayo, or our homemade Vegan Mayonnaise (page 22). (For more information on vegan mayonnaise, see page 22.)

1 Spread tofu on paper towel–lined baking sheet and let drain for 20 minutes. Gently press dry with paper towels and season with salt and pepper.

2 Meanwhile, combine carrots, cucumber, lime juice, and fish sauce substitute in bowl and let sit for 15 minutes. Whisk mayonnaise, Sriracha, and lime zest together in second bowl.

3 Spread cornstarch in shallow dish. Dredge seasoned tofu in cornstarch and transfer to plate. Heat oil in 12-inch nonstick skillet over medium-high heat until just smoking. Add tofu and cook until crisp and browned, about 4 minutes per side; transfer to paper towel–lined plate.

4 Spread mayonnaise mixture evenly over cut sides of each roll. Layer tofu, pickled vegetables (leave liquid in bowl), and cilantro evenly in rolls. Press gently on sandwiches to set. Serve.

burgers, sandwiches, and pizzas

Falafel with Tahini Yogurt Sauce

serves 6 to 8

Why This Recipe Works Falafel is an eastern Mediterranean specialty of savory fried chickpea balls or patties generously seasoned with herbs and spices. And it just might be the perfect vegan meal: It's packed with filling, tasty ingredients, and it features varying textures for lots of appeal—crisp, fried crusts; soft, almost fluffy centers; and creamy sauce. While we like the ease and creamy texture of canned beans in most recipes, starting with dried chickpeas was essential here; using canned chickpeas resulted in mushy falafel that wouldn't hold their shape. We soaked the dried chickpeas overnight in a saltwater solution, which weakened the cell structure of the chickpeas' skins, giving them a softer texture. We then ground the soaked chickpeas with herbs and warm spices: scallions, parsley, cilantro, garlic, cumin, and cinnamon. Shaping the falafel into small disks ensured that the exteriors developed a golden-brown crust while the interiors stayed moist. Both yogurt and tahini sauces are traditional, and tasters liked the two combined into one rich, tangy condiment. The chickpeas in this recipe must be soaked overnight; you cannot substitute canned or quick-soaked chickpeas. Do not use dairy-free Greek-style yogurts, as they make the sauce chalky. Serve the falafel as hors d'oeuvres or in lavash or pita bread with lettuce, tomatoes, red onion, or cucumbers.

FALAFEL

Salt and pepper
12 ounces (2 cups) dried chickpeas, picked over and rinsed
10 scallions, chopped coarse
1 cup fresh parsley leaves
1 cup fresh cilantro leaves
6 garlic cloves, minced
½ teaspoon ground cumin
⅛ teaspoon ground cinnamon
2 cups vegetable oil

SAUCE

⅓ cup tahini
⅓ cup unsweetened plain coconut milk yogurt
3 tablespoons lemon juice
1 garlic clove, minced
Salt and pepper

1 FOR THE FALAFEL Dissolve 3 tablespoons salt in 4 quarts cold water in large container. Add chickpeas and soak at room temperature for at least 8 hours or up to 24 hours. Drain and rinse well.

2 Process chickpeas, scallions, parsley, cilantro, garlic, cumin, cinnamon, 1 teaspoon salt, and 1 teaspoon pepper in food processor until smooth, scraping down sides of bowl as needed, about 1 minute. Working with 2 tablespoons chickpea mixture at time, pinch off and shape into disks, about ½ inch thick and 1 inch wide, and place on parchment paper–lined baking sheet. (Falafel can be refrigerated for up to 3 days.)

3 FOR THE SAUCE Whisk tahini, coconut milk yogurt, lemon juice, garlic, and ¾ teaspoon salt in bowl until combined. Season with salt and pepper to taste; set aside until ready to serve. (Sauce can be refrigerated for up to 4 days.)

4 Adjust oven rack to middle position and heat oven to 200 degrees. Set wire rack in rimmed baking sheet. Heat oil in 12-inch skillet over medium-high heat to 375 degrees. Fry half of falafel until deep golden brown, 2 to 3 minutes per side. Adjust burner, if necessary, to maintain oil temperature of 375 degrees. Using slotted spoon, transfer falafel to prepared wire rack and keep warm in oven. Return oil to 375 degrees and repeat with remaining falafel. Serve with tahini yogurt sauce.

TESTING NOTES **Dairy-Free Yogurts**

OUR FAVORITE Coconut Milk Yogurt

OTHERS TESTED Almond milk yogurt makes the sauce more tart. Soy milk yogurt lends the sauce a distinct soy flavor.

Korean Barbecue Tempeh Wraps
serves 4

¾ cup organic sugar (see page 31)
6 tablespoons soy sauce
6 tablespoons water
5 garlic cloves, minced
1½ tablespoons rice vinegar
1½ teaspoons Sriracha sauce
1½ teaspoons cornstarch
¼ cup vegetable oil
1 pound tempeh, cut crosswise
   into ½-inch-thick strips
4 (10-inch) flour tortillas
2 large heads baby bok choy
   (4 ounces each), sliced thin
   crosswise
1 cup fresh cilantro leaves
3 radishes, trimmed, halved, and
   sliced thin
2 scallions, sliced thin

Why This Recipe Works A boldly flavored, sweet-and-sticky barbecue wrap is always a hit. We were particularly drawn to bold Korean barbecue, so we decided to translate those winning flavors into a delicious vegan wrap. For the protein, we chose tempeh; it has a great firm, chewy texture that stood out once wrapped, and its slight bitterness worked well with a flavor-packed sauce. To give the tempeh a deeply browned crust, we seared it in a skillet before tossing it with a quick sauce made from soy sauce, garlic, sugar, spicy Sriracha sauce, and a shot of rice vinegar, which balanced the flavor of the tempeh with sweetness, tang, and a little heat. Including some cornstarch and simmering the sauce mixture for 5 minutes gave it a thick, velvety consistency, and it clung nicely to the tempeh. For vegetables and herbs to pair with the perfectly cooked tempeh, we chose thinly sliced baby bok choy, radishes, and scallions, and whole cilantro leaves for freshness and cool crunch. We tossed half of the barbecue sauce with the tempeh and then drizzled the other half over the vegetables so the wrap would have great flavors throughout. Tucked into a supple flour tortilla, our sauce-dabbed tempeh proved that a barbecue wrap doesn't need meat to be satisfying and delicious.

1 Whisk sugar, soy sauce, water, garlic, vinegar, Sriracha, and cornstarch together in bowl.

2 Heat 2 tablespoons oil in 12-inch nonstick skillet over medium heat until shimmering. Add half of tempeh and cook until golden brown, 2 to 4 minutes per side; transfer to paper towel–lined plate. Repeat with remaining 2 tablespoons oil and remaining tempeh.

3 Add sugar-soy mixture to now-empty skillet and simmer over medium-low heat until thickened and measures 1 cup, about 5 minutes; transfer to bowl. Toss tempeh with half of sauce in separate bowl.

4 Lay tortillas on counter, arrange tempeh, bok choy, cilantro, radishes, and scallions, in center of each tortilla, then drizzle each with 1 tablespoon sauce. Fold short sides then bottom of tortilla over filling, pulling back firmly to tighten tortilla around filling, then continue to roll tightly. Serve with remaining sauce.

Sizzling Saigon Crêpes (Banh Xeo)

makes 9 crêpes; serves 8

Why This Recipe Works Named for the appetite-inducing sound these crêpes make when the batter hits a hot wok, sizzling Saigon crêpes are best described as paper-thin eggless Vietnamese omelets. These crispy yellow rice flour crêpes are stuffed with fillings, wrapped with lettuce and herbs, and dipped into a sweet-tart sauce. We chose a filling of shredded carrots, onions, and bean sprouts. The batter for the crêpes is simple: just water, rice flour, and coconut milk. To give them a subtle savory flavor, we added scallions and turmeric. And for the dressing, we combined fish sauce substitute with lime juice, sugar, minced fresh chiles, and garlic. White rice flour is available at most supermarkets and can also be found in natural foods stores; you cannot substitute regular flour or cornstarch for the rice flour. For a spicier dish, add the chile ribs and seeds. If you can't find Thai basil, you can substitute regular basil. To allow for practice, the recipe yields one extra crêpe.

DRESSING AND GARNISH

⅓ cup fish sauce substitute (see page 21)

¼ cup warm water

3 tablespoons lime juice (2 limes)

2 tablespoons organic sugar (see page 31)

2 Thai, serrano, or jalapeño chiles, stemmed, seeded, and minced

1 garlic clove, minced

2 heads red or green leaf lettuce, leaves separated (1½ pounds)

1 cup fresh Thai basil leaves

1 cup fresh cilantro leaves

CRÊPES

2¾ cups water

1¾ cups white rice flour

½ cup canned coconut milk

4 scallions, sliced thin
   Salt

1 teaspoon ground turmeric

¼ cup vegetable oil

1 onion, halved and sliced thin

1 pound carrots, peeled and shredded

6 ounces (3 cups) bean sprouts

1 FOR THE DRESSING AND GARNISH Whisk fish sauce substitute, water, lime juice, sugar, chiles, and garlic in bowl until sugar dissolves. Arrange lettuce, basil, and cilantro on platter.

2 FOR THE CRÊPES Adjust oven rack to middle position and heat oven to 200 degrees. Set wire rack in rimmed baking sheet. Whisk water, rice flour, coconut milk, scallions, 1 teaspoon salt, and turmeric in bowl until combined.

3 Heat 1 tablespoon oil in 10-inch nonstick skillet over medium-high heat until shimmering. Add onion and ½ teaspoon salt and cook until onion is softened, 5 to 7 minutes; transfer to bowl. Add carrots to now-empty skillet and cook until tender, about 2 minutes; transfer to bowl with onions and let cool slightly. Stir in bean sprouts.

4 Wipe out skillet with paper towels. Heat 1 teaspoon oil in now-empty skillet over medium-high heat until just smoking. Quickly stir batter to recombine, then pour ½ cup batter into skillet while swirling pan gently to distribute it evenly over pan bottom. Reduce heat to medium and cook crêpe until edges pull away from sides and are deep golden, 3 to 5 minutes.

5 Gently slide spatula underneath edge of crêpe, grasp edge with your fingertips, and flip crêpe. Cook until spotty brown on second side, 2 to 3 minutes. Slide crêpe onto prepared wire rack and keep warm in oven. Repeat with remaining oil and remaining batter. Divide carrot mixture evenly among crêpes and fold crêpes in half. Serve crêpes with dressing, passing garnish platter separately. (To eat, slice off wedge of crêpe, wrap in lettuce leaf, sprinkle with basil and cilantro, and dip into dressing.)

Baja-Style Cauliflower Tacos

serves 4 to 6

3 cups (7½ ounces) coleslaw mix
½ mango, peeled and cut into
    ¼-inch pieces (¾ cup)
1 tablespoon chopped fresh
    cilantro
2 tablespoons lime juice
1 tablespoon minced jalapeño
    chile
    Salt and pepper
1 cup unsweetened shredded
    coconut
1 cup panko bread crumbs
1 cup canned coconut milk
1 teaspoon garlic powder
1 teaspoon ground cumin
¼ teaspoon cayenne
½ head cauliflower (1 pound),
    trimmed and cut into 1-inch
    pieces
8–12 (6-inch) corn tortillas, warmed
1 recipe Cilantro Sauce (page 166)

Why This Recipe Works A true Baja California experience requires sunny, breezy patios and a plate of tacos. We aimed to re-create the feel of a Baja-style fish taco in our home kitchen, instead bringing veggies to the forefront. We thought that battered cauliflower bites, drizzled with a cool and creamy vegan sauce, were the perfect stand-in for the fish. We wanted to avoid the mess of deep-frying, so we cut the cauliflower into large florets and roasted them. To boost their flavor, we dunked the pieces in canned coconut milk seasoned with garlic and spices and then rolled them in a mixture of panko bread crumbs and shredded coconut. Not only did this add richness and the flavors of a cabana-shaded getaway, but it also mimicked the crisp exterior texture of batter-fried fish. A bed of crunchy slaw with juicy mango and spicy jalapeño provided the perfect balance of sweetness and heat. By using equal parts vegan mayonnaise and dairy-free sour cream, plus cilantro and a bit of lime zest, we were able to whip up a vegan *crema* to top it all off. Just add cerveza and sunshine. For a spicier slaw, mince and add the jalapeño ribs and seeds. Serve with lime wedges.

1 Adjust oven rack to middle position and heat oven to 450 degrees. Combine coleslaw mix, mango, cilantro, lime juice, jalapeño, and ¼ teaspoon salt in bowl, cover, and refrigerate.

2 Spray rimmed baking sheet with vegetable oil spray. Combine coconut and panko in shallow dish. Whisk coconut milk, garlic powder, cumin, cayenne, and 1 teaspoon salt together in bowl. Add cauliflower to coconut milk mixture; toss to coat well. Working with 1 piece cauliflower at a time, remove from coconut milk, letting excess drip back into bowl, then coat well with coconut-panko mixture, pressing gently to adhere; transfer to prepared sheet.

3 Bake until cauliflower is tender, golden, and crisp, 20 to 25 minutes, flipping cauliflower and rotating sheet halfway through baking.

4 Divide slaw evenly among warm tortillas and top with cauliflower. Drizzle with cilantro sauce and serve.

Thin-Crust Pizza Dough

makes 1¾ pounds

3 cups (16½ ounces) bread flour
2 tablespoons organic sugar
  (see page 31)
½ teaspoon instant or rapid-rise
  yeast
1⅓ cups ice water
1 tablespoon vegetable oil
1½ teaspoons salt

Why This Recipe Works No matter the topping, pizza is only as good as its dough. Most pizza doughs are hard to work with and impossible to stretch thin without tearing or snapping back. We wanted to produce a New York–style crust—a thin and crisp pizza crust that was both tender and chewy and that would complement any toppings or flavor profiles we threw at it. Using high-protein bread flour resulted in a chewy, nicely tanned crust. Landing on the right ratio of flour to water and yeast gave us a dough that would stretch and would retain moisture as it baked. We kneaded the dough quickly in a food processor and then let it proof in the refrigerator for at least a day (or up to three days) to develop its flavors. The result was an easy-to-stretch dough that was effortless to work with and that baked up brown and crisp. It is important to use ice water in the dough to prevent it from overheating while it's in the food processor.

1 Pulse flour, sugar, and yeast in food processor until combined, about 5 pulses. With processor running, slowly add ice water and process until dough is just combined and no dry flour remains, about 10 seconds. Let dough rest for 10 minutes.

2 Add oil and salt to dough and process until dough forms satiny, sticky ball that clears sides of bowl, 30 to 60 seconds. Transfer dough to lightly oiled counter and knead by hand to form smooth, round ball, about 30 seconds. Place dough seam side down in lightly greased large bowl or container, cover tightly with plastic wrap, and refrigerate for at least 24 hours or up to 3 days.

Whole-Wheat Pizza Dough

makes
1½ pounds

1½ cups (8¼ ounces) whole-wheat
   flour
 1 cup (5½ ounces) bread flour
 2 teaspoons sugar (see page 31)
¾ teaspoon instant or rapid-rise
   yeast
1¼ cups ice water
 2 tablespoons extra-virgin olive oil
1¾ teaspoons salt

Why This Recipe Works Whole-wheat pizza sounds like a great idea: A nutty, wheaty-tasting crust would be a satisfying and flavorful change of pace from the typical parlor pie. Unfortunately, it's nearly impossible to come by a whole-wheat dough that develops the same char and chew of traditional thin-crust pizzas; most are dry and dense. We wanted to find a way to make a flavorful whole-wheat crust that baked up with the same great texture as our Thin-Crust Pizza Dough (page 134). Using whole-wheat flour alone would give us a dense crust, so we incorporated just enough structure-building white bread flour. To help strengthen the gluten network, a highly hydrated dough was particularly important for this pie; the whole-wheat flour's mix of starch, bran, and germ absorbed more water than if we used white flour only. But because our dough was so wet, simply preheating the pizza stone in a 500-degree oven wasn't enough; we found we needed to heat the stone under the broiler's high heat so that the crust would brown before the toppings overcooked. It is important to use ice water in the dough to prevent it from overheating while it's in the food processor.

1 Pulse whole-wheat flour, bread flour, sugar, and yeast in food processor until combined, about 5 pulses. With processor running, slowly add ice water and process until dough is just combined and no dry flour remains, about 10 seconds. Let dough rest for 10 minutes.

2 Add oil and salt to dough and process until dough forms satiny, sticky ball that clears sides of bowl, 45 to 60 seconds. Transfer dough to lightly oiled counter and knead by hand to form smooth, round ball, about 30 seconds. Place dough seam side down in lightly greased large bowl or container, cover tightly with plastic wrap, and refrigerate for at least 18 hours or up to 2 days.

Pesto Pizza with Fennel and Cauliflower

makes two 13-inch pizzas

Why This Recipe Works Tomato sauce pies are great, but to freshen things up, we like pizza spread with garlicky pesto. When we simply omitted the Parmesan from the pesto, we didn't miss it; we got all the savory flavor we desired from the olive oil, pine nuts, and garlic. For a vegetable topper, we thought some sweet, caramelized cauliflower and fragrant fennel would serve as delicious opposing forces to the bold sauce. A sprinkle of more pine nuts and fresh basil was a nice call-out to the pesto below. You can shape the second dough ball while the first pizza bakes, but don't top the pizza until right before you bake it. If you don't have a baking stone, bake the pizzas on an overturned and preheated rimmed baking sheet. Semolina flour is ideal for dusting the peel; use it in place of flour if you have it.

2 cups fresh basil leaves plus 2 tablespoons shredded

½ cup extra-virgin olive oil

6 tablespoons pine nuts, toasted

2 garlic cloves, minced
Salt and pepper

1 recipe Thin-Crust Pizza Dough (page 134) or Whole-Wheat Pizza Dough (page 135)

2 cups chopped cauliflower

1 fennel bulb, stalks discarded, bulb halved, cored, and cut into ½-inch pieces

3 tablespoons water

1 One hour before baking, adjust oven rack to upper-middle position, set baking stone on rack, and heat oven to 500 degrees. Process 2 cups basil leaves, 6 tablespoons oil, ¼ cup pine nuts, garlic, and ½ teaspoon salt in food processor until smooth, scraping down sides of bowl as needed, about 1 minute; transfer to bowl. (Pesto can be refrigerated for up to 4 days.)

2 Remove dough from refrigerator and divide in half. Shape each half into smooth, tight ball. Space dough balls 3 inches apart on lightly oiled baking sheet, cover loosely with greased plastic wrap, and let rest for 1 hour.

3 Meanwhile, heat remaining 2 tablespoons oil in 12-inch non-stick skillet over medium heat until shimmering. Add cauliflower, fennel, water, and ¼ teaspoon salt; cover and cook until vegetables begin to soften, about 5 minutes. Uncover, increase heat to medium-high, and continue to cook until tender and browned around edges, 10 to 12 minutes; transfer to bowl.

4 Heat broiler for 10 minutes. Meanwhile, coat 1 dough ball generously with flour and place on well-floured counter. Using your fingertips, gently flatten dough into 8-inch round, leaving 1 inch of outer edge slightly thicker than center. Using your hands, gently stretch disk into 12-inch round, working along edges and giving disk quarter turns. Transfer dough to well-floured peel and stretch into 13-inch round. Spread half of pesto over dough, leaving ¼-inch border around edge, then sprinkle with half of cauliflower mixture. Slide pizza carefully onto stone and return oven to 500 degrees. Bake until crust is well browned, 10 to 12 minutes, rotating pizza halfway through baking. Transfer pizza to wire rack, let cool for 5 minutes, then sprinkle with 1 tablespoon shredded basil and 1 tablespoon pine nuts. Slice and serve. Repeat shaping, topping, and baking for second pizza.

Mushroom Pizza with Cashew Ricotta

makes two 13-inch pizzas

Why This Recipe Works This pizza is a knockout—tangy, cooling dollops of homemade cashew ricotta top layers of umami-rich mushrooms for a beautiful lesson in texture and flavor contrasts. For the mushroom base, we fortified workhorse cremini with meaty-tasting shiitakes and soy sauce. We made the creamy ricotta by mixing oil, lemon, and salt, plus a little water to loosen, into our multipurpose cashew cheese. You can shape the second dough ball while the first pizza bakes, but don't top the pizza until right before you bake it. If you don't have a baking stone, bake the pizzas on an overturned and preheated rimmed baking sheet. Semolina flour is ideal for dusting the peel; use it in place of flour if you have it.

⅔ cup Cashew Ricotta (page 27)

7 tablespoons extra-virgin olive oil, plus extra for serving

3 tablespoons water

½ teaspoon grated lemon zest plus ¾ teaspoon juice
  Salt and pepper

1 recipe Thin-Crust Pizza Dough (page 134) or Whole-Wheat Pizza Dough (page 135)

12 ounces cremini mushrooms, trimmed and sliced thin

12 ounces shiitake mushrooms, stemmed and sliced thin

3 garlic cloves, minced

2 tablespoons soy sauce

¼ cup chopped fresh parsley

1 One hour before baking, adjust oven rack to upper-middle position, set baking stone on rack, and heat oven to 500 degrees. Combine cashew ricotta, 1 tablespoon oil, water, lemon zest and juice, and ⅛ teaspoon salt in bowl and refrigerate until ready to use. (Cashew ricotta can be refrigerated for up to 1 week.)

2 Remove dough from refrigerator and divide in half. Shape each half into smooth, tight ball. Space dough balls 3 inches apart on lightly oiled baking sheet, cover loosely with greased plastic wrap, and let rest for 1 hour.

3 Meanwhile, heat 2 tablespoons oil in 12-inch nonstick skillet over medium heat until shimmering. Add cremini mushrooms, shiitake mushrooms, and ½ teaspoon salt, cover, and cook until mushrooms have released their liquid, about 8 minutes. Uncover and cook until mushrooms are dry and starting to brown, about 15 minutes longer. Stir in garlic and cook until fragrant, about 30 seconds. Stir in soy sauce, scraping up any browned bits, and cook until well coated and pan is nearly dry, about 30 seconds. Transfer mushrooms to bowl; set aside.

4 Heat broiler for 10 minutes. Meanwhile, coat 1 dough ball generously with flour and place on well-floured counter. Using your fingertips, gently flatten dough into 8-inch round, leaving 1 inch of outer edge slightly thicker than center. Using your hands, gently stretch disk into 12-inch round, working along edges and giving disk quarter turns. Transfer dough to well-floured peel and stretch into 13-inch round. Spread 2 tablespoons oil over dough, leaving ¼-inch border around edge, then sprinkle with half of cooked mushrooms. Slide pizza carefully onto stone and return oven to 500 degrees. Bake until crust is well browned, 10 to 12 minutes, rotating pizza halfway through baking. Transfer pizza to wire rack and dollop half of cashew ricotta over pizza in small spoonfuls. Sprinkle with parsley and drizzle with extra oil. Slice and serve. Repeat shaping, topping, and baking for second pizza.

burgers, sandwiches, and pizzas

main
salads
and
bowls

dish

Kale Caesar Salad

serves 4 to 6

Why This Recipe Works Kale is fast closing in on romaine as the Caesar salad green of choice; the hearty leaves, with their pungent earthiness, pair surprisingly well with the tangy dressing—perhaps even better than romaine. But the success of a Caesar salad made with any green rests on its dressing. And given that Caesar dressing traditionally contains Parmesan and anchovies and gets its rich creaminess from emulsifying egg yolks, a stellar vegan version may seem unthinkable. But really, the vegan pantry offers ways to achieve pungency, depth, and cheese-like richness. For our reimagined dressing, we used creamy vegan mayo as the base. To mimic the flavors that anchovies and Parmesan provide, we incorporated briny capers and umami-boosting nutritional yeast. The result? A luxurious dressing that tasted like an exact replica of classic versions. We found that soaking the kale in a warm water bath for just 10 minutes caused the cell walls of the leaves to break down, tenderizing the hardy vegetable. Our next step: chilling the dressed salad to cool it down and allow the flavors to meld. We strongly prefer our favorite vegan mayonnaise, Just Mayo, or our homemade Vegan Mayonnaise (page 22). (For more information on vegan mayonnaise, see page 22.) Tasters felt that the nutritional yeast provided the requisite cheesy flavor, but you can serve the salad with a sprinkling of our Vegan Parmesan Substitute (page 27), if desired.

SALAD

- 1 pound curly kale, stemmed and cut into 1-inch pieces
- 5 ounces baguette, cut into ¾-inch cubes (4 cups)
- 2 tablespoons extra-virgin olive oil
- ¼ teaspoon pepper
- ⅛ teaspoon salt

DRESSING

- 6 tablespoons vegan mayonnaise
- 1½ tablespoons nutritional yeast
- 1½ tablespoons lemon juice
- 1½ tablespoons capers, rinsed
- 2 teaspoons white wine vinegar
- 2 teaspoons vegan Worcestershire sauce
- 1 garlic clove, minced
- ¾ teaspoon Dijon mustard
- ½ teaspoon salt
- ½ teaspoon pepper
- 3 tablespoons extra-virgin olive oil

1 FOR THE SALAD Place kale in large bowl, cover with warm tap water (about 110 degrees), and let sit for 10 minutes. Dry thoroughly.

2 Adjust oven rack to middle position and heat oven to 350 degrees. Toss baguette with oil, pepper, and salt in bowl. Spread on rimmed baking sheet and bake until golden and crisp, about 15 minutes; set aside and let cool completely, about 15 minutes. (Croutons can be stored at room temperature for up to 24 hours.)

3 FOR THE DRESSING Process mayonnaise, nutritional yeast, lemon juice, capers, vinegar, Worcestershire, garlic, mustard, salt, and pepper in blender until smooth, about 30 seconds. With blender running, slowly add oil until emulsified. Toss kale with dressing in large bowl and refrigerate for at least 20 minutes or up to 6 hours to chill. Toss salad with croutons and serve.

Green Salad with Crispy Spiced Chickpeas and Mustard Vinaigrette

serves 4 to 6

Why This Recipe Works We originally set out to re-create the hearty flavors of a bacon-dressed salad. But calling the star of our vegan salad, spiced chickpeas, a stand-in for bacon does them a disservice, and we were impressed by the smoky flavor and supercrisp texture of our fried chickpeas in their own right. The contrasting flavors (sweet, smoky, sharp) and textures (soft, crunchy, creamy) in this salad made a satisfying vegan main dish. We cooked the chickpeas in hot oil until they were toasty and crisp and then tossed them with smoked paprika, cumin, sugar, salt, and cayenne pepper for some heat. Crushing some of the chickpeas ensured that they clung to the lettuce and didn't roll around the salad bowl when we tried to pick up bites with a fork. A scant teaspoon of vegan mayonnaise whisked with a combination of sharp but fruity cider vinegar, sweet maple syrup, and seedy whole-grain mustard gave us a vinaigrette that was creamy yet not so heavy that it weighed down delicate mesclun leaves. Charring sliced red onion under the broiler brought out its sweetness and added an extra layer of smoke to the salad. We strongly prefer our favorite vegan mayonnaise, Just Mayo, or our homemade Vegan Mayonnaise (page 22). (For more information on vegan mayonnaise, see page 22.)

SALAD

- 1 teaspoon smoked paprika
- 1 teaspoon organic sugar (see page 31)
- ½ teaspoon ground cumin Salt
- ¼ teaspoon cayenne pepper
- ¾ cup plus 1 tablespoon vegetable oil
- 1 (15-ounce) can chickpeas, rinsed and thoroughly dried
- 1 red onion, halved and sliced through root end
- 6 ounces (6 cups) mesclun

DRESSING

- 1½ tablespoons cider vinegar
- 1 tablespoon whole-grain mustard
- 2 teaspoons maple syrup
- 1½ teaspoons grated lemon zest
- ¾ teaspoon vegan mayonnaise
- ¼ teaspoon salt
- ¼ cup extra-virgin olive oil

1 FOR THE SALAD Combine paprika, sugar, cumin, ½ teaspoon salt, and cayenne in bowl. Heat ¾ cup oil in Dutch oven over high heat until just smoking. Add chickpeas, partially cover (to prevent splattering), and cook, stirring occasionally, until deep golden brown and crisp, 10 to 12 minutes.

2 Using slotted spoon, transfer chickpeas to paper towel–lined plate to drain briefly, then toss in bowl with spice mix. Let cool for 5 minutes, then crush half of chickpeas into coarse crumbs.

3 Adjust oven rack 6 inches from broiler element and heat broiler. Toss onion with remaining 1 tablespoon oil and ¼ teaspoon salt and spread on aluminum foil–lined rimmed baking sheet. Broil onion until edges are charred, 6 to 8 minutes, stirring halfway through cooking. Let onion cool slightly, about 5 minutes, then add to spiced chickpeas along with mesclun, tossing to combine.

4 FOR THE DRESSING Whisk vinegar, mustard, maple syrup, lemon zest, mayonnaise, and salt together in large bowl. Whisking constantly, slowly drizzle in oil. Add mesclun mixture and toss to combine. Season with salt and pepper to taste, and serve.

main dish salads and bowls

Garlicky Tofu Tabbouleh
serves 4 to 6

Why This Recipe Works Tabbouleh made from bulgur wheat, tomatoes, lemon, and heaps of fresh herbs is often served as meze. But with just a little help, we thought tabbouleh could have main-dish potential. Enter tofu. A surprising addition, garlicky, savory, sautéed tofu transformed this classic into a summery meal. Rather than using large cubes of tofu, we pulsed it in the food processor to create a texture similar to that of the bulgur; the extra surface area meant it could absorb more flavor from the dressing, too. We started by salting our tomatoes to rid them of excess liquid, and we used their juice (rather than water) to soak the bulgur. Meanwhile, we sautéed our tofu with a hefty dose of toasted garlic. As the tofu cooled, we made a lemony dressing and then tossed everything with liberal amounts of parsley, mint, and scallions and let the whole thing sit for about an hour to let the flavors mingle. When shopping, don't confuse bulgur with cracked wheat, which has a much longer cooking time and will not work in this recipe. You can substitute firm tofu for the extra-firm in this recipe.

3 tomatoes, cored and cut into ½-inch pieces
Salt and pepper
½ cup medium-grind bulgur, rinsed
¼ cup lemon juice (2 lemons)
14 ounces extra-firm tofu, cut into 2-inch pieces
¼ cup extra-virgin olive oil
3 garlic cloves, minced
⅛ teaspoon cayenne pepper
1½ cups minced fresh parsley
½ cup minced fresh mint
2 scallions, sliced thin

1 Toss tomatoes with ¼ teaspoon salt in fine-mesh strainer set over bowl and let drain, tossing occasionally, for 30 minutes; reserve 2 tablespoons drained tomato juice. Toss bulgur with 2 tablespoons lemon juice and reserved tomato juice in bowl and let sit until grains begin to soften, 30 to 40 minutes.

2 Meanwhile, spread tofu on paper towel–lined baking sheet and let drain for 20 minutes. Gently press dry with paper towels and season with salt and pepper. Pulse tofu in food processor until coarsely chopped, 3 to 4 pulses. Line baking sheet with clean paper towels. Spread processed tofu over prepared sheet and press gently with paper towels to dry.

3 Heat 2 teaspoons oil in 12-inch nonstick skillet over medium-high heat until shimmering. Add tofu and cook, stirring occasionally, until tofu is lightly browned, 10 to 12 minutes. (Tofu should start to sizzle after about 1½ minutes; adjust heat as needed.) Push tofu to sides of skillet. Add 1 teaspoon oil and garlic to center and cook, mashing garlic into skillet, until fragrant, about 1 minute. Stir mixture into tofu. Transfer to bowl and let cool for 10 minutes.

4 Whisk remaining 2 tablespoons lemon juice, remaining 3 tablespoons oil, cayenne, and ½ teaspoon salt together in large bowl. Add drained tomatoes, soaked bulgur, cooled tofu, parsley, mint, and scallions and toss to combine. Cover and let sit until bulgur is tender, about 1 hour. Toss to recombine and season with salt and pepper to taste before serving.

Cauliflower Salad with Chermoula and Carrots

serves 4 to 6

Why This Recipe Works Chermoula is a traditional Moroccan marinade made with hefty amounts of cilantro, lemon, and garlic that packs a big flavor punch. While this dressing is traditionally used as a marinade for meat and fish, we decided to make it the flavor base for a zippy cauliflower salad in an effort to dress up a vegetable that can be bland and boring. We focused first on the cooking method of the starring vegetable. Roasting was the best choice to add deep flavor to the cauliflower and balance the bright chermoula. To keep the cauliflower from overbrowning before the interior was cooked, we started it covered and let it steam until barely tender. Then we removed the foil, added sliced onion, and returned the pan to the oven to let both the onion and the cauliflower caramelize. Adding the onion to the pan once the cauliflower was uncovered ensured that they would finish cooking at the same time. Finally, to highlight the natural sweetness of the cooked vegetables, we added shredded carrot and raisins, two traditional North African ingredients. Use the large holes of a box grater to shred the carrot.

SALAD

- 1 head cauliflower (2 pounds), cored and cut into 2-inch florets
- 2 tablespoons extra-virgin olive oil
  Salt and pepper
- ½ red onion, sliced ¼ inch thick
- 1 cup shredded carrot
- ½ cup raisins
- 2 tablespoons chopped fresh cilantro
- 2 tablespoons sliced toasted almonds

CHERMOULA

- ¾ cup fresh cilantro leaves
- ¼ cup extra-virgin olive oil
- 2 tablespoons lemon juice
- 4 garlic cloves, minced
- ½ teaspoon ground cumin
- ½ teaspoon paprika
- ¼ teaspoon salt
- ⅛ teaspoon cayenne pepper

1 FOR THE SALAD Adjust oven rack to lowest position and heat oven to 475 degrees. Toss cauliflower with oil and season with ½ teaspoon salt and ¼ teaspoon pepper. Spread on parchment paper–lined rimmed baking sheet, cover tightly with aluminum foil, and roast until softened, 5 to 7 minutes.

2 Remove foil and scatter onion on sheet. Roast until vegetables are tender, cauliflower is deep golden, and onion slices are charred at edges, 10 to 15 minutes, stirring halfway through roasting. Let cool slightly, about 5 minutes.

3 FOR THE CHERMOULA Process all ingredients in food processor until smooth, about 1 minute, scraping down sides of bowl as needed; transfer to large bowl. Add cauliflower-onion mixture, carrot, and raisins and toss to combine. Season with salt and pepper to taste, sprinkle with cilantro and almonds, and serve warm or at room temperature.

main dish salads and bowls

Asparagus and Arugula Salad with Cannellini Beans

serves 4 to 6

5 tablespoons extra-virgin olive oil
½ red onion, sliced thin
1 pound asparagus, trimmed and cut on bias into 1-inch lengths
Salt and pepper
1 (15-ounce) can cannellini beans, rinsed
2 tablespoons plus 2 teaspoons balsamic vinegar
6 ounces (6 cups) baby arugula

Why This Recipe Works Asparagus is one of our favorite vegetables in the test kitchen: Its deep flavor is similar to that of cruciferous vegetables, yet it's sweeter and more subtle. And with its crisp-tender stalks and frilly tips, its texture is more delicate. To make this standout multipurpose vegetable the center of a bright, fresh salad, choosing the right cooking method was paramount. Steaming produced bland, mushy spears, but sautéing the asparagus over high heat delivered deep flavor and tender texture. We sliced the spears on the bias to expose as much of the inner fibers to the cooking surface as possible. We browned some red onion with olive oil in a hot pan before adding the asparagus pieces. Just 4 minutes of cooking was enough to produce uniformly tender pieces. Creamy cannellini beans provided a subtly nutty flavor and smooth contrast to the asparagus. While the asparagus mixture cooled, we made a simple vinaigrette of balsamic vinegar, olive oil, salt, and pepper. For the greens, we knew peppery arugula would hold up well against the other bold flavors, so we dressed and plated it before tossing the asparagus in the dressing as well. Look for asparagus spears no thicker than ½ inch.

1 Heat 2 tablespoons oil in 12-inch nonstick skillet over high heat until just smoking. Add onion and cook until lightly browned, about 1 minute. Add asparagus, ¼ teaspoon salt, and ¼ teaspoon pepper and cook, stirring occasionally, until asparagus is browned and crisp-tender, about 4 minutes. Transfer to bowl, stir in beans, and let cool slightly, about 5 minutes.

2 Whisk vinegar, ¼ teaspoon salt, and ⅛ teaspoon pepper together in bowl. Whisking constantly, slowly drizzle in remaining 3 tablespoons oil. Toss arugula with 2 tablespoons dressing until coated and season with salt and pepper to taste. Divide arugula among individual plates. Toss asparagus mixture with remaining dressing, arrange over arugula, and serve.

Quinoa, Black Bean, and Mango Salad with Lime Dressing

serves 4 to 6

1½ cups prewashed white quinoa

2¼ cups water

Salt and pepper

5 tablespoons lime juice (3 limes)

½ jalapeño chile, stemmed, seeded, and chopped

¾ teaspoon ground cumin

½ cup extra-virgin olive oil

⅓ cup fresh cilantro leaves

1 red bell pepper, stemmed, seeded, and chopped

1 mango, peeled, pitted, and cut into ¼-inch pieces

1 (15-ounce) can black beans, rinsed

2 scallions, sliced thin

1 avocado, halved, pitted, and sliced thin

Why This Recipe Works Sure, quinoa is a complete protein and is known as a "superfood," so it's a great base for a hearty and healthful main dish salad. But we love it also for its intriguing and delicate texture and nutty flavor. For a quinoa salad that showcased these great qualities, we started by toasting the quinoa to bring out its flavor before adding liquid to the pan and simmering the seeds until nearly tender. We then spread the quinoa on a rimmed baking sheet so that the residual heat would finish cooking it gently as it cooled, giving us perfectly cooked, fluffy grains. Black beans, mango, and bell pepper lent the salad bright flavor, color, and satisfying heft. A simple but intense dressing made with olive oil, lime juice, jalapeño, cumin, and cilantro gave this dish the acidity needed to keep its flavors fresh. Finally, sliced scallions contributed bite, and a generous topping of avocado slices provided a creamy richness that balanced the bright dressing. If you buy unwashed quinoa (or if you are unsure whether it's washed), be sure to rinse it before cooking to remove its bitter protective coating (called saponin). For a spicier dressing, add the jalapeño ribs and seeds.

1 Toast quinoa in large saucepan over medium-high heat, stirring often, until quinoa is very fragrant and makes continuous popping sound, 5 to 7 minutes. Stir in water and ½ teaspoon salt and bring to simmer. Cover, reduce heat to low, and simmer gently until most of water has been absorbed and quinoa is nearly tender, about 15 minutes.

2 Spread quinoa on rimmed baking sheet and let cool completely, about 15 minutes; transfer to large bowl. (Cooled quinoa can be refrigerated for up to 3 days.)

3 Process lime juice, jalapeño, cumin, and 1 teaspoon salt in blender until jalapeño is finely chopped, about 15 seconds. With blender running, add oil and cilantro; continue to process until smooth and emulsified, about 20 seconds.

4 Add bell pepper, mango, beans, scallions, and lime-jalapeño dressing to cooled quinoa and toss to combine. Season with salt and pepper to taste. Serve, topping individual servings with avocado.

Farro Salad with Sugar Snap Peas and White Beans

serves 4 to 6

12 ounces sugar snap peas, strings removed, cut into 1-inch lengths
Salt and pepper
1½ cups whole farro
3 tablespoons extra-virgin olive oil
2 tablespoons lemon juice
2 tablespoons minced shallot
1 teaspoon Dijon mustard
1 (15-ounce) can cannellini beans, rinsed
6 ounces cherry tomatoes, halved
⅓ cup chopped pitted kalamata olives
2 tablespoons chopped fresh dill

Why This Recipe Works We've developed recipes for farro as a warm side dish or cooked risotto-style for a comforting supper, but we wanted to give it a new spin and use it as the base of a hearty, fresh salad. The problem? Traditionally, farro is soaked overnight and then cooked gradually for more than an hour. Could we find a quicker, simpler method? Luckily, this was easy. After testing out a few cooking techniques, we learned that boiling the farro and then draining it (we call this the pasta method), like we do for so many other grains, yielded nicely firm but tender farro—no soaking necessary. We let the grains cool and then tossed them with snap peas that we had cooked first in the boiling water to bring out their vibrant color and crisp-tender bite. A lemon-dill dressing served as a citrusy, herbal complement to the earthy farro and fresh-tasting peas. For a full-flavored finish, we added in some cherry tomatoes and meaty kalamata olives, and we stirred in creamy cannellini beans to make this salad even more of a hearty meal. We prefer the flavor and texture of whole-grain farro; pearled farro can be used, but the texture may be softer. We found a wide range of cooking times among various brands of farro, so start checking for doneness after 10 minutes. Do not use quick-cooking farro in this recipe.

1 Bring 4 quarts water to boil in large pot. Add snap peas and 1 tablespoon salt and cook until crisp-tender, about 2 minutes. Using slotted spoon, transfer snap peas to large plate and let cool completely, about 15 minutes.

2 Add farro to water, return to boil, and cook until grains are tender with slight chew, 15 to 30 minutes. Drain farro, spread on rimmed baking sheet, and let cool completely, about 15 minutes. (Cooled farro can be refrigerated for up to 3 days.)

3 Whisk oil, lemon juice, shallot, mustard, ¼ teaspoon salt, and ¼ teaspoon pepper together in large bowl. Add cooled snap peas, cooled farro, beans, tomatoes, olives, and dill and toss to combine. Season with salt and pepper to taste, and serve.

Wheat Berry Salad with Chickpeas, Spinach, and Orange

serves 4 to 6

1½ cups wheat berries
Salt and pepper
3 oranges
4 teaspoons sherry vinegar
2 teaspoons Dijon mustard
1 garlic clove, minced
¾ teaspoon sweet smoked paprika
3 tablespoons extra-virgin olive oil
1 (15-ounce) can chickpeas, rinsed
3 ounces (3 cups) baby spinach, chopped
1 small red onion, sliced thin
¼ cup minced fresh mint

Why This Recipe Works The earthy, almost sweet flavor and firm chew of wheat berries make them an ideal choice for a filling salad that's dressed to impress. We wanted a wheat berry salad that was interesting but also pantry-friendly. We chose to showcase a classic pair of ingredients from Spanish cuisine—chickpeas and spinach. Along with these, we added juicy orange segments (another popular Spanish ingredient) and piquant red onion slices, and tossed them in a tangy, aromatic vinaigrette made with sherry vinegar, Dijon mustard, garlic, sweet smoked paprika, and extra-virgin olive oil. Minced fresh mint rounded out the dish with a verdant brightness. We found it easiest to cook the wheat berries like pasta, simply boiling them in 4 quarts of water with salt to boost their flavor. Some simply shake a random measure of salt into their pasta pot, but we found that nailing the amount of salt in the boiling water was key to making the wheat berries taste good: With too little salt, the grains were insipid, and with too much salt, they didn't absorb enough water and remained hard and crunchy after cooking. One and a half teaspoons of salt was just right, flavoring the perfectly cooked wheat berries from germ to bran. If using quick-cooking or presteamed wheat berries (read the ingredient list on the package to determine this), you will need to decrease the wheat berry cooking time in step 1.

1 Bring 4 quarts water to boil in large pot. Add wheat berries and 1½ teaspoons salt, return to boil, and cook until tender but still chewy, 1 hour to 1 hour 10 minutes. Drain wheat berries, spread on rimmed baking sheet, and let cool completely, about 15 minutes. (Cooled wheat berries can be refrigerated for up to 3 days.)

2 Meanwhile, cut away peel and pith from oranges. Cut each fruit into quarters, then slice each quarter into ¼-inch-thick pieces. Transfer fruit to bowl.

3 Whisk vinegar, mustard, garlic, paprika, ½ teaspoon salt, and ¼ teaspoon pepper together in large bowl. Whisking constantly, slowly drizzle in oil. Add wheat berries, chickpeas, spinach, onion, oranges, and mint and toss gently to combine. Season with salt and pepper to taste, and serve.

main dish salads and bowls

157

Freekeh Salad with Butternut Squash, Walnuts, and Raisins

serves 4 to 6

1½ cups whole freekeh
  Salt and pepper
1½ pounds butternut squash,
  peeled, seeded, and cut into
  ½-inch pieces (4 cups)
5 tablespoons extra-virgin olive oil
½ teaspoon ground fenugreek
⅓ cup golden raisins
2½ tablespoons lemon juice
2 tablespoons tahini
1 garlic clove, minced
1 cup coarsely chopped cilantro
⅓ cup walnuts, toasted and
  chopped

Why This Recipe Works A commonly used grain across the eastern Mediterranean and North Africa, freekeh has a grassy, slightly smoky flavor that deserves more recognition at home. Here, we pair robust freekeh with subtly sweet butternut squash in a satisfying salad. Roasting the squash resulted in lightly charred, beautifully caramelized edges; to give the squash more dimension, we paired it with fenugreek, a nutty seed with a unique maple-like flavor. To bring the two elements together, we stirred in a rich yet bright tahini-lemon dressing. A little extra sweetness came in the form of plumped raisins. Toasted walnuts offered complementary crunch, and a generous amount—one whole cup—of chopped cilantro gave the salad freshness in spades. We prefer the texture of whole, uncracked freekeh; cracked freekeh can be substituted, but you will need to decrease the freekeh cooking time in step 1.

1 Adjust oven rack to lowest position and heat oven to 450 degrees. Bring 4 quarts water to boil in Dutch oven. Add freekeh and 1 tablespoon salt, return to boil, and cook until grains are tender, 30 to 45 minutes. Drain freekeh, spread over rimmed baking sheet, and let cool completely, about 15 minutes. (Cooled freekeh can be refrigerated for up to 3 days.)

2 Meanwhile, toss squash with 1 tablespoon oil, fenugreek, ¼ teaspoon salt, and ⅛ teaspoon pepper. Spread on rimmed baking sheet and roast until well browned and tender, 30 to 35 minutes, stirring halfway through roasting; let cool completely, about 15 minutes.

3 Combine raisins and ¼ cup hot tap water in small bowl and let sit until softened, about 5 minutes; drain.

4 Whisk lemon juice, tahini, 1 tablespoon water, garlic, ½ teaspoon salt, and ⅛ teaspoon pepper in large bowl until smooth. Whisking constantly, slowly drizzle in remaining ¼ cup oil. Add cooled freekeh, squash, plumped raisins, cilantro, and walnuts and toss to combine. Season with salt and pepper to taste, and serve.

Red Rice and Quinoa Salad

serves 4 to 6

¾ cup red rice
   Salt and pepper
¾ cup prewashed white quinoa
3 tablespoons lime juice (2 limes)
2 oranges
1 small shallot, minced
1 tablespoon minced fresh cilantro
   plus 1 cup leaves
¼ teaspoon red pepper flakes
¼ cup extra-virgin olive oil
6 ounces pitted dates, chopped
   (1 cup)

Why This Recipe Works Regular white rice; aromatic basmati; chewy, healthful brown rice; and even rustic wild rice are common pantry items. But there's one rice variety that doesn't get enough play: red rice. Red rice sports—surprise—a red husk, and it has a nutty flavor and is highly nutritious. For a rice and grain salad that was colorful, hearty, and a little out of the ordinary, we mixed this healthful rice with nutty quinoa, cooking both in the same pot using the pasta method. We gave the rice a 15-minute head start and then added the quinoa to the pot to ensure that both grains were done at the same time. Then we drained them, drizzled them with lime juice to add bright flavor, and let them cool. Next, we looked for ingredients that would make this salad fresh and a little sweet. We added dates and orange segments for sweetness (and used some of the orange juice in our dressing). Cilantro and red pepper flakes added a fresh bite and a bit of spiciness to round it out. If you buy unwashed quinoa (or if you are unsure whether it's washed), be sure to rinse it before cooking to remove its bitter protective coating (called saponin).

1 Bring 4 quarts water to boil in large pot over high heat. Add rice and 1 tablespoon salt and cook, stirring occasionally, for 15 minutes. Add quinoa to pot and continue to cook until grains are tender, 12 to 14 minutes. Drain rice-quinoa mixture, spread over rimmed baking sheet, drizzle with 2 tablespoons lime juice, and let cool completely, about 15 minutes.

2 Meanwhile, cut away peel and pith from oranges. Holding fruit over bowl, use paring knife to slice between membranes to release segments. Cut segments in half crosswise. If needed, squeeze orange membranes to equal 2 tablespoons juice in bowl.

3 Whisk 2 tablespoons orange juice, remaining 1 tablespoon lime juice, shallot, minced cilantro, and pepper flakes together in large bowl. Whisking constantly, slowly drizzle in oil. Add rice-quinoa mixture, dates, orange segments, and remaining 1 cup cilantro leaves, and toss to combine. Season with salt and pepper to taste, and serve.

Chickpea Salad with Carrots, Arugula, and Olives

serves 4 to 6

2 (15-ounce) cans chickpeas, rinsed

¼ cup extra-virgin olive oil

2 tablespoons lemon juice

Salt and pepper

Pinch cayenne pepper

3 carrots, peeled and shredded

1 cup baby arugula, chopped coarse

½ cup pitted kalamata olives, chopped coarse

Why This Recipe Works Creamy, nutty-tasting, filling chickpeas are one of our favorite ingredients, making their way into soups, sandwich fillings, and more. And they should make a great salad. Too often, however, chickpea salads fall flat; the chickpeas are simply tossed with vinaigrette, and the dressing slides off their slippery surfaces. For our chickpea salad, we wanted to infuse each bean with big, bold flavor to the core. We discovered that the key was to warm the chickpeas before mixing them with our lemony and slightly spicy dressing ingredients: The seed coats that cover the chickpeas are rich in pectin, which breaks down when exposed to heat and moisture, creating a more porous inner surface that our flavorful dressing could easily penetrate. Letting the dressed chickpeas rest for 30 minutes put the flavor over the top and allowed the chickpeas to cool. Finally, we focused on choosing complementary add-ins for our salad. Chopped arugula offset the mild chickpeas with peppery bite. For one salad, a combination of sweet carrots—a common partner for chickpeas in salads in the Mediterranean—and briny olives added more contrasting texture and flavor. And a variation featuring crunchy, anise-flavored fennel kept things interesting.

1 Microwave chickpeas in medium bowl until hot, about 2 minutes. Stir in oil, lemon juice, ¾ teaspoon salt, ½ teaspoon pepper, and cayenne and let sit for 30 minutes.

2 Add carrots, arugula, and olives and toss to combine. Season with salt and pepper to taste, and serve.

VARIATION

Chickpea Salad with Fennel and Arugula

Substitute 1 fennel bulb, stalks discarded, bulb halved, cored, and cut into ¼-inch pieces, for carrots and olives.

Spiced Lentil Salad with Winter Squash

serves 4 to 6

Salt and pepper
1 cup black lentils, picked over and rinsed
1 pound butternut squash, peeled, seeded, and cut into ½-inch pieces (3 cups)
5 tablespoons extra-virgin olive oil
2 tablespoons balsamic vinegar
1 garlic clove, minced
½ teaspoon ground coriander
¼ teaspoon ground cumin
¼ teaspoon ground ginger
⅛ teaspoon ground cinnamon
1 teaspoon Dijon mustard
½ cup fresh parsley leaves
¼ cup finely chopped red onion
1 tablespoon raw pepitas, toasted

Why This Recipe Works Lentil salads are highly adaptable: Use your favorite variety; keep them simple or stir in other ingredients; serve them warm or cold. For a unique and balanced lentil salad to add to our repertoire, we paired sophisticated, bold-tasting black lentils with butternut squash; the squash's sweetness was a nice foil to this earthy legume. To accentuate the delicate squash flavor, we tossed small pieces with balsamic vinegar and extra-virgin olive oil and roasted them in a hot oven. Putting the rack in the lowest position encouraged deep, even browning. Satisfied with the squash, we turned to the lentils. We soaked them in a saltwater solution to season them throughout and ensure fewer blowouts. To infuse them with more flavor as they cooked, we chose a mixture of warm, floral spices. We cooked the pot of lentils in the oven rather than on the stove for even cooking. As for the dressing, we echoed the flavor of the squash by using balsamic vinegar. We also added a small amount of Dijon mustard for depth. Parsley and chopped red onion gave the dish some color and freshness, and toasted pepitas provided just the right amount of textural contrast. You can use *lentilles du Puy* (also called French green lentils), brown, or regular green lentils in this recipe, though cooking times will vary. Salt-soaking helps keep the lentils intact, but if you don't have time, they'll still taste good.

1 Dissolve 1 teaspoon salt in 4 cups warm water (about 110 degrees) in bowl. Add lentils and soak at room temperature for 1 hour. Drain well.

2 Meanwhile, adjust oven racks to middle and lowest positions and heat oven to 450 degrees. Toss squash with 1 tablespoon oil, 1½ teaspoons vinegar, ¼ teaspoon salt, and ¼ teaspoon pepper. Spread squash on rimmed baking sheet and roast on lower rack until well browned and tender, 20 to 25 minutes, stirring halfway through roasting. Let cool slightly, about 5 minutes. Reduce oven temperature to 325 degrees.

3 Heat 1 tablespoon oil, garlic, coriander, cumin, ginger, and cinnamon in medium saucepan over medium heat until fragrant, about 1 minute. Stir in 4 cups water and lentils. Cover, transfer saucepan to upper oven rack, and cook until lentils are tender but remain intact, 40 minutes to 1 hour.

4 Drain lentils well. Whisk remaining 3 tablespoons oil, remaining 1½ tablespoons vinegar, and mustard together in large bowl. Add squash, lentils, parsley, and onion and toss to combine. Season with salt and pepper to taste, sprinkle with pepitas, and serve warm or at room temperature.

Multipurpose Sauces

BUILD A BOWL

This chapter includes recipes for unique vegan bowls: meals made from a base of warm grains or noodles topped with various ingredients that provide protein, flavor, and texture. These bowls come together with a drizzle of a vibrant sauce. These are some of our favorite sauces. You can use them on sandwiches, as dipping sauces, and on any plain dish that needs an upgrade.

Cilantro Sauce   makes about ¾ cup

We prefer the flavor and texture of Tofutti Better Than Sour Cream. Other dairy-free sour creams will add their distinctive flavor and you may need to adjust the consistency with water. We strongly prefer our favorite vegan mayonnaise, Just Mayo, or our homemade Vegan Mayonnaise (page 22). (For more information on vegan mayonnaise, see page 22.)

¼ cup vegan mayonnaise
¼ cup dairy-free sour cream
3 tablespoons water
3 tablespoons minced fresh cilantro
¼ teaspoon salt

Whisk all ingredients together in bowl.

Chile Sauce   makes about ½ cup

The Korean chile paste *gochujang* is sold in Asian markets and some supermarkets. If you can't find it, an equal amount of Sriracha sauce can be substituted. But because Sriracha sauce is more watery than *gochujang*, omit the water.

¼ cup gochujang
3 tablespoons water
2 tablespoons toasted sesame oil
1 teaspoon organic sugar (page 31)

Whisk all ingredients in bowl until well combined.

Citrus Sauce   makes about ½ cup

3 tablespoons rice vinegar
2 tablespoons mirin
½ teaspoon organic sugar (see page 31)
3 tablespoons soy sauce
1 teaspoon grated fresh ginger
½ teaspoon grated orange zest plus 1 tablespoon juice
½ teaspoon grated lime zest plus 1 tablespoon juice

Bring vinegar, mirin, and sugar to boil in small saucepan, then remove from heat. Whisk in soy sauce, ginger, orange zest and juice, and lime zest and juice. Transfer sauce to bowl.

Curried Peanut Sauce makes about 1 cup

For a spicier sauce, add the jalapeño ribs and seeds. Unseasoned rice vinegar will work in this recipe if you can't find seasoned.

    1 tablespoon vegetable oil
    2 Thai, serrano, or jalapeño chiles, stemmed, seeded, and minced
    3 garlic cloves, minced
    1 tablespoon grated fresh ginger
 1½ teaspoons curry powder
    ½ cup water, plus extra as needed
    ⅓ cup creamy peanut butter
    3 tablespoons seasoned rice vinegar
    2 tablespoons soy sauce
    1 tablespoon organic sugar (see page 31)

Heat oil in medium saucepan over medium heat until shimmering. Stir in Thai chiles, garlic, ginger, and curry powder and cook until fragrant, about 30 seconds. Stir in water, peanut butter, vinegar, soy sauce, and sugar and bring to simmer. Cook, stirring occasionally, until slightly thickened and flavors meld, about 2 minutes. Adjust consistency as needed with additional water. Transfer sauce to bowl.

Miso-Ginger Sauce makes about ¾ cup

We strongly prefer our favorite vegan mayonnaise, Just Mayo, or our homemade Vegan Mayonnaise (page 22). (For more information on vegan mayonnaise, see page 22.)

    ¼ cup vegan mayonnaise
    3 tablespoons red miso
    2 tablespoons water
    1 tablespoon maple syrup
    1 tablespoon sesame oil
 1½ teaspoons sherry vinegar
 1½ teaspoons grated fresh ginger

Whisk all ingredients in bowl until well combined.

Basmati Rice Bowl with Spiced Cauliflower and Pomegranate

serves 4 to 6

¼ cup extra-virgin olive oil
1 onion, chopped coarse
  Salt and pepper
1½ cups basmati rice, rinsed
4 garlic cloves, minced
½ teaspoon ground cinnamon
½ teaspoon ground turmeric
½ teaspoon ground cumin
2¼ cups water
1 head cauliflower (2 pounds), cored and cut into ¾-inch florets
½ cup pomegranate seeds
1 recipe Cilantro Sauce (page 166)
2 tablespoons chopped fresh cilantro
2 tablespoons chopped fresh mint

Why This Recipe Works Basmati rice is truly something else. Its grains, when cooked properly, are long, slender, distinct, and not at all sticky. What's more, basmati is intensely aromatic. We wanted to use this special grain in a warm-spiced rice bowl that highlighted its virtues. We paired the rice with sweet, earthy roasted cauliflower, which we tossed with a generous amount of black pepper for heat and cumin for depth. Roasting at a high temperature for a short time caramelized and crisped small florets without rendering them limp and mushy. To cook the rice, we toasted it in a flavorful mixture of sautéed onion, garlic, and spices and simmered it until tender and fluffy. To serve, we topped individual portions of the spiced rice with our roasted cauliflower and finished the dish with a burst of sweet, crunchy pomegranate seeds and a mix of fresh herbs. A drizzle of creamy cilantro sauce was a cooling counterpoint to the warm spices that brought the dish together. Long-grain white, jasmine, or Texmati rice can be substituted for the basmati.

1 Adjust oven rack to lowest position and heat oven to 475 degrees. Heat 2 tablespoons oil in large saucepan over medium heat until shimmering. Add onion and ¼ teaspoon salt and cook until softened and lightly browned, 5 to 7 minutes. Stir in rice, garlic, cinnamon, turmeric, and ¼ teaspoon cumin and cook until edges of rice begin to turn translucent, about 3 minutes.

2 Stir in water and bring to simmer. Reduce heat to low, cover, and simmer gently until rice is tender and water is absorbed, 16 to 18 minutes. Remove saucepan from heat, lay clean folded dish towel underneath lid, and let rice sit for 10 minutes. Fluff rice with fork and season with salt and pepper to taste.

3 While rice cooks, toss cauliflower with remaining 2 tablespoons oil, ½ teaspoon salt, ½ teaspoon pepper, and remaining ¼ teaspoon cumin. Spread cauliflower on rimmed baking sheet and roast until just tender, 10 to 15 minutes; set aside.

4 Divide rice among individual bowls, then top with roasted cauliflower and pomegranate seeds. Drizzle with cilantro sauce, sprinkle with cilantro and mint, and serve.

Brown Rice Burrito Bowl

serves 4 to 6

1½ cups long-grain brown rice, rinsed
   Salt and pepper
5 tablespoons extra-virgin olive oil
1 tablespoon lime juice
1½ teaspoons ground cumin
1½ teaspoons ground coriander
2 ears corn, kernels cut from cobs
3 garlic cloves, minced
3 poblano chiles, stemmed,
   seeded, and cut into ½-inch
   pieces
1 onion, chopped
1 (15-ounce) can black beans,
   rinsed
1 recipe Creamy Chipotle Sauce
   (page 120)
¼ cup chopped fresh cilantro

Why This Recipe Works A good burrito is all about the filling; layers of spicy, smoky flavors work together in a cohesive whole. We wanted to take the burrito out of its wrapper and put the filling in a bowl to allow each of its elements to shine in a balanced dish. We chose brown rice as the base of our bowl for its nutty flavor and hearty texture. While the rice boiled away on the stove, we seared our vegetables in batches in a skillet for just the right color and char, building flavor in the pan with each batch. Fresh corn provided sweetness and pops of crunch, and poblano peppers offered a subtle background heat. Black beans, cooked with sautéed aromatics, gave our bowl heft and substance. Seasoning the cooked rice with lime, cumin, and coriander brought classic burrito flavors center stage, and finishing the dish with chipotle sauce lent it creamy, smoky richness. With this warm, hearty bowl, we may never wrap burritos again. Serve with avocado, red onion, pico de gallo, and/or lime wedges.

1 Bring 4 quarts water to boil in large pot. Add rice and 1 tablespoon salt, return to boil, and cook, stirring occasionally, until rice is tender, 25 to 30 minutes. Drain rice. Meanwhile, whisk 2 tablespoons oil, lime juice, ½ teaspoon cumin, ½ teaspoon coriander, ¼ teaspoon salt, and ¼ teaspoon pepper together in large bowl. Stir in hot rice and toss to coat. Cover to keep warm.

2 While rice cooks, heat 1 tablespoon oil in 12-inch nonstick skillet over medium-high heat until shimmering. Stir in corn, ¼ teaspoon salt, and ¼ teaspoon pepper and cook until spotty brown, about 3 minutes. Transfer to second bowl and cover to keep warm.

3 Heat 1 tablespoon oil in now-empty skillet over medium-high heat until shimmering. Stir in 2 teaspoons garlic, remaining 1 teaspoon cumin, and remaining 1 teaspoon coriander and cook until fragrant, about 30 seconds. Stir in poblanos and cook until charred and tender, 6 to 8 minutes. Transfer to third bowl and cover to keep warm.

4 Heat remaining 1 tablespoon oil in now-empty skillet over medium heat until shimmering. Add onion and cook until softened and just beginning to brown, 5 to 7 minutes. Stir in remaining garlic and cook until fragrant, about 30 seconds. Stir in beans, ¼ cup water, and ¼ teaspoon salt and bring to simmer. Reduce heat to medium-low and simmer, stirring occasionally, until beans are warmed through and most of liquid has evaporated, about 2 minutes.

5 Divide rice among individual bowls, then top with poblanos, corn, and beans. Drizzle with chipotle sauce, sprinkle with cilantro, and serve.

Farro Bowl with Tofu, Mushrooms, and Spinach

serves 4 to 6

1½ cups whole farro
   Salt and pepper
2 teaspoons toasted sesame oil
1 teaspoon sherry vinegar
14 ounces firm tofu, sliced
   crosswise into 8 equal slabs
⅓ cup cornstarch
¼ cup vegetable oil, plus extra
   as needed
10 ounces cremini mushrooms,
   trimmed and chopped coarse
1 shallot, minced
2 tablespoons dry sherry
10 ounces (10 cups) baby spinach
1 recipe Miso-Ginger Sauce
   (page 166)
2 scallions, sliced thin

Why This Recipe Works We love that vegetable-and-grain bowls give you the freedom to mix things up—literally and stylistically—at dinnertime. This bowl is a shining example of that. The base of this bowl, hearty, nutty farro, is traditionally associated with Italy and flavor profiles of the western Mediterranean. We wanted to prove that full-flavored and nutritious farro need not be typecast, and we thought it would stand up well to bold Asian ingredients. For toppings, we chose crispy seared tofu planks, which we attractively fanned on top of the grains, along with a simple sauté of mushrooms, shallot, and spinach. We partnered these easy-to-prepare toppings with a potent miso-ginger sauce, which is enhanced with a little vegan mayo for body so it's the perfect drizzlable consistency. We prefer the flavor and texture of whole-grain farro; pearled farro can be used, but the texture may be softer. We found a wide range of cooking times among various brands of farro, so start checking for doneness after 10 minutes. Do not use quick-cooking farro in this recipe.

1 Bring 4 quarts water to boil in large pot. Stir in farro and 1 tablespoon salt, return to boil, and cook until grains are tender with slight chew, 15 to 30 minutes. Drain farro and return to now-empty pot. Drizzle with sesame oil and vinegar, toss to coat, and cover to keep warm.

2 While farro cooks, spread tofu on paper towel–lined baking sheet and let drain for 20 minutes. Gently press dry with paper towels and season with salt and pepper.

3 Spread cornstarch in shallow dish. Coat tofu thoroughly in cornstarch, pressing gently to adhere; transfer to plate. Heat 1 tablespoon vegetable oil in 12-inch nonstick skillet over medium-high heat until just smoking. Add tofu and cook until both sides are crisp and browned, about 4 minutes per side, adding more oil as necessary to prevent charring. Transfer to paper towel–lined plate to drain and tent with aluminum foil.

4 In now-empty skillet, heat 2 tablespoons vegetable oil over medium-high heat until shimmering. Stir in mushrooms, shallot, and ⅛ teaspoon salt and cook until vegetables begin to brown, 5 to 8 minutes. Stir in sherry and cook, scraping up any browned bits, until skillet is nearly dry, about 1 minute; transfer to bowl.

5 Heat remaining 1 tablespoon vegetable oil over medium-high heat in now-empty skillet until shimmering. Add spinach, 1 handful at a time, and cook until just wilted, about 1 minute.

6 Divide farro among individual bowls, then top with tofu, mushrooms, and spinach. Drizzle with miso-ginger sauce, sprinkle with scallions, and serve.

Spicy Peanut Rice Noodle Bowl

serves 4 to 6

1 cup shredded carrots

2 tablespoons seasoned rice vinegar

12 ounces (¼-inch wide) rice noodles

3 tablespoons vegetable oil

1 cup frozen edamame

1 recipe Curried Peanut Sauce
   (see page 166)

1 cup shredded red cabbage

⅓ cup dry-roasted peanuts, chopped

2 tablespoons torn fresh Thai basil
   Lime wedges

Why This Recipe Works This noodle bowl, inspired by the sweet, savory, and spicy flavors of Southeast Asia, is a real stunner, boasting a colorful medley of simple but texturally interesting toppings. We combined tender rice noodles with savory edamame, tangy lightly pickled carrots, and crunchy cabbage, and we draped it all with a rich peanut sauce that's a little spicy, a little sweet, and enlivened with a hint of curry powder for aromatic appeal. Instead of taking the time to pickle our carrots in advance of making the dish, we simply added seasoned rice vinegar to shredded carrots and let them sit while the rice noodles soaked and softened. After the 20-minute noodle soaking period, we started the cooking process by first quickly sautéing the edamame just until it was speckled brown but still maintained a tender-crisp texture and fresh flavor. After removing the edamame from the skillet, we finished cooking the noodles in the same pan with half of our sauce and some water until the noodles were perfectly tender and chewy. Cooking the noodles in the sauce lightly glazed and flavored them. After topping our noodle bowls with the veggies, we added plenty of garnishes—fragrant Thai basil, chopped peanuts, lime wedges, and a light pour of additional sauce were the perfect finish. If you can't find Thai basil you can substitute regular basil. We prefer the flavor of seasoned rice vinegar to pickle the carrots in this recipe.

1 Combine carrots and vinegar in small bowl; set aside. Cover noodles with very hot tap water in large bowl and stir to separate. Let noodles soak until softened, pliable, and limp but not fully tender, about 20 minutes. Drain noodles.

2 Heat 1 tablespoon oil in 12-inch nonstick skillet over medium-high heat until just smoking. Add edamame and cook until spotty brown but still bright green, about 2 minutes; transfer to bowl. In now-empty skillet, heat remaining 2 tablespoons oil over medium heat until shimmering, add drained noodles, 1¼ cups water, and ½ cup peanut sauce and cook until sauce has thickened slightly and noodles are well coated and tender, about 1 minute.

3 Divide noodles among individual serving bowls, then top with carrots, edamame, and cabbage. Drizzle with remaining peanut sauce, sprinkle with peanuts and basil, and serve with lime wedges.

Barley Bowl with Roasted Carrots and Snow Peas

serves 4 to 6

¼ cup extra-virgin olive oil
3 tablespoons minced fresh mint
1 teaspoon grated lemon zest plus
  2 tablespoons juice
1½ cups pearl barley
  Salt and pepper
5 carrots, peeled
¾ teaspoon ground coriander
8 ounces snow peas, strings
  removed, halved lengthwise
⅔ cup raw sunflower seeds
½ teaspoon ground cumin
⅛ teaspoon ground cardamom
½ cup Tahini Sauce (page 120)

Why This Recipe Works Chewy, nutty, pearl barley isn't just for soups. Here, we've made it the star of a hearty bowl that's full of contrasting—and surprising—textures and Middle Eastern flavors, with its warm spices and colorful vegetables. To keep the cooking method easy, we simply boiled the barley. This made the individual grains tender and kept them distinct and light. We tossed the warm barley with a bright lemon-mint dressing so the grains would readily soak it up. While the barley cooked, we pan-roasted coriander-dusted spears of carrots until charred, sweet, and tender. We then threw in crisp snow peas and cooked them until just blistered, so they would retain their green freshness. Toasting sunflower seeds with cumin, cardamom, and a little more coriander gave the dish a warm, aromatic finish. We piled a mound of the dressed barley and vegetables into our bowls, followed by our crunchy seed topping. Finally, to pull all the components of the bowl together, we needed a drizzle of sauce, and our Tahini Sauce was a creamy, zesty addition. Do not substitute hulled barley or hull-less barley in this recipe. If using quick-cooking or presteamed barley (read the ingredient list on the package to determine this), you will need to decrease the barley cooking time in step 1. We also like this bowl topped with avocado.

1 Whisk 2½ tablespoons oil, 2 tablespoons mint, and lemon zest and juice together in large bowl, set aside. Bring 4 quarts water to boil in large pot. Add barley and 1 tablespoon salt, return to boil, and cook until tender, 20 to 40 minutes. Drain barley, transfer to bowl with lemon-mint mixture, and toss to combine. Season with salt and pepper to taste and cover to keep warm.

2 While barley cooks, halve carrots crosswise, then halve or quarter lengthwise to create uniformly sized pieces. Heat 1 tablespoon oil in 12-inch nonstick skillet over medium-high heat until just smoking. Add carrots and ½ teaspoon coriander and cook, stirring occasionally, until lightly charred and just tender, 5 to 7 minutes. Stir in snow peas and cook until spotty brown, 3 to 5 minutes; transfer to second bowl.

3 Heat remaining 1½ teaspoons oil in now-empty skillet over medium heat until shimmering. Add sunflower seeds, cumin, cardamom, remaining ¼ teaspoon coriander, and ¼ teaspoon salt. Cook, stirring constantly, until seeds are toasted, about 2 minutes; transfer to third bowl.

4 Divide barley among individual bowls, then top with carrot–snow pea mixture and sunflower seeds. Drizzle with tahini sauce, sprinkle with remaining 1 tablespoon mint, and serve.

Brown Sushi Rice Bowl with Tofu and Vegetables

serves 6

3½ cups water

2⅓ cups short-grain brown rice, rinsed

¼ cup mirin

3 tablespoons rice vinegar

28 ounces soft tofu, patted dry and cut into 3-inch-long by ½-inch-thick fingers

Salt and pepper

¾ cup cornstarch

¼ cup cornmeal

2 tablespoons vegetable oil

1 (8 by 7½-inch) sheet nori, crumbled (optional)

6 radishes, sliced thin

1 avocado, halved, pitted, and sliced thin

1 cucumber, peeled, halved lengthwise, seeded, and sliced thin

1 recipe Citrus Sauce (page 166)

4 scallions, sliced thin

Why This Recipe Works Rice bowls are popular fare in Japan, so we wanted to add compelling Japanese flavors to our roster of grain bowls. We started by swapping out our go-to long-grain rice for more appropriate sticky short-grain brown rice. To infuse the cooked rice with flavor akin to sushi rice, we tossed it with mirin and rice vinegar. To top off the flavorful sticky rice, we coated soft tofu with cornstarch and crunchy cornmeal, and we cooked it in a skillet. By cutting the tofu into fingers, we were rewarded with four ultracrispy sides that gave way to an appealingly creamy interior. We garnished the bowls with crumbled nori seaweed, spicy sliced radishes, rich avocado, cool cucumber, and scallions, and we dressed the bowls with a potent sauce of soy, ginger, orange, and lime. To save time, prep the tofu and vegetables while the rice cooks. We prefer the creamier texture of soft tofu here, but firm or extra-firm will work. Nori is seaweed that has been dried and pressed into sheets used for rolling sushi; you can find nori in the international foods aisle of the supermarket.

1 Bring water and rice to simmer in large saucepan over high heat. Reduce heat to low, cover, and continue to simmer until rice is tender and water is absorbed, 45 to 50 minutes. Remove pot from heat, lay clean folded dish towel underneath lid, and let sit for 10 minutes. Transfer rice to large bowl. Drizzle with mirin and vinegar, then let cool for 20 minutes, gently tossing with wooden paddle or spoon occasionally.

2 While rice cooks, spread tofu over paper towel–lined baking sheet and let drain for 20 minutes. Gently press tofu dry with paper towels and season with salt and pepper.

3 Adjust oven rack to middle position, place paper towel–lined plate on rack, and heat oven to 200 degrees. Whisk cornstarch and cornmeal together in shallow dish. Working with several pieces of tofu at a time, coat thoroughly with cornstarch mixture, pressing to help coating adhere, and transfer to wire rack set in rimmed baking sheet.

4 Heat 1 tablespoon oil in 12-inch nonstick skillet over medium-high heat until shimmering. Carefully add half of tofu and cook until crisp and lightly golden on all sides, 10 to 12 minutes; transfer to plate in oven. Repeat with remaining 1 tablespoon oil and remaining tofu.

5 Divide rice among individual bowls, then sprinkle with half of nori, if using. Top with browned tofu, radishes, avocado, and cucumber. Drizzle with citrus sauce, sprinkle with scallions, and serve, passing remaining nori separately.

main dish salads and bowls

Why This Recipe Works Korean *dolsot* bibimbap features a crispy rice crust and a variety of lively toppings—some savory, some acidic, some spicy. It just might be the ultimate rice bowl. Some versions include eggs and meat, but with all of the intriguing, fresh ingredients in this dish, we didn't miss them one bit. We did, however, want to add some heft, so we incorporated tempeh; the tempeh's nutty and pleasantly bitter notes played nicely with the dish's parade of sweet and sour flavors. For a quick dinner, prepare the pickles, chile sauce, and vegetables a day ahead (warm the vegetables to room temperature in the microwave before adding them to the rice). You can also substitute store-bought kimchi for the pickles to save time. For a true bibimbap experience, bring the pot to the table before stirring the vegetables and tempeh into the rice in step 8.

PICKLES

1 cup cider vinegar

2 tablespoons organic sugar (see page 31)

1½ teaspoons salt

1 cucumber, peeled, quartered lengthwise, seeded, and sliced thin on bias

4 ounces (2 cups) bean sprouts

RICE

2½ cups short-grain white rice

2½ cups water

¾ teaspoon salt

VEGETABLES AND TEMPEH

2 tablespoons vegetable oil

8 ounces tempeh, cut into ½-inch pieces

¼ cup soy sauce

¼ teaspoon salt

¼ teaspoon pepper

½ cup water

3 scallions, minced

3 garlic cloves, minced

1 tablespoon organic sugar (see page 31)

3 carrots, peeled and shredded (2 cups)

8 ounces shiitake mushrooms, stemmed and sliced thin

10 ounces curly-leaf spinach, stemmed and chopped coarse

BIBIMBAP

2 tablespoons vegetable oil

1 tablespoon toasted sesame oil

1 recipe Chile Sauce (page 166)

1 FOR THE PICKLES Whisk vinegar, sugar, and salt together in bowl. Add cucumber and bean sprouts and toss to combine. Press vegetables to submerge, cover, and refrigerate for at least 30 minutes or up to 24 hours.

2 FOR THE RICE Bring rice, water, and salt to boil in medium saucepan over high heat. Cover, reduce heat to low, and cook for 7 minutes. Remove saucepan from heat and let sit, covered, until rice is tender, about 15 minutes.

3 FOR THE VEGETABLES AND TEMPEH While rice cooks, heat 1 tablespoon oil in 12-inch nonstick skillet over medium-high heat until just smoking. Add tempeh, 1 tablespoon soy sauce, salt, and pepper and cook until well browned, 4 to 6 minutes. Remove from heat and cover to keep warm.

4 Combine water, scallions, garlic, sugar, and remaining 3 tablespoons soy sauce in bowl. Heat 1 teaspoon oil in Dutch oven over high heat until shimmering. Add carrots, stirring to coat. Stir in ⅓ cup scallion mixture and cook until carrots are slightly softened and liquid has evaporated, about 1 minute; transfer to bowl.

5 Heat 1 teaspoon oil in now-empty pot until shimmering. Add mushrooms, stirring to coat. Stir in ⅓ cup scallion mixture and cook until mushrooms are tender and liquid has evaporated, about 3 minutes; transfer mushrooms to second bowl.

6 Heat remaining 1 teaspoon oil in now-empty Dutch oven until shimmering. Stir in spinach and remaining scallion mixture and cook until spinach is just wilted, about 1 minute. Transfer spinach to third bowl, discard any remaining liquid, and wipe out pot with paper towel.

7 FOR THE BIBIMBAP Heat vegetable oil and sesame oil in now-empty pot over high heat until shimmering. Carefully add cooked rice and press into even layer. Cook, without stirring, until rice begins to form crust on bottom of pot, about 2 minutes. Transfer tempeh, carrots, mushrooms, and spinach to pot and arrange in piles to cover surface of rice. Reduce heat to low and cook until golden brown crust forms on bottom of rice, about 5 minutes.

8 Drizzle 2 tablespoons chile sauce over top. Without disturbing crust, stir rice, vegetables, and tempeh until combined. Scrape large pieces of crust from bottom of pot and stir into rice. Serve in individual bowls, passing pickles and remaining chile sauce separately.

new

dinn

favor

er
ites

Creamy Cashew Mac and Cheese

serves 4 to 6

⅓ cup coconut oil (see page 30)
¼ cup nutritional yeast
4 teaspoons dry mustard
1 tablespoon tomato paste
2 garlic cloves, minced
Salt and pepper
½ teaspoon ground turmeric
4½ cups unsweetened almond milk
10 ounces cauliflower florets, cut into ½-inch pieces (3 cups)
1¼ cups raw cashews, chopped
1 pound elbow macaroni
1 tablespoon distilled white vinegar

Why This Recipe Works Homestyle stovetop mac and cheese is a dish you might think you have to live without on a vegan diet—the word "cheese" is in the name, after all. But we were determined to make a creamy vegan macaroni. Existing versions call for pureeing ingredients ranging from squash or potatoes to sunflower seeds and even cannellini beans for the sauce. We found those to largely be vegetal-tasting and sticky. Our winning formula was a mixture of cashews, cauliflower, and almond milk that we simmered together and blended until smooth. The rich fat from the cashews and the light, silken texture of the cauliflower made for a decadent, pasta-coating sauce. Funky nutritional yeast, when combined with mustard powder for bite, tomato paste for sweetness, and vinegar for tang, gave the dish a remarkable cheesy flavor. The sauce will be loose as you add the macaroni, but it will thicken as it finishes cooking and is served. Serve with our Vegan Parmesan Substitute (page 27).

1 Heat oil in large saucepan over medium heat until shimmering. Stir in nutritional yeast, mustard, tomato paste, garlic, 2 teaspoons salt, and turmeric and cook until fragrant, about 30 seconds. Stir in almond milk, scraping up any browned bits, and bring to simmer over medium-high heat. Stir in cauliflower and cashews, reduce heat to medium-low, and cook, partially covered, until cauliflower is very soft and falls apart easily when poked with fork, about 20 minutes.

2 Working in 2 batches, process cauliflower mixture in blender until smooth, about 2 minutes, scraping down sides as needed.

3 Meanwhile, bring 4 quarts water to boil in large pot. Add macaroni and 1 tablespoon salt and cook, stirring often, until nearly tender. Reserve ½ cup cooking water, then drain macaroni and set aside. Transfer pureed cauliflower mixture to now-empty pot and bring to gentle simmer over medium-low heat. Add drained macaroni and vinegar and cook, stirring constantly, until warmed through and sauce is slightly thickened, about 3 minutes. Adjust consistency with reserved cooking water as needed, season with salt and pepper to taste, and serve immediately.

TESTING NOTES **Dairy-Free Milks**
OUR FAVORITE **Almond Milk**
OTHERS TESTED Soy milk yields a less savory mac and cheese and a thicker sauce. Coconut milk makes a flatter-tasting mac and cheese with a thinner consistency. Oat milk is very sweet; do not use.

Return Policy

With a sales receipt or Barnes & Noble.com packing slip, a full refund in the original form of payment will be issued from any Barnes & Noble Booksellers store for returns of undamaged NOOKs, new and unread books, and unopened and undamaged music CDs, DVDs, vinyl records, toys/games and audio books made within 14 days of purchase from a Barnes & Noble Booksellers store or Barnes & Noble.com with the below exceptions:

A store credit for the purchase price will be issued (i) for purchases made by check less than 7 days prior to the date of return, (ii) when a gift receipt is presented within 60 days of purchase, (iii) for textbooks, (iv) when the original tender is PayPal, or (v) for products purchased at Barnes & Noble College bookstores that are listed for sale in the Barnes & Noble Booksellers inventory management system.

Opened music CDs, DVDs, vinyl records, audio books may not be returned, and can be exchanged only for the same title and only if defective. NOOKs purchased from other retailers or sellers are returnable only to the retailer or seller from which they are purchased, pursuant to such retailer's or seller's return policy. Magazines, newspapers, eBooks, digital downloads, and used books are not returnable or exchangeable. Defective NOOKs may be exchanged at the store in accordance with the applicable warranty.

Returns or exchanges will not be permitted (i) after 14 days or without receipt or (ii) for product not carried by Barnes & Noble or Barnes & Noble.com.

Policy on receipt may appear in two sections.

Return Policy

With a sales receipt or Barnes & Noble.com packing slip, a full refund in the original form of payment will be issued from any Barnes & Noble Booksellers store for returns of undamaged NOOKs, new and unread books, and unopened and undamaged music CDs, DVDs, vinyl records, toys/games and audio books made within 14 days of purchase from a Barnes & Noble Booksellers store or Barnes & Noble.com with the below exceptions:

A store credit for the purchase price will be issued (i) for purchases made by check less than 7 days prior to the date of return, (ii) when a gift receipt is presented within 60 days of purchase, (iii) for textbooks, (iv) when the original tender is PayPal, or (v) for products purchased at Barnes & Noble College bookstores that are listed for sale in the Barnes & Noble Booksellers inventory management system.

Opened music CDs, DVDs, vinyl records, audio books

Mushroom Bolognese
serves 4 to 6

2 pounds cremini mushrooms, trimmed and quartered

1 carrot, peeled and chopped

1 small onion, chopped

1 (28-ounce) can whole peeled tomatoes

3 tablespoons extra-virgin olive oil

½ ounce dried porcini mushrooms, rinsed and minced

3 garlic cloves, minced

1 teaspoon organic sugar (see page 31)

2 tablespoons tomato paste

1 cup dry red wine

½ cup vegetable broth

1 tablespoon soy sauce
Salt and pepper

3 tablespoons unsweetened soy creamer

1 pound fettuccine or linguine

Why This Recipe Works A good Bolognese sauce is savory, lush, and decadent. Traditional Bolognese gets its rich flavor from a combination of several types of meat. To mimic the meat sauce's long-cooked richness, we turned to the mighty mushroom. Two types of mushrooms helped us replicate that complexity. Dried porcini delivered depth of flavor while 2 pounds of fresh cremini gave the sauce a satisfying, substantial texture. To further round out the sauce's savory flavor, we added two umami-rich ingredients soy sauce and tomato paste. Red wine lent richness and depth and a little sugar balanced the dish. Bolognese often includes a pour of cream; we found that some soy creamer—just 3 tablespoons—stirred in at the end rounded out the sauce and made it silky. We strongly prefer our favorite vegetable broths, Orrington Farms Vegan Chicken Broth or our homemade Vegetable Broth Base (page 21). (For more information on vegetable broth, see page 21.) Any dairy-free creamer will work in this recipe. Serve with our Vegan Parmesan Substitute (page 27).

1 Working in batches, pulse cremini mushrooms in food processor until pieces are no larger than ½ inch, 5 to 7 pulses; transfer to large bowl. Pulse carrot and onion in now-empty processor until finely chopped, 5 to 7 pulses; transfer to bowl with processed mushrooms. Pulse tomatoes and their juice in now-empty processor until finely chopped, 6 to 8 pulses; set aside separately.

2 Heat oil in Dutch oven over medium heat until shimmering. Add processed vegetables and porcini mushrooms, cover, and cook, stirring occasionally, until they release their liquid, about 5 minutes. Uncover, increase heat to medium-high, and cook until vegetables begin to brown, 12 to 15 minutes.

3 Stir in garlic and sugar and cook until fragrant, about 30 seconds. Stir in tomato paste and cook for 1 minute. Stir in wine and simmer until nearly evaporated, about 5 minutes.

4 Stir in processed tomatoes, broth, soy sauce, ½ teaspoon salt, and ¼ teaspoon pepper, and bring to simmer. Reduce heat to medium-low and simmer until sauce has thickened but is still moist, 8 to 10 minutes. Off heat, stir in soy creamer.

5 Meanwhile, bring 4 quarts water to boil in large pot. Add pasta and 1 tablespoon salt and cook, stirring often, until al dente. Reserve ½ cup cooking water, then drain pasta and return it to pot. Add sauce and toss to combine. Adjust consistency with reserved cooking water as needed, season with salt and pepper to taste, and serve.

Fettuccine Alfredo

serves 4 to 6

2½ cups unsweetened almond milk
⅓ cup coconut oil (see page 30)
3 tablespoons white miso
Salt and pepper
10 ounces cauliflower florets, cut into ½-inch pieces (3 cups)
¾ cup raw cashews, chopped
1 pound fettuccine
Pinch ground nutmeg
2 tablespoons chopped fresh parsley

Why This Recipe Works Classic fettuccine Alfredo is loaded with cream, Parmesan cheese, and butter, so it's usually reserved for enjoying just a few times a year. We were excited for the challenge of veganizing this decadent dish and eating it more often. To replicate the creaminess of the original, we started with the silky base of pureed cauliflower and cashews that we use in our Creamy Cashew Mac and Cheese (page 184). Here we were looking for a more subtly flavored, luxurious sauce, with the slightly sweet notes of traditional Alfredo. We added coconut oil for the richness of a cream sauce and miso paste for savory-sweet balance. Like classic fettuccine Alfredo, the texture of the sauce changes dramatically as the dish stands for a few minutes; serving in warmed bowls helps ensure that it retains its creamy texture while it's being eaten. Adjust the consistency with reserved cooking water as needed. Serve with our Vegan Parmesan Substitute (page 27).

1 Combine almond milk, oil, miso, and 1 teaspoon salt in large saucepan and bring to simmer over medium-high heat, whisking to dissolve miso. Stir in cauliflower and cashews, reduce heat to medium-low, and cook, partially covered, until cauliflower is very soft and falls apart easily when poked with fork, about 20 minutes.

2 Process cauliflower mixture and ½ cup water in blender until smooth, about 2 minutes, scraping down sides as needed. Strain through fine-mesh strainer set over bowl, pressing on solids to extract as much puree as possible; discard solids.

3 Meanwhile, bring 4 quarts water to boil in large pot. Add pasta and 1 tablespoon salt and cook, stirring often, until nearly tender. Reserve ½ cup cooking water, then drain pasta and set aside in colander.

4 Transfer pureed cauliflower mixture to now-empty pot. Whisk in nutmeg and bring to gentle simmer over medium-low heat. Add drained pasta and cook, stirring constantly, until warmed through and sauce is slightly thickened, about 3 minutes. Adjust consistency with reserved cooking water as needed, season with salt and pepper to taste, sprinkle with parsley, and serve immediately.

TESTING NOTES **Dairy-Free Milks**
OUR FAVORITE **Almond Milk**
OTHERS TESTED: Coconut milk was slightly more vegetal. Soy milk made a thicker fettuccine with a distinct soy flavor. Oat milk is very sweet; do not use.

Why This Recipe Works How could we develop a stick-to-your-ribs vegan vegetable lasagna if a good one features layer upon layer of cheese? We tested our way through dairy-free béchamel sauces (pasty and off-tasting), tofu-based fillings (strong soy flavor), and vegan mozzarella-style cheeses (artificial taste and plasticky texture), and we found that our winning combination of cashews and cauliflower gave our lasagna the right creaminess. However, this time we used this duo to mimic the texture of ricotta, not a sauce: We axed the almond milk, drained the mixture of excess liquid after cooking, and processed it in a food processor to achieve a slightly grainy, ricotta-like texture. Be sure to let the lasagna cool for the full 25 minutes. Not all no-boil lasagna noodles are vegan, so check ingredient lists carefully.

TOMATO SAUCE

1 (28-ounce) can crushed tomatoes
1 (14.5-ounce) can diced tomatoes, drained
¼ cup chopped fresh basil
3 tablespoons extra-virgin olive oil
2 garlic cloves, minced
1 teaspoon organic sugar
   (see page 31)
½ teaspoon salt
¼ teaspoon red pepper flakes

FILLING

8 ounces cauliflower florets, cut into ½-inch pieces (2¼ cups)
1½ cups raw cashews, chopped
   Salt and pepper
¼ cup extra-virgin olive oil
1 tablespoon chopped fresh basil

VEGETABLES

1 pound eggplant, peeled and cut into ½-inch pieces
1 pound white mushrooms, trimmed and sliced thin
3 tablespoons extra-virgin olive oil
1 garlic clove, minced
   Salt
1 pound zucchini, cut into ½-inch pieces

LASAGNA

12 no-boil lasagna noodles
1 tablespoon extra-virgin olive oil
1 tablespoon chopped fresh basil

1 FOR THE TOMATO SAUCE Process tomatoes, basil, oil, garlic, sugar, salt, and pepper flakes in food processor until smooth, scraping down sides of bowl as needed, about 30 seconds. Transfer sauce to bowl and set aside. (Sauce can be refrigerated for up to 1 day.)

2 FOR THE FILLING Bring 3 quarts water to boil in large saucepan. Add cauliflower florets, cashews, and 2 teaspoons salt and cook until cauliflower is very soft and falls apart easily when poked with fork, about 20 minutes. Drain cauliflower mixture in colander and let cool slightly, about 5 minutes.

3 Process cauliflower mixture, 3 tablespoons oil, and ¼ cup water in clean, dry food processor until smooth, scraping down sides of bowl as needed, about 2 minutes (mixture will be slightly grainy). Season with salt and pepper to taste. Transfer ¼ cup mixture to bowl and stir in remaining 1 tablespoon oil and basil; set aside for topping. (Mixtures can be refrigerated for up to 3 days.)

4 FOR THE VEGETABLES Adjust oven rack to upper-middle position and heat oven to 450 degrees. Toss eggplant and mushrooms with 2 tablespoons oil, garlic, and ½ teaspoon salt in bowl, then spread on rimmed baking sheet. Toss zucchini with remaining 1 tablespoon oil, and ¼ teaspoon salt in now-empty bowl. Roast eggplant-mushroom mixture until beginning to wilt, about 15 minutes. Remove sheet from oven, stir zucchini into vegetables, and continue to roast, stirring occasionally, until mushrooms are lightly browned, eggplant and zucchini are tender, and most of juices have evaporated, 15 to 20 minutes. Set aside. (Cooked vegetables can be refrigerated for up to 1 day.)

5 FOR THE LASAGNA Adjust oven rack to middle position and heat oven to 375 degrees. Grease 13 by 9-inch baking dish. Spread 1⅓ cups tomato sauce over bottom of dish. Arrange 4 noodles on top. Spread half of cauliflower filling over noodles, followed by half of vegetables. Spread 1⅓ cups tomato sauce over vegetables. Repeat layering with 4 noodles, remaining cauliflower filling, and remaining vegetables. Arrange remaining 4 noodles on top, and cover completely with remaining tomato sauce.

6 Cover dish with aluminum foil and bake until edges are bubbling, 45 to 50 minutes, rotating dish halfway through baking. Dollop lasagna evenly with 8 to 10 spoonfuls of reserved cauliflower topping, and let cool for 25 minutes. Drizzle with oil, sprinkle with remaining 1 tablespoon basil, and serve.

Spaghetti and Meatless Meatballs

serves 4 to 6

Why This Recipe Works To make a vegan meatball that had the savory flavor and heft of a classic one, we turned to vegan protein crumbles, which provided structure and chew. A full pound of meaty cremini mushrooms, pulsed fine in a food processor and deeply browned in a skillet, boosted the savory flavor and meaty texture. Both of these ingredients are crumbly, so we needed a strong binder. Stirring panko bread crumbs and aquafaba into the mix helped, but the meatballs still lacked cohesiveness. We found that 4 ounces of chopped eggplant, sautéed with the mushrooms, provided a lovely silky texture without too strong a flavor. To make the porcini powder, grind the dried porcini mushrooms in a spice grinder until they are reduced to fine dust. Serve with our Vegan Parmesan Substitute (page 27).

SAUCE AND PASTA

- 2 (28-ounce) cans crushed tomatoes
- 2 tablespoons extra-virgin olive oil
- 1 onion, chopped fine
  Salt and pepper
- 4 garlic cloves, minced
- 1 tablespoon tomato paste
- ¼ cup dry red wine
- ½ cup chopped fresh basil
- ½ teaspoon organic sugar (see page 31)
- 1 pound spaghetti

MEATLESS MEATBALLS

- 1 pound cremini mushrooms, trimmed and quartered
- 4 ounces eggplant, cut into 1-inch pieces (1¾ cups)
- 1 onion, chopped
- 4 garlic cloves, minced
- 2 tablespoons extra-virgin olive oil
- ⅛ ounce dried porcini mushrooms, finely ground (1 tablespoon)
  Salt and pepper
- 12 ounces vegan protein crumbles, broken into small pieces
- 1 cup panko bread crumbs
- ¼ cup chopped fresh parsley
- 3 tablespoons aquafaba (see page 34)

1 FOR THE SAUCE Process tomatoes in food processor until smooth, about 30 seconds. Heat oil in large pot over medium heat until shimmering. Add onion, 1 teaspoon salt, and ¼ teaspoon pepper and cook until onion is softened and just beginning to brown, 5 to 7 minutes.

2 Stir in garlic and tomato paste and cook until fragrant, about 30 seconds. Stir in wine and cook, scraping up any browned bits, until evaporated, about 1 minute. Stir in processed tomatoes and bring to boil. Reduce heat to low and simmer gently until sauce is slightly thickened, 10 to 15 minutes. Off heat, stir in ¼ cup basil and sugar. Season with salt and pepper to taste; cover to keep warm. (Sauce can be refrigerated for up to 1 day.)

3 FOR THE MEATBALLS Meanwhile, adjust oven rack to upper-middle position and heat oven to 400 degrees. Line rimmed baking sheet with parchment paper and spray with vegetable oil spray. Pulse cremini mushrooms in clean, dry food processor until pieces are no larger than ¼ inch, 5 to 7 pulses; transfer to bowl. Pulse eggplant, onion, and garlic in now-empty processor until chopped fine, 6 to 8 pulses; transfer to bowl with mushrooms.

4 Heat oil in 12-inch nonstick skillet over medium heat until shimmering. Add processed vegetables, ground porcini mushrooms, 1 teaspoon salt, and ¼ teaspoon pepper, cover, and cook, stirring occasionally, until vegetables have released their liquid, about 5 minutes. Uncover, increase heat to medium-high, and cook until vegetables are well browned, about 15 minutes; transfer to large bowl.

5 Add protein crumbles, panko, parsley, and aquafaba to bowl with browned vegetables and toss to combine. Using your hands, knead mixture well until cohesive and sticky, about 1 minute.

6 Shape mushroom mixture into 24 meatballs (about 2 table-spoons each) and space evenly on prepared sheet. Bake until browned and firm, 25 to 30 minutes, gently turning meatballs and rotating sheet halfway through baking.

7 Meanwhile, bring 4 quarts water to boil in large pot. Add pasta and 1 tablespoon salt and cook, stirring often, until al dente. Drain pasta and return it to pot. Measure out 4 cups sauce and toss with pasta to combine. Top individual portions of spaghetti with meatballs and sprinkle with remaining ¼ cup basil. Serve, passing remaining sauce separately.

Why This Recipe Works Italians have a knack for transforming humble ingredients into remarkable meals, and the rustic trio of pasta, greens, and beans is a fine example. For our hearty dish, we combined whole-wheat spaghetti with curly-leaf spinach, creamy cannellini beans, and sweet diced tomatoes. We wanted the pasta to have a strong savory presence without using cheese, so we employed a one-two punch of umami with white miso and cheesy-tasting nutritional yeast. To ensure everything would fit in one pan, we wilted half of the spinach before adding the rest with the tomatoes and vegetable broth. Then we braised the spinach in the broth and followed by adding the beans and some kalamata olives for a briny pop of flavor. This mixture had to simmer with the pasta for just a couple minutes to create a harmonious dish. The skillet will be very full once you add all the spinach in step 2, but will become more manageable as it wilts. We strongly prefer our favorite vegetable broths, Orrington Farms Vegan Chicken Broth or our homemade Vegetable Broth Base (page 21). (For more information on vegetable broth, see page 21.) Serve with our Vegan Parmesan Substitute (page 27).

¼ cup extra-virgin olive oil, plus extra for serving

8 garlic cloves, peeled (5 sliced thin, 3 minced)

Salt and pepper

1 onion, chopped fine

½ teaspoon red pepper flakes

1¼ pounds curly-leaf spinach, stemmed and cut into 1-inch pieces

2 tablespoons white miso

2 tablespoons nutritional yeast

¾ cup vegetable broth

1 (14.5-ounce) can diced tomatoes, drained

1 (15-ounce) can cannellini beans, rinsed

¾ cup pitted kalamata olives, chopped coarse

1 pound whole-wheat spaghetti

1 Cook 3 tablespoons oil and sliced garlic in 12-inch skillet over medium heat, stirring often, until garlic turns golden but not brown, about 3 minutes. Using slotted spoon, transfer garlic to paper towel–lined plate; season lightly with salt.

2 Add onion to oil left in pan and cook over medium heat until softened and just beginning to brown, 5 to 7 minutes. Stir in minced garlic and pepper flakes and cook until fragrant, about 30 seconds. Add half of spinach and cook, tossing occasionally, until starting to wilt, about 2 minutes. Whisk miso and nutritional yeast into broth to combine, then add to pan with remaining spinach, tomatoes, and ¾ teaspoon salt. Bring to simmer, then cover and cook, tossing occasionally, until spinach is completely wilted, about 10 minutes (mixture will be somewhat loose and watery at this point). Stir in beans and olives, then remove pan from heat and cover to keep warm.

3 Meanwhile, bring 4 quarts water to boil in large pot. Add pasta and 1 tablespoon salt and cook, stirring often, until nearly tender. Reserve ½ cup cooking water, then drain pasta and return it to pot. Stir in spinach mixture and cook over medium heat, tossing to combine, until pasta is tender and most of liquid is absorbed, about 2 minutes.

4 Off heat, stir in remaining 1 tablespoon oil. Adjust consistency with reserved cooking water as needed and season with salt and pepper to taste. Serve, garnishing individual portions with garlic chips and drizzling with oil.

Almost Hands-Free Mushroom Risotto

serves 6

4 cups vegetable broth

3 cups water

⅓ cup white miso

¼ cup extra-virgin olive oil

1 pound cremini mushrooms, trimmed and sliced ¼ inch thick

Salt and pepper

1 onion, chopped fine

4 garlic cloves, minced

1 ounce dried porcini mushrooms, rinsed and minced

2 cups Arborio rice

½ cup dry white wine

¼ cup chopped fresh parsley

Why This Recipe Works The ideal risotto is beloved for its plush creaminess, derived in part from copious amounts of butter and Parmesan. Our challenge was to replicate the test kitchen's classic Almost Hands-Free Risotto without the dairy. Our starting point, cashew cheese, turned the risotto sticky and pasty. Some recipes call for chia seeds, but they speckled the rice with unappealing globules. Simply stirring in olive oil made the risotto greasy, and store-bought vegan Parmesan imparted a plasticky sheen. We thought creamy vegan risotto wasn't meant to be until we stumbled upon the use of miso, and it was a breakthrough. We add miso to dishes for its savory notes; here it also acted as a thickener, giving the risotto a satiny gloss. To make our risotto a meal, we added savory cremini mushrooms and dried porcini. This more hands-off method requires precise timing, so we highly recommend using a timer. We strongly prefer our favorite vegetable broths, Orrington Farms Vegan Chicken Broth or our homemade Vegetable Broth Base (page 21). (For more information on vegetable broth, see page 21.) Serve with our Vegan Parmesan Substitute (page 27).

1 Bring broth, water, and miso to boil in large saucepan over high heat; reduce heat to medium-low and simmer, whisking occasionally, until miso is dissolved, about 5 minutes. Cover and keep warm over low heat.

2 Meanwhile, heat 1 tablespoon oil in Dutch oven over medium heat until shimmering. Add cremini mushrooms and ¼ teaspoon salt, cover, and cook until mushrooms have released their liquid, about 5 minutes. Uncover and continue to cook until well browned, 10 to 12 minutes longer; transfer to bowl.

3 Heat 2 tablespoons oil in now-empty pot over medium heat until shimmering. Stir in onion and ¼ teaspoon salt and cook until softened, about 5 minutes. Add garlic and porcini mushrooms and cook until fragrant, about 30 seconds. Add rice and cook, stirring frequently, until grains are translucent around edges, about 3 minutes. Add wine and cook, stirring constantly, until fully absorbed, about 2 minutes. Stir in 5 cups hot broth mixture; reduce heat to medium-low, cover, and simmer until almost all liquid has been absorbed and rice is just al dente, 16 to 19 minutes, stirring twice during cooking.

4 Add ¾ cup hot broth mixture and browned cremini mushrooms, and stir gently and constantly until risotto becomes creamy, about 3 minutes. Remove pot from heat, cover, and let stand for 5 minutes. Stir in parsley and remaining 1 tablespoon oil and season with salt and pepper to taste. Before serving, adjust consistency with additional broth mixture as needed.

Almost Hands-Free Fennel Risotto

Omit porcini mushrooms. Substitute 1 large fennel bulb, stalks discarded, bulb halved, cored, and chopped, for cremini mushrooms. In step 2, reduce uncovered cooking time to 7 to 10 minutes, then add 1 tablespoon Pernod and continue to cook until completely evaporated, about 1 minute, before transferring to bowl.

Vegan Shepherd's Pie

serves 4 to 6

2 pounds russet potatoes, peeled
and cut into 1-inch pieces
Salt and pepper
⅓ cup unsweetened almond milk
5 tablespoons extra-virgin olive oil
¼ cup minced fresh chives
1 onion, chopped
4 ounces white mushrooms,
trimmed and chopped
1 tablespoon tomato paste
2 garlic cloves, minced
2 tablespoons Madeira or ruby port
2 tablespoons all-purpose flour
2½ cups vegetable broth
2 carrots, peeled and chopped
2 teaspoons vegan Worcestershire
sauce
2 sprigs fresh thyme
1 bay leaf
12 ounces vegan protein crumbles,
broken into small pieces

Why This Recipe Works Shepherd's pie has universal appeal, with its rich, satisfying filling and its playful fluff of mashed potato topping. Neither the filling nor the topping is vegan-friendly, but we were determined to make a vegan version to please palateson the coldest of nights. We first looked to the gravy. Sautéing umami-rich mushrooms and tomato paste with onion and garlic created lots of flavor-boosting fond; we then deglazed the pan with Madeira wine before adding the broth. This gravy gave us a backbone of meaty flavor, but the biggest key to success was using vegan protein crumbles. When cooked in our gravy, they added depth and an appealing chew. For the topping, we whipped up some mashed potatoes, adding almond milk for creaminess. Using a fork, we created ridges in the potato topping that would brown under the broiler. We strongly prefer our favorite vegetable broths, Orrington Farms Vegan Chicken Broth or our homemade Vegetable Broth Base (page 21). (For more information on vegetable broth, see page 21.)

1 Cover potatoes with water in large saucepan. Add 1 tablespoon salt, bring to simmer over medium-high heat, and cook until potatoes are tender, 8 to 10 minutes.

2 Drain potatoes and return to now-empty saucepan. Using potato masher, mash potatoes until smooth, then stir in almond milk, ¼ cup oil, and chives. Season with salt and pepper to taste; cover and set aside.

3 Heat remaining 1 tablespoon oil in broiler-safe 10-inch skillet over medium heat until shimmering. Add onion, mushrooms, and ¼ teaspoon pepper and cook until softened, about 5 minutes. Stir in tomato paste and garlic and cook until bottom of skillet is dark brown, about 2 minutes.

4 Stir in Madeira and cook, scraping up any browned bits, until evaporated, about 1 minute. Stir in flour and cook for 1 minute. Stir in broth, carrots, Worcestershire, thyme sprigs, and bay leaf and bring to boil, scraping up any browned bits. Reduce heat to medium-low and simmer gently until carrots and mushrooms are tender, 10 to 15 minutes. Discard thyme sprigs and bay leaf, stir in protein crumbles, and season with salt and pepper to taste.

5 Adjust oven rack 5 inches from broiler element and heat broiler. Transfer mashed potatoes to 1-gallon zipper-lock bag, seal top, and snip off bottom corner to make 1-inch opening. Pipe potatoes evenly over filling to cover. Smooth potatoes with back of spoon, then make ridges over surface with fork. Place skillet on rimmed baking sheet and broil until potatoes are golden and crusty, 5 to 10 minutes. Let cool for 10 minutes before serving.

Pinto Bean and Swiss Chard Enchiladas

serves 4 to 6

¼ cup vegetable oil
2 onions, chopped fine
  Salt and pepper
3 tablespoons chili powder
2 teaspoons ground cumin
2 teaspoons organic sugar (see page 31)
6 garlic cloves, minced
2 (8-ounce) cans tomato sauce
½ cup water
1 pound Swiss chard, stemmed and sliced into ½-inch-wide strips
2 green bell peppers, stemmed, seeded, and cut into ½-inch pieces
1 (15-ounce) can pinto beans, rinsed
12 (6-inch) corn tortillas, warmed
1 recipe Cilantro Sauce (page 166)
1 avocado, halved, pitted, and cut into ½-inch pieces
¼ cup fresh cilantro leaves
  Lime wedges

Why This Recipe Works Making enchiladas can be cumbersome—churning out sauces, fillings, toppings, warming tortillas, assembling, and then baking. We wanted hearty, delicious vegetable enchiladas that were streamlined but with tons of flavor. Cheese fillings and shredded meat are common, but we kept things green by wilting some flavorsome Swiss chard and crisp, slightly bitter green peppers with garlic and onions. To add creamy cohesiveness and heft, we mashed half a can of pinto beans and mixed in our greens; we stirred in the rest of the beans whole for contrasting texture. This clean-tasting filling needed a robust sauce to round out the flavors; a quick simmer of canned tomato sauce with aromatics and spices did the trick. Traditional recipes call for frying the tortillas one at a time, but we found that brushing them with oil and microwaving worked just as well—and without the mess. Store-bought dairy-free cheeses weighed down our enchiladas and added off-flavors. A topping of a *crema*-like cilantro sauce and avocado was ideal: tangy, creamy, fresh-tasting, and rich.

1 Adjust oven rack to middle position and heat oven to 450 degrees. Heat 1 tablespoon oil in large saucepan over medium heat until shimmering. Add half of onions and ½ teaspoon salt and cook until softened, about 5 minutes. Stir in chili powder, cumin, sugar, and half of garlic and cook until fragrant, about 30 seconds. Stir in tomato sauce and water, bring to simmer, and cook until slightly thickened, about 7 minutes. Season with salt and pepper to taste; set aside.

2 Meanwhile, heat 1 tablespoon oil in Dutch oven over medium heat until shimmering. Add remaining onions and ¼ teaspoon salt and cook until softened and just beginning to brown, 5 to 7 minutes. Add remaining garlic and cook until fragrant, about 30 seconds. Add chard and bell peppers, cover, and cook until chard is tender, 6 to 8 minutes. Using potato masher, coarsely mash half of beans in large bowl. Stir in chard-pepper mixture, ¼ cup sauce, and remaining whole beans.

3 Spread ½ cup sauce over bottom of 13 by 9-inch baking dish. Brush both sides of tortillas with remaining 2 tablespoons oil. Stack tortillas, wrap in damp dish towel, and place on plate; microwave until warm and pliable, about 1 minute. Working with 1 warm tortilla at a time, spread ¼ cup chard filling across center. Roll tortilla tightly around filling and place seam side down in baking dish; arrange enchiladas in 2 columns across width of dish. Cover completely with remaining sauce.

4 Cover dish tightly with aluminum foil and bake until enchiladas are heated through, 15 to 20 minutes. Let enchiladas cool for 10 minutes. Drizzle with cilantro sauce and sprinkle with avocado and cilantro. Serve with lime wedges.

Cauliflower Steaks with Salsa Verde

serves 4

1½ cups fresh parsley leaves
½ cup fresh mint leaves
½ cup extra-virgin olive oil
2 tablespoons water
1½ tablespoons white wine vinegar
1 tablespoon capers, rinsed
1 garlic clove, minced
Salt and pepper
2 heads cauliflower (2 pounds each)
Lemon wedges

Why This Recipe Works Our favorite thing about plant-based cooking is that it allows us to reimagine what we put in the center of our plates. Case in point: cauliflower steaks. When you cook thick planks of cauliflower, they develop a substantial, meaty texture and become nutty, sweet, and caramelized. Recipes for cauliflower steaks abound, but many of them involve fussy transitions between stovetop and oven. We wanted to find a simple way to produce four perfectly cooked cauliflower steaks simultaneously, so we opted for a rimmed baking sheet and a scorching oven. Steaming the cauliflower briefly by covering the baking sheet with foil, followed by high-heat uncovered roasting on the lowest oven rack produced dramatic-looking, caramelized seared steaks with tender interiors. To elevate the cauliflower to centerpiece status, we paired it with a vibrant Italian-style *salsa verde*—a blend of parsley, mint, capers, olive oil, and white wine vinegar. We brushed the hot steaks with the salsa verde so they'd soak up its robust flavor. Look for fresh, firm, bright white heads of cauliflower that feel heavy for their size and are free of blemishes or soft spots; florets are more likely to separate from older heads of cauliflower. Serve with our Vegan Parmesan Substitute (page 27).

1 Pulse parsley, mint, ¼ cup oil, water, vinegar, capers, garlic, and ⅛ teaspoon salt in food processor until mixture is finely chopped but not smooth, about 10 pulses, scraping down sides of bowl as needed. Transfer sauce to small bowl and set aside. (Sauce can be refrigerated for up to 2 days.)

2 Adjust oven rack to lowest position and heat oven to 500 degrees. Working with 1 head cauliflower at a time, discard outer leaves of cauliflower and trim stem flush with bottom florets. Halve cauliflower lengthwise through core. Cut one 1½-inch-thick slab lengthwise from each half, trimming any florets not connected to core. Repeat with remaining cauliflower. (You should have 4 steaks; reserve remaining cauliflower for another use. For more information on how to cut cauliflower steaks, see page 6.)

3 Place steaks on rimmed baking sheet and drizzle with 2 tablespoons oil. Sprinkle with ¼ teaspoon salt and ⅛ teaspoon pepper and rub to distribute. Flip steaks and repeat.

4 Cover baking sheet tightly with foil and roast for 5 minutes. Remove foil and roast until bottoms of steaks are well browned, 8 to 10 minutes. Gently flip and continue to roast until tender and second sides are well browned, 6 to 8 more minutes.

5 Transfer steaks to platter and brush evenly with ¼ cup salsa verde. Serve with lemon wedges and remaining salsa verde.

Chile-Rubbed Butternut Squash Steaks with Ranch Dressing

serves 4

¼ cup extra-virgin olive oil
2 teaspoons organic sugar (see page 31)
2 teaspoons smoked paprika
1½ teaspoons salt
½ teaspoon chipotle chile powder
1 teaspoon garlic powder
½ teaspoon pepper
2 (3-pound) butternut squashes
1 recipe Ranch Dressing (page 262)

Why This Recipe Works We had a lot of fun making our cauliflower steaks (page 202), so we wanted to add another vegetable steak to our repertoire. Butternut squash's dense texture gives it a meaty bite, and its sweet, mild flavor can handle bold seasonings. To create thick slabs, we used the necks of large butternuts, carefully peeling them and slicing them lengthwise. Looking to steak-cooking technique, we tried searing the steaks in a hot skillet before transferring them to the oven, but this made our crust soggy. Flipping the process and roasting the steaks before searing ensured the interior was tender, and it dried out the exterior so it could then develop a crust in the skillet. We scored the surface of the squash in a crosshatch pattern to create more surface area for absorbing our spice rub, speed up the process of drying out the exterior, and give our steaks the appearance of quadrillage-style grill marks. A bold-tasting Southwestern rub made from smoked paprika, chipotle chile powder, garlic powder, sugar, salt, pepper, and olive oil made our squash remind tasters of blackened steak. Ranch dressing provides a bright, refreshing foil to the spicy intensity of the steaks. Look for butternut squashes with necks at least 5 inches in length and 2½ to 3½ inches in diameter.

1 Adjust oven rack to middle position and heat oven to 450 degrees. Combine 3 tablespoons oil, sugar, paprika, salt, chile powder, garlic powder, and pepper in bowl; set aside.

2 Working with 1 squash at a time, cut crosswise into 2 pieces at base of neck; reserve bulb for another use. Peel away skin and fibrous threads just below skin (squash should be completely orange, with no white flesh), then carefully cut each piece in half lengthwise. Cut one, ¾-inch-thick slab lengthwise from each half. Repeat with remaining squash. (You should have 4 steaks; reserve remaining squash for another use. For more information on how to cut butternut squash steaks, see page 8.)

3 Place steaks on wire rack set in rimmed baking sheet. Cut ¹⁄₁₆-inch-deep slits on both sides of steaks, spaced ½ inch apart, in crosshatch pattern, and brush evenly with spice mixture. Flip steaks and brush second side with spice mixture. Roast until nearly tender and knife inserted into steaks meets with some resistance, 15 to 17 minutes; remove from oven.

4 Heat remaining 1 tablespoon oil in 12-inch nonstick skillet over medium-high heat until just smoking. Carefully place steaks in skillet and cook, without moving, until well browned and crisp on first side, about 3 minutes. Flip steaks and continue to cook until well browned and crisp on second side, about 3 minutes. Transfer steaks to platter and serve with ranch dressing.

Pan-Seared Tempeh Steaks with Chimichurri Sauce

serves 4

Why This Recipe Works We use tempeh as a protein-boosting ingredient in breakfast, lunch, and dinner dishes. Made from whole fermented soybeans and a mix of grains, tempeh has a firmer, chewier texture than tofu, but it is just as good at soaking up flavor. We thought it deserved top billing at dinner as rich steaks. Marinating the tempeh in a seasoned vinegar-and-water base infused it with flavor. Patting the marinated tempeh dry and pan-searing it created a delectably crisp edge and made the texture more cohesive. We wanted to balance the tempeh's earthy flavor by serving it with a bright herb sauce. Chimichurri sauce is a traditional condiment for steak that combines parsley, wine vinegar, oil, lots of garlic, oregano, and a good dose of red pepper flakes. It paired perfectly with our tempeh, lending bright flavor and richness to the impressive seared steaks.

5 tablespoons red wine vinegar
¼ cup water
4 garlic cloves, minced
1½ teaspoons dried oregano
½ teaspoon red pepper flakes
1 pound tempeh, cut into 3½-inch-long by ⅜-inch-thick slabs
1 cup fresh parsley leaves
½ cup extra-virgin olive oil
Salt and pepper

1 Combine ¼ cup vinegar, water, half of garlic, 1 teaspoon oregano, and ¼ teaspoon pepper flakes in 1-gallon zipper-lock bag. Add tempeh, press out air, seal, and toss to coat. Refrigerate tempeh for at least 1 hour or up to 24 hours, flipping bag occasionally.

2 Pulse parsley, ¼ cup oil, ½ teaspoon salt, remaining 1 tablespoon vinegar, remaining garlic, remaining ½ teaspoon oregano, and remaining ¼ teaspoon pepper flakes in food processor until coarsely chopped, about 10 pulses, scraping down sides of bowl as needed. Transfer to bowl and season with salt and pepper to taste.

3 Remove tempeh from marinade and pat dry with paper towels. Heat 2 tablespoons oil in 12-inch nonstick skillet over medium heat until shimmering. Add 4 pieces tempeh and cook until golden brown on first side, 2 to 4 minutes.

4 Flip tempeh, reduce heat to medium-low, and continue to cook until golden brown on second side, 2 to 4 minutes; transfer to platter. Wipe out skillet with paper towels and repeat with remaining 2 tablespoons oil and remaining tempeh. Serve with parsley sauce.

VARIATION
Pan-Seared Tempeh Steaks with Chermoula Sauce
Omit oregano. Substitute lemon juice for red wine vinegar, ¼ teaspoon cayenne pepper for red pepper flakes, and cilantro for parsley. Add ½ teaspoon ground cumin and ½ teaspoon paprika to tempeh marinade. Add ½ teaspoon ground cumin and ½ teaspoon paprika to sauce.

Crispy Orange Seitan

serves 4

Why This Recipe Works Crispy orange chicken is takeout comfort food that we were amazed didn't miss a beat when we ditched the meat. That's because the real star of the classic is that crispy crust and sweet, tangy sauce. Seitan, a protein made from wheat gluten, was the best protein option; its chewy interior provided a perfect contrast to a crispy coating. To make sure our coating kept its crunch under the sauce, we would typically dip the protein in egg, dredge it in cornstarch, and fry it. To replace the egg wash, we dunked our seitan pieces in canned coconut milk. And we added cornmeal to the cornstarch coating for a rough surface to hold on to our quick-to-make, vibrant orange juice–based sauce. Use cubed or block seitan, not ground or strips in this recipe. For a spicier dish, increase the cayenne added to the sauce to ½ teaspoon. The bird chiles are added for appearance only and can be omitted. Stir them into the sauce at the end of cooking; allowing them to sit in the sauce for too long will turn the sauce unpalatably spicy. We strongly prefer our favorite vegetable broths, Orrington Farms Vegan Chicken Broth or our homemade Vegetable Broth Base (page 21). (For more information on vegetable broth, see page 21.) Serve over rice and with steamed broccoli.

SAUCE

½ cup vegetable broth
¼ cup packed organic dark brown sugar (page 31)
3 tablespoons distilled white vinegar
3 tablespoons soy sauce
2 garlic cloves, minced
1 teaspoon grated orange zest, plus 6 (2-inch) strips zest, plus ½ cup juice
¾ teaspoon grated fresh ginger
⅛ teaspoon cayenne pepper
4 teaspoons cold water
1 tablespoon cornstarch
6 dried bird chiles (optional)
1 scallion, sliced thin

SEITAN

1½ cups cornstarch
½ cup cornmeal
1 cup canned coconut milk
1 pound seitan, drained, patted dry, and cut into 1-inch pieces
3 cups vegetable oil
Salt

1 FOR THE SAUCE Bring broth, sugar, vinegar, soy sauce, garlic, grated orange zest and juice, ginger, and cayenne to boil in large saucepan over high heat. Whisk cold water and cornstarch together in bowl, then whisk into boiling sauce. Reduce heat to medium-low and simmer, stirring occasionally, until slightly thickened, about 1 minute (you should have about 1½ cups sauce). Remove from heat and cover to keep warm.

2 FOR THE SEITAN Adjust oven rack to middle position, place paper towel–lined plate on rack, and heat oven to 200 degrees.

3 Combine cornstarch and cornmeal in shallow dish. Combine coconut milk and seitan in bowl; turn to coat. Working with 1 piece seitan at a time, remove from coconut milk, letting excess drip back into bowl, then coat well with cornstarch mixture, pressing gently to adhere; transfer to large plate. Repeat with remaining seitan.

4 Add oil to 12-inch nonstick skillet and heat over medium-high heat to 350 degrees. Add half of seitan and cook until golden brown on all sides, flipping as necessary, 7 to 11 minutes. Using slotted spoon, transfer to plate in oven. Return oil to 350 degrees and repeat with remaining seitan.

5 Add strips orange zest; chiles, if using; and seitan to sauce in pot and toss to coat well. Season with salt to taste, transfer to platter, sprinkle with scallions, and serve.

Teriyaki Tofu

serves 4 to 6

½ cup water
½ cup soy sauce
½ cup organic sugar (see page 31)
2 tablespoons mirin
1 garlic clove, minced
1 teaspoon cornstarch
½ teaspoon grated fresh ginger
28 ounces extra-firm tofu, sliced crosswise into ¾-inch-thick slabs
Pepper
2 scallions, green parts only, sliced thin
Lime wedges

Why This Recipe Works Teriyaki sauce and tofu are a perfect weeknight-friendly match: The sauce is easy to make from a few pantry ingredients, and the mild tofu readily soaks up the potent teriyaki flavors. To make the teriyaki sauce, we simmered a mixture of soy sauce, sugar, mirin, garlic, ginger, and some cornstarch for thickening. To encourage the tofu to absorb as much flavor as possible from our sauce, we cut the tofu into slabs, laid them in a baking dish, and covered them with the sauce before cooking them slowly in the gentle heat of the oven. But we were disappointed to find that the liquid released from the tofu during cooking had watered down the sauce, even after draining the tofu for a full 20 minutes before cooking. Since it was impossible to drain the tofu of all its liquid, we decided not to drain it at all here; instead, we accounted for the inevitable released liquid by overreducing the sauce to start. As the tofu baked, it released water into the super-concentrated sauce, diluting it to just the right flavor and thickness. You can substitute firm tofu for the extra-firm in this recipe. Serve over rice.

1 Adjust oven rack to middle position and heat oven to 350 degrees. Whisk water, soy sauce, sugar, mirin, garlic, cornstarch, and ginger in small saucepan until smooth. Bring sauce to boil over medium-high heat, whisking occasionally, then reduce heat to medium-low and simmer vigorously until sauce is thickened and reduced to ¾ cup, 12 to 15 minutes.

2 Arrange tofu in even layer in 13 by 9-inch baking dish and pour sauce evenly over top. Cover with aluminum foil and bake until flavors have melded and tofu is warmed through, about 30 minutes, flipping tofu and replacing foil halfway through cooking.

3 Transfer tofu to platter. Season sauce with pepper to taste, pour over tofu, and sprinkle with scallions. Serve with lime wedges.

Thai-Style Tofu and Basil Lettuce Cups

serves 4

14 ounces extra-firm tofu, cut into 2-inch pieces
Salt and pepper
2 cups fresh basil leaves
3 garlic cloves, peeled
6 green or red Thai chiles, stemmed
2 tablespoons fish sauce substitute (see page 21), plus extra as needed
1 tablespoon vegan oyster sauce
1 tablespoon organic sugar (see page 31)
1 teaspoon distilled white vinegar, plus extra as needed
3 shallots, halved and sliced thin
2 tablespoons vegetable oil
¼ cup dry-roasted peanuts, chopped
2 heads Bibb lettuce (1 pound), leaves separated
Red pepper flakes

Why This Recipe Works We took inspiration from the sweet, savory, and spicy flavors of Thai cuisine and made a stir-fried tofu filling to serve in crisp, cool lettuce cups. The Thai low-temperature method of stir-frying involves sautéing the aromatics slowly over moderate heat. The aromatics infuse the oil as they cook, which gives the finished dish layers of complexity. We thought this technique would be perfect for packing mild tofu with great flavor. For the aromatics, we combined garlic, basil, and Thai chiles. We reserved a portion of this mixture and added fish sauce substitute, vegan oyster sauce, sugar, and vinegar to make a balanced, savory stir-fry sauce. We added the oil, remaining aromatics, sliced shallot, and tofu (which we pulsed in a food processor and then pressed dry) to a cold skillet and cooked everything over medium heat until the tofu and shallots turned golden brown. At the end, we stirred in the sauce and more fresh basil leaves until wilted and then added some crunchy peanuts. You can use either firm or extra-firm tofu in this recipe. If fresh Thai chiles are unavailable, substitute two serranos or one jalapeño. For a milder dish, remove the seeds and ribs from the chiles. Serve with rice, if desired.

1 Spread tofu over paper towel–lined baking sheet and let drain for 20 minutes. Gently press dry with paper towels and season with salt and pepper.

2 Meanwhile, process 1 cup basil, garlic, and chiles in food processor until finely chopped, 6 to 10 pulses, scraping down sides of bowl as needed. Transfer 1 tablespoon basil mixture to small bowl and stir in fish sauce substitute, oyster sauce, sugar, and vinegar. Transfer remaining basil mixture to 12-inch nonstick skillet.

3 Pulse tofu in now-empty food processor until coarsely chopped, 3 to 4 pulses. Line baking sheet with clean paper towels. Spread processed tofu over prepared baking sheet and press gently with paper towels to dry.

4 Stir dried tofu, shallots, and oil into skillet with basil mixture and cook over medium heat, stirring occasionally, until tofu and shallots are browned, 10 to 15 minutes. (Mixture should start to sizzle after about 1½ minutes; adjust heat as needed.)

5 Add reserved basil mixture and continue to cook, stirring constantly, until well coated, about 1 minute. Stir in remaining 1 cup basil and cook, stirring constantly, until wilted, 30 to 60 seconds. Off heat, stir in peanuts. Transfer mixture to platter and serve with lettuce leaves, pepper flakes, extra fish sauce substitute, and extra vinegar.

Barbecue Tempeh, Mushroom, and Bell Pepper Skewers

serves 4

2 cups ketchup

6 tablespoons molasses

2 tablespoons cider vinegar

2 teaspoons hot sauce

¼ teaspoon liquid smoke (optional)

¼ cup vegetable oil

¼ cup water

1 pound tempeh, cut into 1½-inch-thick pieces

1 pound cremini mushrooms, trimmed

2 red bell peppers, stemmed, seeded, and cut into 1½-inch pieces

Why This Recipe Works We've long known that the grill is good for more than cooking cuts of meat, and it imparts smoky flavor to vegetable dishes as well. We wondered if our backyard buddy could do the same for protein-packed tempeh kebabs. Cubes of tempeh took on great char and stayed intact on the grill. Tasters craved the familiar flavors of sweet, tomatoey barbecue, so we paired the tempeh with a tangy, molasses-y pantry sauce, which tempered the slightly bitter tempeh. Firm, sweet red bell peppers and juicy, savory mushrooms turned out to be great contrasting companions. We thinned a portion of our sauce with oil and water for a simple marinade that infused the tempeh with barbecue flavor and made it pleasingly soft and moist. After we got good char on our skewers, we brushed on more sauce as they cooked for a syrupy glaze and applied another coat when they were hot off the grill. You will need eight 12-inch metal skewers for this recipe.

1 Whisk ketchup, molasses, vinegar, hot sauce, and liquid smoke, if using, together in bowl. Whisk 1 cup sauce, oil, and water together in second bowl, then transfer to 1-gallon zipper-lock bag. Set aside remaining sauce. Add tempeh and vegetables to bag with marinade, press out air, seal, and toss to coat. Refrigerate for at least 1 hour or up to 24 hours, flipping bag occasionally.

2 Remove tempeh and vegetables from marinade and thread in alternating order onto eight 12-inch metal skewers. Pat dry with paper towels.

3a FOR A CHARCOAL GRILL Open bottom vent completely. Light large chimney starter filled with charcoal briquettes (6 quarts). When top coals are partially covered with ash, pour evenly over grill. Set cooking grate in place, cover, and open lid vent completely. Heat grill until hot, about 5 minutes.

3b FOR A GAS GRILL Turn all burners to high, cover, and heat grill until hot, about 15 minutes. Leave all burners on high.

4 Clean and oil cooking grate. Place skewers on grill and cook (covered if using gas), turning as needed, until tempeh is well browned and vegetables are tender and slightly charred, 8 to 12 minutes. Brush 1 side of skewers with ¼ cup reserved sauce, turn skewers sauced side down, and cook until sizzling and well browned, about 1 minute. Brush second side with ¼ cup reserved sauce, turn skewers sauced side down, and continue to cook until sizzling and well browned, about 1 minute longer. Transfer skewers to platter and brush with additional ¼ cup reserved sauce. Remove tempeh and vegetables from skewers, and serve, passing remaining sauce separately.

Stir-Fried Tofu, Shiitakes, and Green Beans

serves 4

Why This Recipe Works There are many reasons to love stir-fries: They're quick, healthful, and open to endless variations. We wanted to develop a classic stir-fry that captured our infatuation with the dish, so we refreshed ourselves on the wisdom we've collected over the years. For a cooking vessel, we use a nonstick skillet; a wok is designed for a pit-style stove. Patience is on our ingredient list; despite the name, if you overstir your stir-fry, you'll lose that coveted sear. And the process is fast; you must have your ingredients ready before you start cooking. We paired sturdy green beans and meaty shiitake mushrooms, with cornstarch-coated tofu, which developed a slightly crunchy sheath. Although we often cook the vegetables in batches, here we were able to stir-fry them at the same time; the moisture released from the mushrooms nicely steamed the green beans. For a balanced brown sauce, we combined soy sauce, sesame oil, rice vinegar, and a touch of sugar and pepper flakes, and we thickened it with cornstarch. We strongly prefer our favorite vegetable broths, Orrington Farms Vegan Chicken Broth or our homemade Vegetable Broth Base (page 21). (For more information on vegetable broth, see page 21.) Serve over rice.

SAUCE

- ¾ cup vegetable broth
- 3 tablespoons soy sauce
- 2 tablespoons rice vinegar
- 1 tablespoon packed organic brown sugar (see page 31)
- 2 teaspoons cornstarch
- 1 teaspoon toasted sesame oil
- ⅛ teaspoon red pepper flakes

STIR-FRY

- 14 ounces extra-firm tofu, cut into ¾-inch pieces
- ⅓ cup cornstarch
- 3 tablespoons vegetable oil
- 2 scallions, white and green parts separated and sliced thin on bias
- 3 garlic cloves, minced
- 1 tablespoon grated fresh ginger
- 12 ounces green beans, trimmed and cut on bias into 1-inch lengths
- 12 ounces shiitake mushrooms, stemmed and quartered
- 1 tablespoon toasted sesame seeds (optional)

1 FOR THE SAUCE Whisk all ingredients together in bowl.

2 FOR THE STIR-FRY Spread tofu on paper towel–lined baking sheet and let drain for 20 minutes. Gently pat dry with paper towels. Toss drained tofu with cornstarch in bowl, then transfer to fine-mesh strainer and shake gently to remove excess cornstarch.

3 Combine 1 teaspoon oil, scallion whites, garlic, and ginger in bowl. Heat 2 tablespoons oil in 12-inch nonstick skillet over high heat until shimmering. Add tofu and cook, turning as needed, until crisp and well browned on all sides, 12 to 15 minutes; transfer to paper towel–lined plate to drain.

4 Add remaining 2 teaspoons oil to now-empty skillet and heat over medium-high heat until shimmering. Add green beans and mushrooms, cover, and cook until mushrooms release their liquid and green beans are bright green and beginning to soften, 4 to 5 minutes. Uncover and continue to cook until vegetables are spotty brown, about 3 minutes.

5 Push vegetables to sides of skillet. Add garlic mixture to center and cook, mashing mixture into pan, until fragrant, about 30 seconds. Stir garlic mixture into vegetables. Add browned tofu and stir to combine. Whisk sauce to recombine, then add to skillet and cook, stirring constantly, until sauce is thickened, about 30 seconds. Transfer to platter; sprinkle with scallion greens and sesame seeds, if using; and serve.

Stir-Fried Tempeh, Napa Cabbage, and Carrots

serves 4

Why This Recipe Works The stir-fry skillet is a place to get creative—pick your favorite vegetables and your favorite flavors, and if you cook each component just right, anything you can dream up, you can cook up. Unfortunately, when we dreamed up a tempeh and napa cabbage stir-fry, we initially produced pale, unappealing chunks of tempeh amidst soggy, mushy greens—not exactly our vision of golden-brown tempeh and crisp, fresh cabbage in a lustrous, tangy-sweet sauce. First we perfected the tempeh, searing it in a hot skillet with soy sauce to give it a flavor boost and a crisp brown crust. We decided to add carrots for a sweet element and crunch, cranking the heat to high for good caramelization. Napa cabbage can go from tender-crisp to limp and watery in a matter of seconds, so we cooked it just until it achieved a little browning and was heated through. Pairing these ingredients with the right sauce took some experimentation. While we knew we wanted the sauce to have an orange flavor, many orange stir-fry sauces were too light to stand up to the heartiness of the tempeh. Full-flavored and full-bodied orange sweet-and-sour sauce tamed the tempeh's slight bitterness. And the sauce's bright acidity complemented the sweet carrots and mild cabbage. Serve over rice.

SAUCE

- 6 tablespoons red wine vinegar
- 6 tablespoons orange juice
- 6 tablespoons organic sugar (see page 31)
- 3 tablespoons ketchup
- 1 teaspoon cornstarch
- ½ teaspoon salt

STIR-FRY

- 3 tablespoons vegetable oil
- 4 scallions, white and green parts separated and sliced thin on bias
- 3 garlic cloves, minced
- 1 tablespoon grated fresh ginger
- ½ teaspoon red pepper flakes
- 12 ounces tempeh, cut into ½-inch pieces
- 2 tablespoons soy sauce
- 3 carrots, peeled and sliced on bias ¼ inch thick
- ½ head napa cabbage (about 1 pound), cored and cut into 1½-inch pieces

1 FOR THE SAUCE Whisk all ingredients together in bowl.

2 FOR THE STIR-FRY Combine 1 teaspoon oil, scallion whites, garlic, ginger, and pepper flakes in bowl. Heat 2 tablespoons oil in 12-inch nonstick skillet over high heat until just smoking. Add tempeh and soy sauce, and cook, stirring occasionally, until well browned, 4 to 6 minutes; transfer to plate.

3 Heat remaining 2 teaspoons oil in now-empty skillet over high heat until shimmering. Add carrots and cook, stirring occasionally, until spotty brown, about 4 minutes. Stir in cabbage and cook until vegetables are crisp-tender, about 4 minutes.

4 Push vegetables to sides of skillet. Add garlic mixture to center and cook, mashing mixture into pan, until fragrant, about 30 seconds. Stir garlic mixture into vegetables. Add browned tempeh and stir to combine. Whisk sauce to recombine, then add to skillet and cook, stirring constantly, until sauce is thickened, about 2 minutes. Transfer to platter, sprinkle with scallion greens, and serve.

Stir-Fried Eggplant with Garlic-Basil Sauce

serves 4

Why This Recipe Works Eggplant is a powerhouse vegetable; it has a robust flavor, its texture can range from silky to meaty, and it's filling. Its only shortcoming? It can have a spongy texture that soaks up a lot of oil if it isn't rid of excess moisture before cooking. To account for this eggplant issue we sometimes pretreat it with salt. The technique works great, but it's a pain if you want a quick dinner. That's why eggplant makes a great star ingredient in a vegan stir-fry; a scorching hot skillet is enough to quickly evaporate the moisture—no pretreatment necessary. We started by cooking the eggplant pieces for a full 8 minutes over high heat. In that time we were able to simultaneously drive off moisture and brown the eggplant. We didn't peel the eggplant; leaving the skin on helped the pieces hold together during cooking and gave them nice texture. To complement the earthy eggplant, we added a sweet red bell pepper to the skillet. We tested adding other vegetables, but anything more felt superfluous and obscured the great flavor and texture of the eggplant. Looking to give our stir-fried eggplant a Thai flavor profile, we used a simple combination of water and fish sauce substitute flavored with brown sugar, lime, and red pepper flakes for the sauce. Stirring in a generous amount of basil and scallions made our quick stir-fry fresh-tasting and aromatic. Serve over rice.

SAUCE

½ cup water
¼ cup fish sauce substitute (see page 21)
2 tablespoons packed organic brown sugar (see page 31)
2 teaspoons grated lime zest plus 1 tablespoon juice
2 teaspoons cornstarch
⅛ teaspoon red pepper flakes

STIR-FRY

2 tablespoons plus 1 teaspoon vegetable oil
6 garlic cloves, minced
1 tablespoon grated fresh ginger
1 pound eggplant, cut into ¾-inch pieces
1 red bell pepper, stemmed, seeded, and cut into ¼-inch pieces
½ cup fresh basil leaves, torn into ½-inch pieces
2 scallions, sliced thin

1 FOR THE SAUCE Whisk all ingredients together in bowl.

2 FOR THE STIR-FRY Combine 1 teaspoon oil, garlic, and ginger in bowl. Heat remaining 2 tablespoons oil in 12-inch nonstick skillet over high heat until shimmering. Add eggplant and bell pepper and cook, stirring often, until well browned and tender, 8 to 10 minutes.

3 Push vegetables to sides of skillet. Add garlic mixture to center and cook, mashing mixture into pan, until fragrant, about 30 seconds. Stir garlic mixture into vegetables. Whisk sauce to recombine, then add to skillet and cook, stirring constantly, until sauce is thickened, about 30 seconds. Off heat, stir in basil and scallions and serve.

Thai Red Curry with Cauliflower

serves 4

1 (13.5-ounce) can coconut milk

3 tablespoons fish sauce substitute (see page 21)

1 tablespoon packed organic light brown sugar (see page 31)

2 teaspoons Thai red curry paste

1 teaspoon grated lime zest plus 1 tablespoon juice

⅛ teaspoon red pepper flakes

2 tablespoons plus 1 teaspoon vegetable oil

2 garlic cloves, minced

1 teaspoon grated fresh ginger

1 large head cauliflower (3 pounds), cored and cut into ¾-inch florets

¼ cup water

¼ teaspoon salt

¼ cup fresh basil leaves, torn into rough ½-inch pieces

Why This Recipe Works Cauliflower is a good candidate for a vegetable curry because it's hearty and filling. Thai red curries feature big, eye-opening flavors, so we'd need to develop the cauliflower's deep, nutty flavor so it could shine. Typically we turn to oven roasting to achieve this, but this felt like an unnecessary step for a curry dish that could otherwise be on the table in about 15 minutes. Instead, we confined ourselves to the skillet. Achieving tender, golden-brown cauliflower without scorching was a two-step process. First, we cooked the cauliflower with water in a covered skillet for about 5 minutes, steaming it until it was just tender; then, we uncovered the skillet to finish the cooking. This uncovered cooking time drove off any remaining water, tenderized the cauliflower further, and allowed it to brown without charring. It took just a few minutes in the skillet at the very end of cooking for the red curry sauce to thicken and for its flavors to bloom. Not all brands of red curry paste are vegan, so read labels carefully. Serve over rice.

1 Whisk coconut milk, fish sauce substitute, sugar, curry paste, lime zest and juice, and pepper flakes together in bowl. Combine 1 teaspoon oil, garlic, and ginger in second bowl.

2 Heat remaining 2 tablespoons oil in 12-inch nonstick skillet over high heat until shimmering. Add cauliflower, water, and salt, cover, and cook until cauliflower is just tender and translucent, about 5 minutes. Uncover and continue to cook, stirring occasionally, until liquid is evaporated and cauliflower is tender and well browned, 8 to 10 minutes.

3 Push cauliflower to sides of skillet. Add garlic mixture to center and cook, mashing mixture into pan, until fragrant, about 30 seconds. Stir garlic mixture into cauliflower and reduce heat to medium-high. Whisk coconut milk mixture to recombine, then add to skillet and simmer until slightly thickened, about 4 minutes. Off heat, stir in basil and serve.

VARIATION

Thai Red Curry with Bell Peppers and Tofu

Omit cauliflower, water, and salt. Spread 14 ounces tofu, cut into ¾-inch cubes, on paper towel–lined baking sheet and let drain for 20 minutes. Gently press dry with paper towels. Toss tofu with ⅓ cup cornstarch; transfer to fine-mesh strainer and shake gently to remove excess cornstarch. Add coated tofu to heated oil in step 2 and cook until crisp and well browned on all sides, 12 to 15 minutes; transfer to bowl. Add 2 red bell peppers, cut into 2-inch-long matchsticks, to oil left in skillet and cook until crisp-tender, about 2 minutes, before adding garlic mixture. Return tofu to skillet with sauce.

Saag Tofu (Tofu and Spinach)

serves 4 to 6

Why This Recipe Works *Saag paneer*, cubes of fresh cheese in a spicy sauce of pureed stewed spinach, is an Indian classic. The mildly flavored cheese reminded us of firm tofu and we thought a tofu rendition would make a great vegan version. We built layers of flavor by frying spices and caramelizing onion, jalapeño, garlic, ginger, and tomatoes. In addition to the spinach, mustard greens added heft and pungency to the sauce. Cashews, both pureed into the sauce and sprinkled on top before serving, added body and buttery richness. All we needed to do with the tofu cubes was heat them until they took on a creamy consistency. We prefer firm tofu here, but you can substitute extra-firm tofu in a pinch; do not use soft tofu. For a spicier dish, include the ribs and seeds from the jalapeño. Serve over rice.

14 ounces firm tofu, cut into
½-inch pieces
Salt and pepper
12 ounces curly-leaf spinach,
stemmed
12 ounces mustard greens, stemmed
3 tablespoons vegetable oil
1 teaspoon cumin seeds
1 teaspoon ground coriander
1 teaspoon paprika
½ teaspoon ground cardamom
¼ teaspoon ground cinnamon
1 onion, chopped fine
1 jalapeño chile, stemmed, seeded,
and minced
3 garlic cloves, minced
1 tablespoon grated fresh ginger
1 (14.5-ounce) can diced tomatoes,
drained and chopped
1½ cups unsweetened almond milk
½ cup roasted cashews, chopped
1 teaspoon organic sugar
(see page 31)
1½ tablespoons lemon juice
3 tablespoons minced fresh cilantro

1 Spread tofu on paper towel–lined baking sheet and let drain for 20 minutes. Gently press dry with paper towels and season with salt and pepper.

2 Meanwhile, microwave spinach in bowl, covered, until wilted, about 3 minutes; transfer ½ cup spinach to blender. Chop remaining spinach; set aside. Microwave mustard greens in now-empty bowl, covered, until wilted, about 4 minutes; transfer ½ cup to blender with spinach. Chop remaining mustard greens; set aside.

3 Heat oil in 12-inch skillet over medium-high heat until shimmering. Add cumin seeds, coriander, paprika, cardamom, and cinnamon and cook until fragrant, about 30 seconds. Add onion and ¾ teaspoon salt and cook, stirring frequently, until softened, about 3 minutes. Stir in jalapeño, garlic, and ginger and cook until lightly browned and just beginning to stick to pan, about 3 minutes. Stir in tomatoes, scraping up any browned bits, and cook until pan is dry and tomatoes are beginning to brown, about 4 minutes.

4 Transfer half of onion-tomato mixture, ¾ cup almond milk, ¼ cup cashews, and sugar to blender with greens and process until smooth, about 1 minute. Add pureed greens, chopped greens, lemon juice, and remaining ¾ cup almond milk to skillet with remaining onion-tomato mixture and bring to simmer over medium-high heat. Reduce heat to low and season with salt and pepper to taste. Stir in tofu and cook until warmed through, about 2 minutes. Transfer to serving dish, sprinkle with cilantro and remaining ¼ cup cashews, and serve.

TESTING NOTES **Dairy-Free Milks**
OUR FAVORITE **Almond Milk**
OTHERS TESTED Coconut milk gives the saag a more acidic flavor. Soy milk imparts a subtle soy flavor. Oat milk is very sweet; do not use.

Indian-Style Curry with Sweet Potatoes, Eggplant, and Chickpeas

serves 4 to 6

Why This Recipe Works We wanted a recipe for the ultimate weeknight vegetable curry. We started with the sauce. Toasting store-bought curry powder and garam masala increased their dimension substantially. We cooked the spices and aromatics with our vegetables—an interesting combination of sweet potatoes; savory, meaty eggplant; and earthy green beans; plus a can of chickpeas—so they permeated every bite of the dish. Rounding out the sauce was a combination of water, pureed canned tomatoes, and a splash of coconut milk. We served it with an herb-packed cilantro and mint chutney. We prefer the richer flavor of regular coconut milk here; however, light coconut milk can be substituted. For a spicier curry, include the ribs and seeds from the serrano. Serve over rice.

CHUTNEY

2 cups fresh cilantro leaves

1 cup fresh mint leaves

⅓ cup almond-milk yogurt

¼ cup finely chopped onion

1 tablespoon lime juice

1½ teaspoons sugar

½ teaspoon ground cumin

¼ teaspoon salt

CURRY

1 (14.5-ounce) can diced tomatoes

3 tablespoons vegetable oil

4 teaspoons curry powder

1½ teaspoons garam masala

2 onions, chopped fine

12 ounces sweet potatoes, peeled and cut into 1-inch pieces
Salt and pepper

3 garlic cloves, minced

1 serrano chile, stemmed, seeded, and minced

1 tablespoon grated fresh ginger

1 tablespoon tomato paste

1 pound eggplant, cut into ½-inch pieces

8 ounces green beans, trimmed and cut into 1-inch lengths

1½ cups water

1 (15-ounce) can chickpeas, rinsed

½ cup canned coconut milk

¼ cup minced fresh cilantro

1 FOR THE CHUTNEY Process all ingredients in food processor until smooth, about 20 seconds, scraping down sides of bowl as needed. (Chutney can be refrigerated for up to 1 day.)

2 FOR THE CURRY Pulse diced tomatoes and their juice in clean, dry food processor until nearly smooth, with ¼-inch pieces visible, about 3 pulses. Heat oil in Dutch oven over medium-high heat until shimmering. Add curry powder and garam masala and cook until fragrant, about 10 seconds. Stir in onions, sweet potatoes, and ¼ teaspoon salt and cook, stirring occasionally, until onions are browned and potatoes are golden brown at edges, about 10 minutes.

3 Reduce heat to medium. Stir in garlic, serrano, ginger, and tomato paste and cook until fragrant, about 30 seconds. Add eggplant and green beans and cook, stirring constantly, until vegetables are coated with spices, about 2 minutes.

4 Gradually stir in water, scraping up any browned bits. Stir in chickpeas and tomatoes; bring to simmer. Cover, reduce heat to medium-low, and simmer gently until vegetables are tender, 20 to 25 minutes. Uncover, stir in coconut milk, and cook until warmed through, 1 to 2 minutes. Off heat, stir in cilantro, season with salt and pepper to taste, and serve with chutney.

VARIATION

Indian-Style Curry with Potatoes, Cauliflower, and Chickpeas

Substitute 12 ounces red potatoes, unpeeled and cut into ½-inch pieces, for sweet potatoes. Substitute ½ head of cauliflower (1 pound), cored and cut into 1-inch florets, for eggplant and green beans. Stir in 1½ cups of frozen peas with coconut milk in step 4.

Potato Vindaloo

serves 6

2 tablespoons vegetable oil

2 onions, chopped fine

1 pound red potatoes, unpeeled, cut into ½-inch pieces

1 pound sweet potatoes, peeled and cut into ½-inch pieces
   Salt and pepper

10 garlic cloves, minced

4 teaspoons paprika

1 teaspoon ground cumin

¾ teaspoon ground cardamom

½ teaspoon cayenne pepper

¼ teaspoon ground cloves

2½ cups water

2 bay leaves

1 tablespoon mustard seeds

1 (28-ounce) can diced tomatoes

2½ tablespoons red wine vinegar

¼ cup minced fresh cilantro

Why This Recipe Works Vindaloo is a complex, spicy dish that blends Portuguese and Indian cuisines into a potent braise featuring warm spices, wine vinegar, tomatoes, onions, garlic, and mustard seeds. It's often made with lamb or chicken, but we set out to translate its comfort food appeal into a hearty vegan version. Centering our dish around potatoes seemed right; the hearty potatoes have substance and hold up well during low, slow simmering. A combination of red and sweet potatoes gave our stew both earthy and sweet notes. However, we found that after a whopping 45 minutes of simmering the potatoes with our braising liquid, they still weren't fully cooked. After taking a second look at our ingredients, we thought we knew why: The acidic environment created by the tomatoes and vinegar was preventing our potatoes from becoming tender. To test our theory, we whipped up another batch, this time cooking the potatoes with just the water and leaving out the tomatoes and vinegar until the end, simmering them just enough to mellow their flavors. Sure enough, after just 15 minutes, our potatoes were perfectly tender. To give our vindaloo exceptionally deep flavor, we used a mix of Indian spices plus bay leaves and simmered them with the potatoes, which soaked up the flavors as they cooked. Serve over rice.

1 Heat oil in Dutch oven over medium heat until shimmering. Add onions, red potatoes, sweet potatoes, and ½ teaspoon salt and cook, stirring occasionally, until onions are softened and potatoes begin to soften at edges, 10 to 12 minutes.

2 Stir in garlic, paprika, cumin, cardamom, cayenne, and cloves and cook until fragrant and vegetables are well coated, about 2 minutes. Gradually stir in water, scraping up any browned bits. Stir in bay leaves, mustard seeds, and 1 teaspoon salt and bring to simmer. Cover, reduce heat to medium-low, and cook until potatoes are tender, 15 to 20 minutes.

3 Stir in tomatoes and their juice and vinegar and simmer until flavors are blended and sauce has thickened slightly, about 15 minutes. Discard bay leaves, stir in cilantro, and season with salt and pepper to taste. Serve.

Shiitake Ramen

serves 4 to 6

4 ounces (2 cups) bean sprouts

3 tablespoons soy sauce

4 teaspoons toasted sesame oil

1 tablespoon seasoned rice vinegar

1 onion, chopped

1 (3-inch) piece ginger, peeled and sliced ¼ inch thick

5 garlic cloves, smashed and peeled

4 cups vegetable broth

8 ounces shiitake mushrooms, stems removed and reserved, caps sliced thin

¼ cup mirin

½ ounce kombu

2 tablespoons red miso
   Salt

12 ounces dried ramen noodles, seasoning packets discarded

2 scallions, sliced thin on bias

1 tablespoon toasted black sesame seeds

Why This Recipe Works Our ideal ramen is a big hearty bowl of steaming noodles in a powerful broth, layered with savory flavors; we were thrilled to find we could achieve this in a vegan ramen just as well as we have with pork stock–based versions. We added *kombu,* a type of Japanese seaweed commonly used in stocks and soups, to a brew of browned aromatics, water, and vegetable broth; supplementing the kombu with shiitake mushroom stems and soy sauce provided a triple hit of umami. To round out this savory profile, we poured in some mirin, a sweet Japanese rice wine. Finally, red miso added smoky complexity and body. Instant noodles are handily vegan and maintained a desirable chew in our ramen. (We threw away the lackluster seasoning packet.) Next up: garnishes. We stirred in the delicate caps of the shiitakes until they were just cooked. Lightly dressed bean sprouts were a crisp contrast, and sliced scallions and toasty sesame seeds topped things off. A sprinkling of *shichimi togarashi* (a common Japanese spice mix) tastes good on the ramen; you can buy it in the international aisle of the grocery store or make your own (see page 23). We strongly prefer our favorite vegetable broths, Orrington Farms Vegan Chicken Broth or our homemade Vegetable Broth Base (page 21). (For more information on vegetable broth, see page 21.)

1 Combine bean sprouts, 1 teaspoon soy sauce, 1 teaspoon oil, and vinegar in small bowl; set aside. Heat remaining 1 tablespoon oil in large saucepan over medium-high heat until shimmering. Stir in onion and cook until softened and lightly browned, 5 to 7 minutes. Add ginger and garlic and cook until lightly browned, about 2 minutes.

2 Stir in broth, 4 cups water, mushroom stems, mirin, kombu, and remaining soy sauce and bring to boil. Reduce heat to low, cover, and simmer until flavors meld, about 1 hour.

3 Strain broth through fine-mesh strainer into large bowl, pressing on solids to extract as much broth as possible; discard solids. Wipe saucepan clean with paper towels and return strained broth to now-empty saucepan. Whisk miso into broth and bring to gentle simmer over medium heat, whisking to dissolve miso completely. Stir in mushroom caps and cook until warmed through, about 1 minute; season with salt to taste. Remove from heat and cover to keep warm.

4 Meanwhile, bring 4 quarts water to boil in large pot. Add ramen noodles and 1 tablespoon salt and cook, stirring often, until al dente. Drain noodles and divide evenly among individual bowls. Ladle soup over noodles, garnish with bean sprouts, scallions, and sesame seeds, and serve.

stir-fries, curries, and noodles

Tofu Pad Thai

serves 4

Why This Recipe Works With its sweet-sour-salty-spicy sauce, tender rice noodles, and bits of scrambled egg, pad thai is Thailand's most well-known noodle dish. We wanted a great vegan version that featured crispy tofu. Getting the noodles right is paramount: We soaked rice noodles in hot tap water for 20 minutes before stir-frying for tender but not sticky noodles. To create the punchy but balanced flavor profile, we combined vegan fish sauce substitute, sugar, cayenne, and vinegar. We added tamarind paste for the bright, fruity, pleasantly sour taste essential to this dish. Chopped peanuts, bean sprouts, thinly sliced scallions, and lime wedges completed our authentic-tasting pad thai. For an accurate measurement of boiling water, bring a full kettle of water to a boil and then measure out the desired amount. This dish comes together very quickly; make sure to prep all your ingredients before you start cooking.

SAUCE

- 3 tablespoons tamarind paste
- ¾ cup boiling water
- ¼ cup fish sauce substitute (see page 21)
- 3 tablespoons organic sugar (see page 31)
- 2 tablespoons rice vinegar
- 1 tablespoon vegetable oil
- ⅛ teaspoon cayenne pepper

NOODLES, TOFU, AND GARNISH

- 8 ounces (¼-inch-wide) rice noodles
- 14 ounces extra-firm tofu, cut into ¾-inch cubes
- ⅓ cup cornstarch
- ¼ cup vegetable oil
- 1 shallot, minced
- 3 garlic cloves, minced
- 6 ounces (3 cups) bean sprouts
- 4 scallions, sliced thin on bias
  Salt
- ¼ cup minced fresh cilantro
- 2 tablespoons chopped dry-roasted peanuts
  Lime wedges

1 FOR THE SAUCE Soak tamarind paste in boiling water until softened, about 10 minutes. Strain mixture through fine-mesh strainer, pressing on solids to extract as much pulp as possible; discard solids. Whisk fish sauce substitute, sugar, vinegar, oil, and cayenne into tamarind liquid.

2 FOR THE NOODLES, TOFU, AND GARNISH Cover noodles with very hot tap water in large bowl and stir to separate. Let noodles soak until softened, pliable, and limp but not fully tender, about 20 minutes. Drain noodles. Meanwhile, spread tofu on paper towel–lined baking sheet and let drain for 20 minutes. Gently pat dry with paper towels.

3 Toss drained tofu with cornstarch in bowl, then transfer to fine-mesh strainer and shake gently to remove excess cornstarch. Heat 3 tablespoons oil in 12-inch nonstick skillet over medium-high heat until just smoking. Add tofu and cook, turning as needed, until crisp and browned on all sides, 12 to 15 minutes; transfer to paper towel–lined plate to drain.

4 Heat remaining 1 tablespoon oil in now-empty skillet over medium heat until shimmering. Add shallot and garlic and cook until lightly browned, about 2 minutes.

5 Whisk sauce to recombine. Add noodles and sauce to skillet, increase heat to high, and cook, tossing gently, until noodles are evenly coated, about 1 minute. Add browned tofu, bean sprouts, and scallions and cook, tossing gently, until tofu is warmed through and noodles are tender, about 2 minutes. Season with salt to taste, sprinkle with cilantro and peanuts, and serve with lime wedges.

Udon Noodles with Mustard Greens and Shiitake-Ginger Sauce

serves 4 to 6

1 tablespoon vegetable oil
8 ounces shiitake mushrooms, stemmed and sliced thin
¼ cup mirin
3 tablespoons rice vinegar
3 tablespoons soy sauce
2 garlic cloves, smashed and peeled
1 (1-inch) piece ginger, peeled, halved, and smashed
½ ounce dried shiitake mushrooms, rinsed and minced
1 teaspoon toasted sesame oil
1 teaspoon Asian chili-garlic sauce
1 pound mustard greens, stemmed and chopped into 2-inch pieces
Salt and pepper
1 pound fresh udon noodles

Why This Recipe Works Noodles and greens are a common pairing in Asia. We thought this partnership was a great way to create a vegan noodle dish that was delicate yet filling, and we set out to develop a recipe that married the spicy bite of mustard greens with rustic udon noodles. Udon are fat, chewy noodles made of wheat flour that are sold dried or semi-dried. Since they're starchy and a bit sweet, they stand up well to savory sauces, so we made a highly aromatic and flavorful broth from Asian pantry staples, first browning meaty shiitake mushrooms for flavor and then adding water and mirin along with rice vinegar, soy sauce, cloves of garlic, and a chunk of fresh ginger. Dried shiitake mushrooms, sesame oil, and chili-garlic sauce rounded out the flavors. After this mixture simmered and reduced, we had a sauce that was light and brothy but super savory— perfect for pairing with our cooked noodles and greens. Because fresh noodles cook so quickly, we made sure to add the greens to the pot before the noodles. Do not substitute other types of noodles for the udon noodles here.

1 Heat vegetable oil in Dutch oven over medium-high heat until shimmering. Add fresh mushrooms and cook, stirring occasionally, until softened and lightly browned, about 5 minutes. Stir in 2 cups water, mirin, vinegar, soy sauce, garlic, ginger, dried mushrooms, sesame oil, and chili-garlic sauce and bring to simmer. Reduce heat to medium-low and simmer until liquid has reduced by half, 8 to 10 minutes. Off heat, discard garlic and ginger; cover pot to keep warm.

2 Meanwhile, bring 4 quarts water to boil in large pot. Add mustard greens and 1 tablespoon salt and cook until greens are nearly tender, about 5 minutes. Add noodles and cook until greens and noodles are tender, about 2 minutes. Reserve ⅓ cup cooking water, drain noodles and greens, and return them to pot. Add sauce and reserved cooking water, and toss to combine. Cook over medium-low heat, tossing constantly, until sauce clings to noodles, about 1 minute. Season with salt and pepper to taste, and serve.

Sesame Soba Noodles with Snow Peas, Radishes, and Cilantro

serves 4

Why This Recipe Works Sesame noodles are a real treat, but they're traditionally made with Chinese egg noodles. To use this rich sauce in a vegan noodle dish, we substituted soba noodles for the egg noodles. This pairing may not be traditional, but it sure was delicious; the earthy buckwheat soba tasted great with the nutty sauce. Chunky peanut butter and toasted sesame seeds, ground together in the blender, made the perfect stand-in for hard-to-find Asian sesame paste. Garlic, ginger, soy sauce, rice vinegar, hot sauce, and brown sugar rounded out the flavors. To avoid the pitfalls of most sesame noodle recipes—gummy noodles and bland, pasty sauce—we rinsed the soba noodles after cooking to rid them of excess starch. Tossing the noodles with sesame oil separately, before adding the sauce, also helped keep them from absorbing too much sauce and becoming pasty. We added in snow peas, radishes, and celery to provide a sweet, fresh crunch, and we topped the dish with fragrant cilantro and additional toasted sesame seeds to drive home the sesame flavor. We like conventional chunky peanut butter here; it tends to be sweeter than natural or old-fashioned versions. If you cannot find soba noodles, substitute 12 ounces dried spaghetti or linguine.

SAUCE

- ¼ cup soy sauce
- 3 tablespoons chunky peanut butter
- 3 tablespoons toasted sesame seeds
- 1½ tablespoons rice vinegar
- 1½ tablespoons packed organic light brown sugar (see page 31)
- 1 tablespoon grated fresh ginger
- 1 garlic clove, minced
- ¾ teaspoon hot sauce

NOODLES AND VEGETABLES

- 12 ounces soba noodles
  Salt
- 10 radishes, trimmed, halved, and sliced thin
- 6 ounces snow peas, strings removed and halved lengthwise
- 1 celery rib, sliced thin on bias
- 2 tablespoons toasted sesame oil
- ½ cup fresh cilantro leaves
- 1 tablespoon toasted sesame seeds

1 FOR THE SAUCE Process soy sauce, peanut butter, sesame seeds, vinegar, sugar, ginger, garlic, and hot sauce in blender until smooth and mixture has consistency of heavy cream, about 1 minute (adjust consistency with warm water, 1 tablespoon at a time, as needed). (Sauce can be refrigerated for up to 3 days; add warm water as needed to loosen before using.)

2 FOR THE NOODLES AND VEGETABLES Bring 4 quarts water to boil in large pot. Add noodles and 1 tablespoon salt and cook, stirring often, until al dente. Drain noodles, rinse with cold water, and drain again.

3 Transfer noodles to large bowl and toss with radishes, snow peas, celery, sauce, and oil to coat well. Sprinkle with cilantro and sesame seeds and serve.

Spicy Basil Noodles with Crispy Tofu, Bok Choy, and Bell Peppers

serves 4 to 6

12 ounces (⅜-inch-wide) rice noodles

14 ounces firm tofu, cut into ¾-inch pieces
Salt and pepper

6 Thai, serrano, or jalapeño chiles, stemmed and seeded

4 shallots, peeled

6 garlic cloves, peeled

2 cups vegetable broth

¼ cup fish sauce substitute (see page 21)

¼ cup packed organic brown sugar (see page 31)

3 tablespoons lime juice (2 limes)

⅓ cup cornstarch

5 tablespoons vegetable oil

4 heads baby bok choy (4 ounces each), stalks sliced on bias ¼ inch thick, greens sliced ½ inch thick

1 red bell pepper, stemmed, seeded, sliced ¼ inch thick, and halved crosswise

2 cups fresh Thai basil leaves

Why This Recipe Works As the name suggests, this dish of tender rice noodles in a spicy sauce is all about the basil. And we didn't skimp; we used a whopping 2 cups of licorice-y Thai basil, stirring it in at the end of cooking to keep its flavor fresh. We infused our dish with heat by creating a paste of chiles, garlic, and shallots in the food processor. Cooking the mixture briefly deepened its flavor and mellowed the harshness of the raw aromatics. Fish sauce substitute, brown sugar, lime juice, and vegetable broth added sweet and savory flavors. Pan-fried tofu, coated with a light layer of cornstarch, offered both creamy and crispy textures. Stir-fried baby bok choy and red bell pepper added crunch and bright pops of color. We strongly prefer our favorite vegetable broths, Orrington Farms Vegan Chicken Broth or our homemade Vegetable Broth Base (page 21). (For more information on vegetable broth, see page 21.) Do not substitute other types of noodles for the rice noodles; however, you can substitute ¼-inch-wide dried flat rice noodles and reduce the soaking time to 20 minutes. If you can't find Thai basil, you can substitute regular basil. For a spicier dish, reserve, mince, and add the ribs and seeds from the chiles.

1 Cover noodles with very hot tap water in large bowl and stir to separate. Let noodles soak until softened, pliable, and limp but not fully tender, 35 to 40 minutes. Drain noodles. Meanwhile, spread tofu on paper towel–lined baking sheet and let drain for 20 minutes. Gently pat dry with paper towels and season with salt and pepper.

2 Meanwhile, pulse chiles, shallots, and garlic in food processor to smooth paste, about 20 pulses, scraping down sides of bowl as needed. Whisk broth, fish sauce substitute, sugar, and lime juice together in bowl; set aside.

3 Toss drained tofu with cornstarch in bowl, then transfer to fine-mesh strainer and shake gently to remove excess cornstarch. Heat 2 tablespoons oil in 12-inch nonstick skillet over medium-high heat until shimmering. Add tofu and cook, turning as needed, until crisp and well browned on all sides, 12 to 15 minutes; transfer to paper towel–lined plate to drain.

4 Heat 1 tablespoon oil in now-empty skillet over high heat until shimmering. Add bok choy stalks and bell pepper and cook until crisp-tender and lightly browned, 3 to 4 minutes. Stir in bok choy leaves and cook until beginning to wilt, about 30 seconds; transfer to bowl.

5 Heat remaining 2 tablespoons oil in now-empty skillet over medium-high heat until shimmering. Add processed chile mixture and cook until moisture evaporates and color deepens,

3 to 5 minutes. Add noodles and broth mixture to skillet and cook, tossing gently, until sauce has thickened slightly and noodles are well coated and tender, about 5 minutes.

6 Stir in browned vegetables and basil and cook until warmed through, about 1 minute. Top with crispy tofu and serve.

snac
and
apps

ks

Kale Chips

serves 4

12 ounces Lacinato kale, stemmed and torn into 3-inch pieces
1 tablespoon extra-virgin olive oil
1 teaspoon kosher salt

Why This Recipe Works Is there anything kale can't do? Braised, the earthy green is a simple side dish. Simmered in soup, its leaves become tender and add heft. It serves as the base of a reinvented Caesar salad (see page 142) and even fortifies our breakfast smoothies (see page 74). One of our favorite things to do with this versatile brassica is to turn it into a crisp, earthy-tasting (and healthful) snack. Most homemade kale chips turn limp after baking. We wanted something we didn't need to eat immediately. We found there were three key steps to getting ultracrisp kale chips. First, we made sure that we started with completely dry leaves. Second, we used a very low oven to ensure that the kale would dry out but not burn, and we baked the chips for an hour or more to ensure that all of the moisture evaporated. Finally, we baked the leaves on a wire rack to let the oven air circulate all around the kale. Tossed with olive oil and seasoned lightly with crunchy kosher salt, these crisp kale chips were a supersatisfying snack. We prefer to use Lacinato (Tuscan) kale in this recipe, but curly-leaf kale can be substituted; chips made with curly-leaf kale will taste a bit chewy at the edges and won't hold up as well.

1 Adjust oven racks to upper-middle and lower-middle positions and heat oven to 200 degrees. Set wire racks in 2 rimmed baking sheets. Dry kale thoroughly between clean dish towels, transfer to large bowl, and toss with oil.

2 Arrange kale in single layer on prepared racks, making sure leaves overlap as little as possible. Sprinkle kale with salt and bake until very crisp, 1 to 1¼ hours, switching and rotating sheets halfway through baking.

3 Let chips cool completely on racks, about 10 minutes. Serve. (Kale chips can be stored in paper towel–lined airtight container for up to 1 day.)

VARIATIONS
Ranch-Style Kale Chips
Combine 2 teaspoons dried dill, 1 teaspoon garlic powder, and 1 teaspoon onion powder with salt before sprinkling over kale.

Spicy Sesame-Ginger Kale Chips
Substitute 1 tablespoon sesame oil for olive oil. Combine 2 teaspoons toasted sesame seeds, 1 teaspoon ground ginger, and ¼ teaspoon cayenne pepper with salt before sprinkling over kale.

snacks and apps

Crispy Spiced Chickpeas

serves 6

1 teaspoon smoked paprika
1 teaspoon organic sugar
  (see page 31)
½ teaspoon salt
¼ teaspoon pepper
1 cup extra-virgin olive oil
2 (15-ounce) cans chickpeas,
  rinsed and patted dry

Why This Recipe Works Chickpeas aren't just for salads and curries anymore. Tossed in oil and cooked, these beans become ultracrisp and deeply nutty in flavor—the perfect cocktail snack. Most recipes call for roasting chickpeas in the oven, but we found they never became crisp enough to satisfy us. Switching to the stovetop and frying the chickpeas in olive oil gave us the big crunch factor we were seeking in our snack. A quick toss in a sweet-and-savory mixture of sugar and smoked paprika made our chickpeas incredibly addictive. Make sure to dry the chickpeas thoroughly with paper towels before placing them in the oil. In order to get crisp chickpeas, it's important to keep the heat high enough to ensure the oil is simmering the entire time. After about 12 minutes, test for doneness by removing a few chickpeas and placing them on a paper towel to cool slightly before tasting. If they are not quite crisp yet, continue to cook 2 to 3 minutes longer, checking occasionally for doneness.

1 Combine paprika, sugar, salt, and pepper in large bowl. Heat oil in Dutch oven over high heat until just smoking. Add chickpeas and cook, stirring occasionally, until deep golden and crisp, 12 to 15 minutes.

2 Using slotted spoon, transfer chickpeas to paper towel–lined baking sheet to drain briefly, then toss in bowl with spice mix. Serve. (Chickpeas can be kept at room temperature for up to 2 hours.)

Whipped Cashew Dip with Roasted Red Peppers and Olives

makes about 2 cups

1½ cups raw cashews
½ cup jarred roasted red peppers, rinsed, patted dry, and chopped
3 tablespoons extra-virgin olive oil
3 tablespoons lemon juice
Salt and pepper
1 garlic clove, minced
½ cup minced fresh parsley
½ cup pitted kalamata olives, chopped

Why This Recipe Works What's a party without a big bowl of creamy, crowd-pleasing dip? We were up to the challenge of creating a flavorful dip that was as good as any dairy-based one. Once again, cashews were the ideal starting point. Soaked and pureed, they were creamy and neutral-tasting. We found that we needed to soak the raw cashews for at least 12 hours; any less, and the dip turned out grainy. Next, we turned to a variety of simple vegan pantry ingredients to amp up the flavor of the dip. For our first combination, tasters liked the mildly smoky flavor of roasted red peppers with the briny, salty depth of chopped kalamata olives. A bit of olive oil and lemon juice boosted the flavor further and thinned the dip to a perfect spreadable consistency. Some parsley, stirred in with the olives after processing, provided welcome freshness. Since our dip had come together so quickly and easily, we decided to create two more flavorful variations, one using smoky chipotle, tangy lime juice, and fresh cilantro, and another with sweet sun-dried tomatoes and earthy rosemary. You can substitute an equal amount of slivered almonds for the cashews; however, the dip will have a slightly coarser consistency. Serve with chips, crackers, or crudités.

1 Place cashews in bowl and add cold water to cover by 1 inch. Let sit at room temperature for at least 12 hours or up to 24 hours. Drain and rinse well.

2 Process soaked cashews, red peppers, 3 tablespoons water, oil, lemon juice, ¾ teaspoon salt, ½ teaspoon pepper, and garlic in food processor until smooth, about 2 minutes, scraping down sides of bowl as needed.

3 Transfer cashew mixture to bowl, stir in parsley and olives, and season with salt and pepper to taste. Cover with plastic wrap and let sit at room temperature until flavors meld, about 30 minutes. Serve. (Dip can be refrigerated for up to 5 days; stir in 1 tablespoon warm water to loosen dip if necessary before serving.)

VARIATIONS
Whipped Cashew Dip with Chipotle and Lime
Omit red peppers and olives. Add ½ teaspoon chipotle chile powder and ½ teaspoon ground cumin to processor with soaked cashews and increase water to 6 tablespoons in step 2. Substitute ¼ cup lime juice (2 limes) for lemon juice and ⅓ cup minced fresh cilantro for parsley.

Whipped Cashew Dip with Sun-Dried Tomatoes and Rosemary
Omit red peppers and parsley. Add 2 teaspoons minced fresh rosemary to processor with soaked cashews and increase water to 6 tablespoons in step 2. Substitute ½ cup finely chopped oil-packed sun-dried tomatoes for olives.

Hummus with Smoked Paprika

makes about 2 cups

¼ cup water

3 tablespoons lemon juice

6 tablespoons tahini

2 tablespoons extra-virgin olive oil, plus extra for drizzling

1 (15-ounce) can chickpeas, rinsed

1 small garlic clove, minced

1 teaspoon smoked paprika

½ teaspoon salt

Pinch cayenne pepper

2 tablespoons toasted pine nuts

1 scallion, sliced thin

Why This Recipe Works Hummus is everyone's favorite bean dip. And when it's good, it's really good: light—almost as if it's whipped—and silky-smooth in texture. Unfortunately, we've eaten way too many wan, gritty versions of the dish. For our recipe, we'd settle for nothing less than the ideal—and we wanted to dress it up with different flavors so it was something more than the mildly flavored dip that's ubiquitous. In theory, the best way to guarantee a creamy texture is to remove the chickpeas' tough skins, but we couldn't find an approach that wasn't tedious or futile. Instead, we made the food processor do all the work. When we pureed the chickpeas alone before adding the other ingredients, the hummus was grainy. Instead, we made an emulsion: We started by grinding just the chickpeas and then slowly added in a small amount of water and lemon juice. Then we whisked the olive oil and a generous amount of tahini together and drizzled the mixture into the chickpeas while processing; this created a lush, light, and flavorful puree. To elevate our base puree, we blended in a generous amount of smoked paprika, which contributed great flavor and a beautiful ruddy tone. A garnish of toasted pine nuts and sliced scallion gave our hummus a serious upgrade. Serve with Pita Chips (page 254), bread, or crudités.

1 Combine water and lemon juice in small bowl. Whisk tahini and oil together in second bowl.

2 Process chickpeas, garlic, paprika, salt, and cayenne in food processor until almost fully ground, about 15 seconds; scrape down sides of bowl. With machine running, add lemon juice mixture in steady stream. Scrape down sides of bowl and continue to process for 1 minute. With machine running, add tahini mixture in steady stream and process until hummus is smooth and creamy, about 15 seconds, scraping down sides of bowl as needed.

3 Transfer hummus to bowl, cover with plastic wrap, and let sit at room temperature until flavors meld, about 30 minutes. Sprinkle with pine nuts and scallion, drizzle with oil, and serve. (Hummus can be refrigerated for up to 5 days; refrigerate garnishes separately. Stir in 1 tablespoon warm water to loosen if necessary before serving.)

Sweet Potato Hummus

makes about 2 cups

1 pound sweet potatoes, unpeeled
¼ cup tahini
3 tablespoons extra-virgin olive oil, plus extra for drizzling
¾ cup water
2 tablespoons lemon juice
Salt and pepper
1 garlic clove, minced
1 teaspoon paprika
½ teaspoon ground coriander
¼ teaspoon ground cumin
¼ teaspoon chipotle chile powder
1 tablespoon toasted sesame seeds (optional)

Why This Recipe Works Hummus is all about chickpeas, right? We love traditional hummus, but we wanted to turn it on its head, keeping the accompanying flavorings (tahini, olive oil, garlic, and lemon juice) but losing the chickpeas. In their place, we turned to earthy, vibrant sweet potatoes. We aimed to bring out the sweet potatoes' subtle flavor by figuring out the best cooking method as well as the ideal balance of complementary ingredients. To keep things simple, we opted to microwave the sweet potatoes—dip shouldn't take more than an hour to make. Happily, microwaving the potatoes resulted in flavor that was nearly as intense as when we roasted them. Just ¼ cup of tahini was enough to stand up to the sweet potatoes without overwhelming the hummus. To round out the flavor of the hummus, we added warm spices: paprika, coriander, and cumin. The addition of chipotle and a clove of garlic curbed the sweetness and accented the spices, while a couple tablespoons of lemon juice brought the flavors into focus. We liked this hummus so much we developed a variation with another root: earthy, floral-tasting parsnips. Serve with crackers, chips, or crudités.

1 Prick sweet potatoes several times with fork, place on plate, and microwave until very soft, about 12 minutes, flipping potatoes halfway through microwaving. Let potatoes cool for 5 minutes. Combine tahini and oil in small bowl.

2 Slice potatoes in half lengthwise and scoop flesh from skins; discard skins. Process sweet potato, water, lemon juice, ¾ teaspoon salt, garlic, paprika, coriander, cumin, and chile powder in food processor until completely smooth, about 1 minute, scraping down sides of bowl as needed. With processor running, add tahini mixture in steady stream and process until hummus is smooth and creamy, about 15 seconds, scraping down bowl as needed. Season with salt and pepper to taste.

3 Transfer hummus to bowl, cover with plastic wrap, and let sit at room temperature until flavors meld, about 30 minutes. Drizzle with oil and sprinkle with sesame seeds, if using. Serve. (Hummus can be refrigerated for up to 5 days; stir in 1 tablespoon warm water to loosen if necessary before serving.)

VARIATION
Parsnip Hummus
Look for tender, thin parsnips; large parsnips can taste bitter.

Substitute 1 pound parsnips, peeled and cut into 1-inch lengths, for sweet potatoes. Microwave parsnips in covered bowl until tender, about 10 minutes. Transfer parsnips to food processor and proceed with recipe.

snacks and apps

Muhammara

makes about 2 cups

1½ cups jarred roasted red peppers, rinsed and patted dry
1 cup walnuts, toasted
¼ cup plain wheat crackers, crumbled
3 tablespoons lemon juice
2 tablespoons extra-virgin olive oil
1 tablespoon molasses
1 teaspoon organic sugar (see page 31)
¾ teaspoon salt
½ teaspoon ground cumin
⅛ teaspoon cayenne pepper
1 tablespoon minced fresh parsley (optional)

Why This Recipe Works Muhammara is a hearty, sweet-and-savory Middle Eastern red pepper and walnut dip that's bursting with flavor. It's a truly multipurpose recipe: It's delicious served with bread, or vegetables, and even used as a thick sauce. We wanted to add this unique and versatile vegan dip to our repertoire. Our version is quick and simple but full of authentic flavors. Whirring the roasted red peppers in the food processor created a smooth, velvety consistency for the base of our dip. We flavored the dip with cumin, cayenne, and lemon juice and added smoky molasses and a touch of sugar for sweetness. The toasted walnuts plus some crumbled wheat crackers, both ground with the peppers, lent complexity and richness, amplifying the sweet, smoky, and savory flavors that are unique to this dip. They also bulk up the dip so that it's more filling than your average. Not all crackers are vegan, so check ingredient lists carefully. Serve with Pita Chips (recipe follows) or thinly sliced baguette.

Pulse red peppers, walnuts, crackers, lemon juice, oil, molasses, sugar, salt, cumin, and cayenne in food processor until smooth, 10 to 15 pulses. Transfer to bowl, cover, and refrigerate for 15 minutes. (Dip can be refrigerated for up to 1 day; let sit at room temperature for 30 minutes and season with extra lemon juice, salt, and cayenne to taste before serving.) Sprinkle with parsley, if using, and serve.

Pita Chips serves 8

Use whole-wheat pita bread, if you like. You can also substitute vegetable oil for the olive oil.

4 (8-inch) pita breads
½ cup extra-virgin olive oil
1 teaspoon kosher salt

1 Adjust oven racks to upper-middle and lower-middle positions and heat oven to 350 degrees. Using kitchen shears, cut around perimeter of each pita and separate into 2 thin rounds.

2 Working with 1 round at a time, brush cut side generously with oil and sprinkle with salt. Stack rounds on top of one another, cut side up, as you go. Using chef's knife, cut pita stack into 8 wedges. Spread wedges, cut side up and in single layer, on 2 rimmed baking sheets. Bake until wedges are golden brown and crisp, about 15 minutes, rotating and switching sheets halfway through baking. Let cool before serving.

Guacamole with Habanero and Mango

makes about 3 cups

3 ripe avocados, pitted and cut into ½-inch pieces

¼ cup chopped fresh cilantro

1 habanero chile, stemmed, seeded, and minced

2 tablespoons finely chopped onion

2 tablespoons lime juice

2 garlic cloves, minced
Salt

½ teaspoon ground cumin

½ mango, peeled and cut into ¼ inch pieces

Why This Recipe Works Avocados have become food celebrities; everyone loves the rich, buttery fruit, and no party is complete without a serving of guacamole. We wanted to perfect guacamole but also add some intriguing additions to prevent the much adored dip from ever becoming boring. Our guacamole is all about bold flavor and great texture; no pasty, bland guac here. We think guacamole should be chunky and rustic but smooth enough that it can be scooped on a chip. So for the base, we mashed one avocado and then gently folded in two diced avocados to keep the mixture cohesive but nice and chunky. We flavored our guacamole with the traditional players—onion, fresh herbs, lime juice, and spices—and then we had some fun. For a fresh, tropical twist, we stirred in juicy pieces of mango. The fresh fruit brightened the rich base. With this added sweetness, we wanted to crank up the heat, so we turned to a habanero chile instead of the standard jalapeño; this powerful chile's floral, fruity notes complemented the mango beautifully.

Using fork, mash 1 avocado with cilantro, habanero, onion, lime juice, garlic, ¾ teaspoon salt, and cumin in bowl until mostly smooth. Gently fold in mango and remaining 2 diced avocados. Season with salt to taste, and serve. (Guacamole can be refrigerated, with plastic wrap pressed directly to its surface to prevent browning, for up to 24 hours. Bring to room temperature before serving.)

Nacho Dip

makes about 2 cups

12 ounces russet potatoes, peeled and cut into 1-inch pieces

1 small carrot, peeled and cut into ½-inch pieces (⅓ cup)

3 tablespoons vegetable oil

1½ tablespoons nutritional yeast

1½ teaspoons distilled white vinegar

1 teaspoon salt

⅓ cup finely chopped onion

⅓ cup minced poblano chile

1 garlic clove, minced

½ teaspoon minced canned chipotle chile in adobo sauce

⅛ teaspoon ground cumin

⅛ teaspoon mustard powder

Why This Recipe Works This creamy, gooey, tangy, downright cheesy sauce is sure to score a home run with vegans and non-vegans alike. What's more, it's incredibly easy to make from pantry-friendly ingredients. We experimented with the familiar cast of characters used to develop vegan cheese-like sauces—cashews, nutritional yeast, and miso, along with various vegetables. Tasters were largely distracted by their vegetal flavors and pasty textures. The most neutral-tasting ingredient in the lot was potato, and we had a revelation when we broke a cardinal kitchen rule: We whirred boiled potatoes in the blender at high speed to release as much gummy, gluey starch as possible. While this would make the most unappealing mashed potatoes, the sticky mixture was the ideal base for a cheese-like sauce with stretch. We blended in a few other key ingredients—carrot for a hint of sweetness and a color, nutritional yeast for funky depth, and a bit of vegetable oil for richness and fluidity—and ended up with a sauce with a pleasing orange color, mildly earthy flavor, and ultracreamy texture. We stirred in a combination of sautéed poblano pepper, onion, garlic, chipotle chile, cumin, and mustard powder for Tex-Mex appeal. Serve with corn chips or crudités. To rewarm cooled nacho dip, microwave, covered, in 30-second bursts, whisking at each interval and thinning with water as needed, or rewarm on the stovetop, whisking occasionally, and thinning with water as needed.

1 Bring 2 quarts water to boil in medium saucepan over high heat. Add potatoes and carrot and cook until tender, about 12 minutes; drain in colander.

2 Combine cooked vegetables, ⅓ cup water, 2 tablespoons oil, nutritional yeast, vinegar, and salt in blender. Pulse until chopped and combined, about 10 pulses, scraping down sides of blender jar as needed. (You will need to stop processing to scrape down sides of blender jar several times for mixture to come together.) Process mixture on high speed until very smooth, about 2 minutes.

3 Meanwhile, heat remaining 1 tablespoon oil in now-empty saucepan over medium-high heat until shimmering. Add onion and poblano and cook until softened and lightly browned, 3 to 5 minutes. Stir in garlic, chipotle, cumin, and mustard and cook until fragrant, about 30 seconds; remove from heat.

4 Stir processed potato mixture into onion-poblano mixture in saucepan and bring to brief simmer over medium heat to heat through. Transfer to bowl and serve immediately.

Loaded Nachos

serves 4 to 6

Why This Recipe Works We set out to create a big, bold, party-ready platter of vegan nachos that would deliver an exciting combination of flavors and textures to satisfy even the most voracious case of the munchies. Since our Nacho Dip (page 258) was such a crowd-pleasing success, we decided to use that as our starting point. Rather than default to the usual tomato-based salsa as a complementary topping, we opted for a quick-cooked salsa made with tangy, vibrant fresh tomatillos sautéed with sweet corn (frozen kernels were ideal for year-round convenience). Garlic, oregano, and coriander provided a bold, aromatic backbone and made the fresh flavor of the tomatillos pop. To avoid soggy chips, we cooked the tomatillo mixture until all the moisture had evaporated. We wanted to add a protein-rich component to our nachos, but refried beans weighed down the nachos with too much moisture. We opted for whole canned pinto beans instead, sprinkling them between each layer of chips. Jalapeños added freshness and heat to our nachos. Once we had layered all of our ingredients, it took just 5 minutes in the oven to heat the components and brown the top—any more and the chips became soggy. Serve with your favorite store-bought guacamole or our homemade Guacamole with Habanero and Mango (page 256). You can substitute your favorite corn salsa for the tomatillo-corn salsa in this recipe; be sure to drain the salsa through a fine-mesh strainer for 5 minutes before layering it in the nachos in step 2.

TOMATILLO-CORN SALSA

1 tablespoon vegetable oil

1 onion, chopped fine

1 teaspoon salt

3 garlic cloves, minced

2 teaspoons minced fresh oregano or ½ teaspoon dried

1 teaspoon ground coriander

12 ounces tomatillos, husks and stems removed, rinsed well, dried, and cut into ½-inch pieces

1 cup frozen corn, thawed

NACHOS

8 ounces tortilla chips

1 recipe Nacho Dip (page 258), warmed

1 (15-ounce) can pinto beans, rinsed

2 jalapeño chiles, stemmed and sliced thin

3 radishes, trimmed and sliced thin
Lime wedges

1 FOR THE TOMATILLO-CORN SALSA Adjust oven rack to middle position and heat oven to 450 degrees. Heat oil in 12-inch nonstick skillet over medium heat until shimmering. Add onion and salt and cook until softened, about 5 minutes. Stir in garlic, oregano, and coriander and cook until fragrant, about 30 seconds. Add tomatillos and corn, reduce heat to medium-low, and cook until tomatillos are softened, have released their moisture, and mixture is nearly dry, about 10 minutes. Let cool slightly, about 5 minutes.

2 FOR THE NACHOS Spread half of tortilla chips evenly into 13 by 9-inch baking dish. Drizzle 1 cup nacho dip evenly over chips, then top with half of tomatillo-corn salsa, followed by half of beans and, finally, half of jalapeños. Repeat layering with remaining chips, nacho dip, tomatillo-corn salsa, beans, and jalapeños. Bake until warmed through and edges of chips on top layer are beginning to brown, 5 to 8 minutes.

3 Let nachos cool for 2 minutes, then sprinkle with radishes; serve immediately with lime wedges.

Buffalo Cauliflower Bites

serves 4 to 6

BUFFALO SAUCE
¼ cup coconut oil (see page 30)
½ cup hot sauce
1 tablespoon packed organic
 dark brown sugar (see page 31)
2 teaspoons cider vinegar

CAULIFLOWER
1–2 quarts peanut or vegetable oil
¾ cup cornstarch
¼ cup cornmeal
 Salt and pepper
⅔ cup canned coconut milk
1 tablespoon hot sauce
1 pound cauliflower florets, cut
 into 1½-inch pieces
1 recipe Ranch Dressing
 (recipe follows)

Why This Recipe Works Deemed "better than wings" by our tasters, these crunchy, tangy, spicy, and just plain addictive cauliflower bites will be the new star of your game day table. The key was to come up with a flavorful, crunchy coating that would hold up under the Buffalo sauce. A mixture of cornstarch and cornmeal gave us the ultracrisp exterior we wanted. But because cauliflower is not naturally moist (like chicken), the mixture didn't adhere; we dunked the florets in canned coconut milk first, which had the right viscosity. We got decent results when we baked our bites, but we absolutely flipped over the crackly crust and tender interior we achieved through frying. We served our bites with an herby ranch dressing, a cooling foil to the kick of the bites. We used Frank's Red Hot Original Cayenne Pepper Sauce but other hot sauces can be used. Use a Dutch oven that holds 6 quarts or more for this recipe.

1 FOR THE BUFFALO SAUCE Melt coconut oil in small saucepan over low heat. Whisk in hot sauce, brown sugar, and vinegar until combined. Remove from heat and cover to keep warm; set aside.

2 FOR THE CAULIFLOWER Line platter with triple layer of paper towels. Add oil to large Dutch oven until it measures about 1½ inches deep and heat over medium-high heat to 400 degrees. While oil heats, combine cornstarch, cornmeal, ½ teaspoon salt, and ¼ teaspoon pepper in small bowl. Whisk coconut milk and hot sauce together in large bowl. Add cauliflower; toss to coat well. Sprinkle cornstarch mixture over cauliflower; fold with rubber spatula until thoroughly coated.

3 Fry half of cauliflower, adding 1 or 2 pieces to oil at a time, until golden and crisp, gently stirring as needed to prevent pieces from sticking together, about 3 minutes. Using slotted spoon, transfer fried cauliflower to prepared platter.

4 Return oil to 400 degrees and repeat with remaining cauliflower. Transfer ½ cup sauce to clean large bowl, add fried cauliflower and gently toss to coat. Serve immediately with dressing and remaining sauce.

Ranch Dressing   makes about ½ cup
We strongly prefer our favorite vegan mayonnaise, Just Mayo, or our homemade Vegan Mayonnaise (page 22). (For more information on vegan mayonnaise, see page 22.)

½ cup vegan mayonnaise
2 tablespoons unsweetened plain coconut milk yogurt
1 teaspoon white wine vinegar
1½ teaspoons minced fresh chives

1½ teaspoons minced fresh dill
¼ teaspoon garlic powder
⅛ teaspoon salt
⅛ teaspoon pepper

Whisk all ingredients in bowl until smooth. (Dressing can be refrigerated for up to 4 days.)

Marinated Cauliflower with Chickpeas and Saffron

serves 6 to 8

½ head cauliflower (1 pound),
  cored and cut into 1-inch florets
  Salt and pepper
⅛ teaspoon saffron threads,
  crumbled
⅓ cup extra-virgin olive oil
5 garlic cloves, smashed and peeled
1½ teaspoons organic sugar
  (see page 31)
1½ teaspoons smoked paprika
1 small sprig fresh rosemary
2 tablespoons sherry vinegar
1 cup canned chickpeas, rinsed
½ lemon, sliced thin
1 tablespoon minced fresh parsley

Why This Recipe Works The hallmark flavors of saffron, smoked paprika, and sherry vinegar enliven this elegant tapas-style appetizer of creamy chickpeas and earthy cauliflower marinated in a boldly flavored dressing. First we blanched the cauliflower, softening it so that it would readily absorb the dressing. We established the marinade's base by blooming saffron in hot water to coax out more of its distinct, complex flavors. Heating smashed garlic cloves in olive oil infused the oil with flavor and tamed the garlic's harsh edge. Along with the saffron, smoked paprika gave the marinade a striking brick-red hue, and a sprig of rosemary provided earthy, aromatic flavor. Thin slices of lemon lent a bright citrus note and made for a pretty presentation. We stirred together our marinade, adding the saffron and some flavor-boosting sherry vinegar off the heat. We combined our marinade with the chickpeas and cauliflower and transferred the mixture to the refrigerator to rest, allowing the flavors to meld and deepen. After 4 hours, the chickpeas and cauliflower emerged with a golden hue, brimming with deep, complex flavor. Use a small sprig of rosemary, or its flavor will be overpowering. The garlic will become soft over time. This dish can be served cold or at room temperature.

1 Bring 2 quarts water to boil in large saucepan. Add cauliflower and 1 tablespoon salt and cook until florets begin to soften, about 3 minutes. Drain florets and transfer to paper towel–lined baking sheet to drain.

2 Meanwhile, combine ¼ cup hot water and saffron in bowl; set aside. Heat oil and garlic in small saucepan over medium-low heat until fragrant and beginning to sizzle but not brown, 4 to 6 minutes. Stir in sugar, paprika, and rosemary sprig and cook until fragrant, about 30 seconds. Off heat, stir in saffron mixture, vinegar, 1½ teaspoons salt, and ¼ teaspoon pepper.

3 Combine florets, chickpeas, lemon, and saffron mixture in large bowl. Cover and refrigerate, stirring occasionally, for at least 4 hours or up to 3 days. To serve, discard rosemary sprig, transfer cauliflower and chickpeas to serving bowl with slotted spoon, and sprinkle with parsley.

snacks and apps

265

Socca with Swiss Chard, Pistachios, and Apricots

makes 5;
serves 6 to 8

Why This Recipe Works Socca is a satisfying, savory flatbread made with chickpea flour that is popular in southern France—and it's naturally vegan. The loose, pancake-like batter comes together in less than a minute: Simply whisk together chickpea flour, water, olive oil, turmeric, salt, and pepper. Traditionally the batter is poured into a cast-iron skillet and baked in a wood-burning oven to make a large socca with a blistered top and a smoky flavor. But in a home oven, this technique produced socca that was dry and limp. So we ditched the oven for the higher heat of the stovetop, which gave us crispy, golden-brown socca. But flipping the skillet-size socca wasn't as easy as we'd hoped. We solved this problem by making several smaller flatbreads instead. As an added bonus, these elegant flatbreads had a higher ratio of crunchy crust to tender interior. To complement our savory flatbreads, we came up with a flavorful topping of Swiss chard, dried apricots, and toasted pistachios that was earthy, sweet, and delicious. We used the warm spices cumin and allspice to balance the bright notes of the chickpea flour.

BATTER

- 1½ cups (6¾ ounces) chickpea flour
- ½ teaspoon salt
- ½ teaspoon pepper
- ½ teaspoon turmeric
- 1½ cups water
- 6 tablespoons plus 1 teaspoon extra-virgin olive oil

TOPPING

- 1 tablespoon extra-virgin olive oil
- 1 onion, chopped fine
- 2 garlic cloves, minced
- ¾ teaspoon ground cumin
  Salt and pepper
- ⅛ teaspoon allspice
- 12 ounces Swiss chard, stemmed and chopped
- 3 tablespoons finely chopped dried apricots
- 2 tablespoons finely chopped toasted pistachios
- 1 teaspoon white wine vinegar

1 FOR THE BATTER Adjust oven rack to middle position and heat oven to 200 degrees. Set wire rack in rimmed baking sheet and place in oven. Whisk chickpea flour, salt, pepper, and turmeric together in bowl. Slowly whisk in water and 3 tablespoons oil until combined and smooth.

2 Heat 2 teaspoons oil in 8-inch nonstick skillet over medium-high heat until shimmering. Add ½ cup batter to skillet, tilting pan to coat bottom evenly. Reduce heat to medium and cook until crisp at edges and golden brown on bottom, 3 to 5 minutes. Flip socca and continue to cook until second side is browned, about 2 minutes. Transfer to wire rack in warm oven and repeat, working with 2 teaspoons oil and ½ cup batter at a time.

3 FOR THE TOPPING Heat oil in 12-inch nonstick skillet over medium heat until shimmering. Add onion and cook until softened, about 5 minutes. Stir in garlic, cumin, ¼ teaspoon salt, and allspice and cook until fragrant, about 30 seconds. Stir in Swiss chard and apricots and cook until chard is wilted, 4 to 6 minutes. Off heat, stir in pistachios and vinegar and season with salt and pepper to taste. Top each cooked socca with ⅓ cup chard mixture, slice, and serve.

Polenta Fries with Creamy Chipotle Sauce

serves 4

4 cups water
  Salt and pepper
1 cup instant polenta
2 teaspoons minced fresh oregano
  or ½ teaspoon dried
1 teaspoon grated lemon zest
½ cup vegetable oil
1 recipe Creamy Chipotle Sauce
  (page 120)

Why This Recipe Works Sure, we like a bowl of creamy polenta, but we think the porridge reaches its full potential when made into fries—perfect for an appetizer or served next to a sandwich or burger. If you cook polenta and then chill it until firm, it slices easily into sticks that become crisp when fried and boast a creamy interior. We began our testing using instant polenta, to minimize time on the stove. Stirring oregano and lemon zest into the fully cooked polenta lent an aromatic backbone to our fries and helped brighten the flavor. We then poured our flavored polenta into a straight-sided 13 by 9-inch baking pan and let it set up in the refrigerator before slicing. Once our fries were cut, we looked at methods for cooking them. Deep frying resulted in fries that clumped together and stuck to the bottom of the pot, but pan frying in a skillet resulted in perfectly crisp fries with a tender and fluffy interior. We seasoned the fries lightly with salt as they came out of the pan. It's hard not to like traditional potato French fries, but these delicious polenta fries give them a run for their snack-time money. This recipe uses instant polenta, which has a much shorter cooking time than traditional polenta; do not substitute traditional polenta. We had good luck using Pastene Instant Polenta in this recipe. We like to serve these fries with our Creamy Chipotle Sauce (page 120), but they also taste good with marinara sauce or ketchup.

1 Line 13 by 9-inch baking pan with parchment paper and grease parchment. Bring water to boil in large saucepan over high heat and add 1 teaspoon salt. Slowly add polenta in steady stream while stirring constantly with wooden spoon. Reduce heat to low and cook, stirring often, until polenta is soft and smooth, 3 to 5 minutes.

2 Off heat, stir in oregano and lemon zest and season with salt and pepper to taste. Pour polenta into prepared pan. Refrigerate, uncovered, until firm and sliceable, about 1 hour. (Polenta can be refrigerated, covered, for up to 1 day.)

3 Gently flip chilled polenta out onto cutting board and discard parchment. Cut polenta in half lengthwise, then slice each half crosswise into sixteen ¾-inch-wide fries. (You will have 32 fries total.)

4 Adjust oven rack to middle position and heat oven to 200 degrees. Set wire rack in rimmed baking sheet. Heat oil in 12-inch nonstick skillet over medium heat until shimmering and edge of polenta sizzles when dipped in oil. Working in batches, fry half of polenta until crisp and beginning to brown, 6 to 7 minutes per side. Transfer to prepared rack, season lightly with salt, and keep warm in oven. Repeat with remaining polenta and serve warm with chipotle sauce.

erts

Chocolate Chip Cookies

makes 16 cookies

2 cups (10 ounces) all-purpose flour
1½ teaspoons baking powder
¼ teaspoon baking soda
½ teaspoon salt
1⅓ cups packed (9⅓ ounces) organic light brown sugar (see page 31)
½ cup coconut oil, melted and cooled (see page 30)
6 tablespoons water, room temperature
⅓ cup unsalted creamy almond butter
2 teaspoons vanilla extract
1¼ cups (7½ ounces) semisweet chocolate chips or chunks

Why This Recipe Works When it came to developing a vegan version of the classic chocolate chip cookie, we'd settle for nothing less than perfection; the recipe had to produce a cookie that would be moist and chewy on the inside and crisp at the edges, with deep notes of toffee. We started by baking 11 popular recipes, and we were shocked at the assortment of hockey pucks in front of us. Some cookies didn't spread at all, while others melted into greasy wafers; some tasted like cardboard, while others had funky off-flavors; and some were gelatinous, while others crumbled apart. We had our work cut out for us. Starting with the test kitchen's classic recipe, we removed the egg and found that we simply didn't need a substitute for it. While many cookie recipes call for a mix of white and brown sugars, we opted to use all brown; it gave the cookies a richer flavor and its moisture provided a softer center. But tasters wanted more chew. As it turned out, to achieve a chewier cookie, we had to leave it alone. Letting the mixed dough rest for 1 to 4 hours (no longer) gives the proteins and starches in the flour a jump start at breaking down; meanwhile, the sugar dissolves, hydrates, and later retains this moisture better during baking, preventing the cookie from becoming brittle. Lastly, the surprising addition of a little almond butter added the toffee-like richness that butter typically provides a cookie. Not all semisweet chocolate chips are vegan, so check ingredient lists carefully. Use processed almond butter for the best texture; natural almond butter will make the cookies too greasy, and they will spread too much.

1 Whisk flour, baking powder, baking soda, and salt together in bowl. Whisk sugar, melted oil, water, almond butter, and vanilla in large bowl until well combined and smooth. Using rubber spatula, stir flour mixture into oil mixture until just combined; fold in chocolate chips.

2 Cover bowl with plastic wrap and let rest at room temperature for at least 1 hour or up to 4 hours. (Dough can be refrigerated for up to 24 hours; let sit at room temperature for 30 minutes before portioning.)

3 Adjust oven rack to middle position and heat oven to 350 degrees. Line 2 rimmed baking sheets with parchment paper. Divide dough into 16 portions, each about 3 tablespoons, then arrange dough mounds 2 inches apart on prepared sheets.

4 Bake, 1 sheet at a time, until light golden and edges have begun to set but centers are still soft, 12 to 14 minutes, rotating sheet halfway through baking. Let cookies cool completely on sheet. Serve. (Cookies can be stored at room temperature for up to 3 days.)

Chocolate Chip Oatmeal Cookies
Do not use quick or instant oats in this recipe.

Adjust oven rack to middle position and heat oven to 350 degrees. Spread 1¼ cups old-fashioned rolled oats on rimmed baking sheet and bake until fragrant and lightly browned, about 10 minutes, stirring halfway through baking; let cool completely. Reduce flour to 1⅔ cups and chocolate chips to ¾ cup. Fold oats into dough with chocolate chips in step 1.

Peanut Butter Cookies

makes 24 cookies

1½ cups (7½ ounces) all-purpose flour
1 teaspoon baking soda
½ teaspoon salt
1¼ cups creamy peanut butter
1 cup packed (7 ounces) organic
  light brown sugar (see page 31)
½ cup light corn syrup
¼ cup coconut oil, melted and
  cooled (see page 30)
3 tablespoons water
1 teaspoon vanilla extract
⅓ cup dry-roasted peanuts,
  chopped fine

Why This Recipe Works Chewy peanut butter cookies bring back fond memories of bake sales and childhood lunch boxes. Peanut butter is a staple ingredient in our vegan pantry, so we wanted a vegan peanut butter cookie that conjured that nostalgia. We needed to start by eliminating the eggs in the recipe. We were happy to find that simply adding more peanut butter bound the cookies nicely—and gave them deeper peanut flavor to boot. And a little bit of water—3 tablespoons—made up for the loss of moisture. The softest, chewiest peanut butter cookie recipes we tried included a form of liquid sweetener like molasses or maple syrup in addition to the sugar, but we found those flavors overbearing. Light corn syrup was a better bet; it helped the cookies retain moisture without overshadowing the peanut flavor. A full teaspoon of baking soda reacted quickly with the acidic brown sugar, causing the cookies to puff up and deflate before their structure had time to set. This left the centers pleasingly soft and chewy—just as we like our peanut butter cookies. Use processed peanut butter for the best texture; natural peanut butter will make the cookies too dry and tough. The dough is quite soft, so keep it chilled until you are ready to form and bake the cookies.

1 Whisk flour, baking soda, and salt together in bowl. Whisk peanut butter, sugar, corn syrup, melted oil, water, and vanilla in large bowl until well combined and smooth. Using rubber spatula, stir flour mixture into peanut butter mixture until just combined.

2 Cover bowl with plastic wrap and refrigerate until firm, at least 2 hours or up to 24 hours.

3 Adjust oven rack to middle position and heat oven to 350 degrees. Line 2 rimmed baking sheets with parchment paper. Working with 2 tablespoons dough at a time, roll into balls and space 2 inches apart on prepared sheets. Using bottom of greased drinking glass, press dough to ½-inch thickness, sprinkle with chopped peanuts, and press lightly to adhere.

4 Bake, 1 sheet at a time, until puffed and edges have begun to set but centers are still soft, 12 to 14 minutes, rotating sheet halfway through baking. Let cookies cool on sheet for 5 minutes, then transfer to wire rack. Let cookies cool completely before serving. (Cookies can be stored at room temperature for up to 3 days.)

Aquafaba Meringues

makes 48 cookies

¾ cup (5¼ ounces) organic sugar (see page 31)

4 ounces (½ cup) aquafaba (see page 34)

2 teaspoons cornstarch

¾ teaspoon vanilla extract

¼ teaspoon cream of tartar

⅛ teaspoon salt

Why This Recipe Works Aquafaba is the liquid found in a can of chickpeas, and while we use it in a lot of vegan recipes, we think its most magical property is its ability to whip like egg whites. We hoped whipped aquafaba would bake into ethereal vegan meringues. Unfortunately, our early attempts weren't uplifting. Our meringues deflated and developed a mottled surface and hollow centers. We could attribute some of our trouble to the organic sugar, which is generally coarser than conventional table sugar, so it wasn't fully dissolving. Looking for a solution, we reminded ourselves that while aquafaba might behave like egg whites under some circumstances, it's not the same ingredient. So instead of whipping the aquafaba to soft peaks before adding the sugar, as with egg whites, we heated the aquafaba, dissolved the sugar in it, and then whipped the mixture to stiff peaks. This eliminated the mottling. Then, since we also didn't need to worry about overwhipping, we experimented with long mixing times. Taking the mixture beyond just "stiff peaks" and to a denser, taffy-like texture gave us tunnel-free cookies that held their shape during baking. These meringues rivaled their egg-based counterpart for delicacy and elegance—and outdid them for ease. Do not use Progresso brand chickpeas for the aquafaba; it doesn't whip consistently.

1 Adjust oven racks to upper-middle and lower-middle positions and heat oven to 225 degrees. Line 2 rimmed baking sheets with parchment paper. Microwave sugar and aquafaba in bowl, whisking occasionally, until sugar is completely dissolved, 30 to 60 seconds (mixture should not begin to bubble). Let mixture cool slightly, about 10 minutes, then whisk in cornstarch.

2 Using stand mixer fitted with whisk, whip aquafaba mixture, vanilla, cream of tartar, and salt on high speed until glossy, stiff peaks form, and mixture is sticky and taffy-like, 9 to 15 minutes. Place meringue in pastry bag fitted with ½-inch plain tip or large zipper-lock bag with ½ inch of corner cut off. Pipe meringues into 1¼-inch-wide mounds about 1 inch high on prepared sheets.

3 Bake for 1 hour, switching and rotating sheets halfway through baking. Turn off oven and let meringues cool in oven for at least 1 hour. Remove from oven and let cool completely before serving, about 10 minutes. (Cooled meringues can be stored in single layer in airtight container at room temperature for up to 2 weeks.)

VARIATION

Almond Aquafaba Meringues

Substitute ½ teaspoon almond extract for vanilla extract.

Fudgy Brownies

makes 24 brownies

2 cups (10 ounces) all-purpose flour
1 teaspoon baking powder
¾ teaspoon salt
1 cup boiling water
3 ounces unsweetened chocolate, chopped fine
¾ cup (2¼ ounces) Dutch-processed cocoa powder
1½ teaspoons instant espresso powder (optional)
2½ cups (17½ ounces) organic sugar (see page 31)
½ cup vegetable oil
1 tablespoon vanilla extract
½ cup (3 ounces) bittersweet or semisweet chocolate chips

Why This Recipe Works Chewy, fudgy, ultrachocolaty brownies take very little work for an immensely satisfying reward. Could we make decadent brownies without ingredients like butter and eggs? Happily, we found we could whip up a batch of fudgy vegan brownies just as easily as we do conventional ones. Neutral-flavored vegetable oil was a quick swap for the butter. We typically don't add chemical leavener to a fudgy brownie; however, we found that a small amount of baking powder gave our brownies the perfect amount of lift and structure—without the need for a replacement for the eggs. For sinfully rich brownies, we used three forms of chocolate. We whisked chopped unsweetened chocolate for intensity and cocoa powder for added complexity into boiling water, the heat of which unlocked their flavor compounds. Stirring chocolate chips into the batter created pockets of gooey goodness. Not all semisweet chocolate chips are vegan, so check ingredient lists carefully. It's important to let the brownies cool thoroughly before cutting. If you use a glass baking dish, let the brownies cool for 10 minutes and then remove them from the dish. (The superior heat retention of glass can lead to overbaking.) For an accurate measurement of boiling water, bring a full kettle of water to a boil and then measure out the desired amount.

1 Adjust oven rack to lowest position and heat oven to 350 degrees. Make foil sling for 13 by 9-inch baking pan by folding 2 long sheets of aluminum foil; first sheet should be 13 inches wide and second sheet should be 9 inches wide. Lay sheets of foil in pan perpendicular to each other, with extra foil hanging over edges of pan. Push foil into corners and up sides of pan, smoothing foil flush to pan. Grease foil.

2 Whisk flour, baking powder, and salt together in bowl. Whisk boiling water, unsweetened chocolate, cocoa, and espresso powder, if using, in large bowl until well combined and chocolate is melted. Whisk in sugar, oil, and vanilla. Using rubber spatula, stir flour mixture into chocolate mixture until combined; fold in chocolate chips.

3 Scrape batter into prepared pan and smooth top. Bake until toothpick inserted halfway between edge and center comes out with few moist crumbs attached, 30 to 35 minutes. Let brownies cool in pan on wire rack for 2 hours.

4 Using foil overhang, lift brownies from pan. Return brownies to wire rack and let cool completely, about 1 hour. Cut into squares and serve. (Brownies can be stored at room temperature for up to 4 days.)

Raspberry Streusel Bars

makes
24 bars

2½ cups (12½ ounces) all-purpose
    flour
⅔ cup (4⅔ ounces) organic
    granulated sugar (see page 31)
½ teaspoon salt
¾ cup plus 2 tablespoons coconut
    oil (see page 30)
3 tablespoons water
½ cup (1½ ounces) old-fashioned
    rolled oats
½ cup pecans, toasted and
    chopped fine
¼ cup packed (1¾ ounces) organic
    light brown sugar (see page 31)
¾ cup raspberry jam
3¾ ounces (¾ cup) fresh raspberries
1 tablespoon lemon juice

Why This Recipe Works For the very best vegan raspberry bars, we needed to strike the right balance among bright, tangy fruit filling, tender shortbread crust, and crumbly topping. Traditionally, shortbread is all about the butter; for a vegan base that was just as rich and tender while also firm and sturdy, we found coconut oil to be a terrific alternative. This rich dough did double duty as both the crust and the base of our streusel topping. After pressing part of the flour mixture into the pan, we added oats, brown sugar, and pecans to the remaining mixture and pinched it into clumps to create our topping. These additions made a topping that was light and dry enough to adhere to the filling. For a filling that stayed neatly sandwiched between the base and topping, we combined fresh raspberries with raspberry jam. A squeeze of lemon juice brightened the mix. Prebaking the bottom crust before adding the filling and streusel prevented soggy shortbread. Frozen raspberries can be substituted for fresh, but be sure to defrost them before using. Do not use quick or instant oats in this recipe.

1 Adjust oven rack to middle position and heat oven to 375 degrees. Make foil sling for 13 by 9-inch baking pan by folding 2 long sheets of aluminum foil; first sheet should be 13 inches wide and second sheet should be 9 inches wide. Lay sheets of foil in pan perpendicular to each other, with extra foil hanging over edges of pan. Push foil into corners and up sides of pan, smoothing foil flush to pan. Grease foil.

2 Process flour, granulated sugar, and salt in food processor until combined. Pinch off 1-inch pieces of oil into flour mixture, sprinkle water over top, then pulse until mixture resembles damp sand, about 20 pulses; set aside 1¼ cups of flour mixture for topping. Sprinkle remaining flour mixture into prepared pan and press into even layer using bottom of dry measuring cup. Bake until edges of crust begin to brown, 14 to 18 minutes, rotating pan halfway through baking.

3 Meanwhile, stir oats, pecans, and brown sugar into reserved flour mixture and pinch into clumps of streusel. Mash jam, raspberries, and lemon juice with fork in small bowl until few berry pieces remain.

4 Spread berry mixture evenly over hot crust, then sprinkle evenly with streusel. Bake until filling is bubbling and topping is golden brown, 22 to 25 minutes, rotating pan halfway through baking. Let bars cool completely in pan on wire rack, about 2 hours. Using foil overhang, lift bars from pan. Cut into squares and serve.

desserts

Dark Chocolate Cupcakes

makes 12 cupcakes

Why This Recipe Works Cupcakes aren't just for kids, and there's nothing more grown-up than ultrarich chocolate cake. The ultimate dark chocolate cupcake, vegan or not, needs to be rich and tender with deep chocolate flavor. To make vegan chocolate cupcakes that fit this description, we took a cue from the success of our Blueberry Muffins (page 58) and folded whipped aquafaba, stabilized with cream of tartar, into our cupcake batter. This helped us achieve a light, fluffy crumb—just as if we'd folded in whipped egg whites. Next we focused on complex chocolate flavor, which we got with bittersweet chocolate. But when we added enough to satisfy our chocolate cravings, our cupcakes took on a chalky texture. The culprit? The cocoa butter in the bittersweet chocolate. Once melted and resolidified, this fat takes on a very stable crystalline structure that was detectable in our delicate cupcakes. So to fortify the dark chocolate flavor without overloading our cupcakes with cocoa butter, we added a generous ½ cup of cocoa powder to the mix, which kept our cupcakes tender. Not all brands of bittersweet chocolate are vegan, so check ingredient lists carefully. Do not use natural cocoa powder in this recipe; it gives the cupcakes a rubbery, spongy texture. The cupcakes are best served the day they are made.

1⅓ cups (6⅔ ounces) all-purpose flour
1 cup (7 ounces) organic sugar (see page 31)
¾ teaspoon baking powder
¼ teaspoon baking soda
½ teaspoon salt
1 cup water
½ cup (1½ ounces) Dutch-processed cocoa powder
1 ounce bittersweet chocolate, chopped
¼ cup coconut oil (see page 30)
¾ teaspoon vanilla extract
¼ cup aquafaba (see page 34)
1 teaspoon cream of tartar
½ recipe Creamy Chocolate Frosting (page 285)

1 Adjust oven rack to middle position and heat oven to 400 degrees. Line 12-cup muffin tin with paper or foil liners. Whisk flour, sugar, baking powder, baking soda, and salt together in large bowl.

2 Microwave water, cocoa, chocolate, oil, and vanilla in second bowl at 50 percent power, whisking occasionally, until melted and smooth, about 2 minutes; set aside to cool slightly.

3 Meanwhile, using stand mixer fitted with whisk, whip aquafaba and cream of tartar on high speed until stiff foam that clings to whisk forms, 3 to 9 minutes. Using rubber spatula, stir chocolate mixture into flour mixture until batter is thoroughly combined and smooth (batter will be thick). Stir one-third of whipped aquafaba into batter to lighten, then gently fold in remaining aquafaba until no white streaks remain.

4 Divide batter evenly among prepared muffin cups. Bake until tops are set and spring back when pressed lightly, 16 to 20 minutes, rotating muffin tin halfway through baking.

5 Let cupcakes cool in muffin tin for 10 minutes, then transfer to wire rack and let cool completely, about 1 hour. Spread frosting evenly over cupcakes and serve.

Yellow Layer Cake

serves 10 to 12

1¾ cups unsweetened oat milk, room temperature

½ cup coconut oil, melted and cooled (see page 30)

1½ tablespoons vanilla extract

5 tablespoons aquafaba (see page 34)

1 teaspoon cream of tartar

4 cups (16 ounces) cake flour

1¾ cups (12¼ ounces) organic sugar (see page 31)

1 tablespoon baking powder

1 teaspoon salt

1 recipe Creamy Chocolate Frosting (recipe follows)

Why This Recipe Works Our vegan yellow layer cake stands tall for any celebration. But nailing the recipe was one of our biggest challenges. After all, none of the ingredients that give yellow cake structure or lightness are vegan. And unlike with our Dark Chocolate Cupcakes (page 282), yellow layer cake features only mild vanilla notes; there's nowhere for off-flavors to hide. The vegan cake recipes we tried were far from cake-like: Tasters described one as a grease bomb, while another was foamy and anemic-gray. One had a candied exterior and a gelatinous interior. For a light, downy crumb, we turned to cake flour. Then, once again, we folded whipped aquafaba into our batter to create a fluffy treat with no off-flavors. To enhance fluffiness more, we baked the cake in a hot oven—400 degrees—to boost oven spring (the rise that baked goods experience when they hit the oven). And a lengthy baking time of 25 to 30 minutes helped dry out the layers just enough so there was no pastiness. Using oat milk in our batter further promoted browning thanks to its sugar content. Our cake was much improved, but without the supporting structure of eggs, it was delicate. To prevent slices from crumbling, we omitted baking soda, which makes batter alkaline, weakening the gluten structure and producing a porous crumb. To achieve adequate rise without it, we increased the baking powder to a whopping tablespoon. We frost the cake with a classic: chocolate frosting.

1 Adjust oven rack to middle position and heat oven to 400 degrees. Grease two 9-inch round cake pans, line with parchment paper, and grease parchment.

2 Whisk oat milk, melted oil, and vanilla together in bowl. Using stand mixer fitted with whisk, whip aquafaba and cream of tartar on high speed until stiff foam that clings to whisk forms, 3 to 9 minutes; transfer to clean bowl.

3 Return now-empty bowl to mixer and mix flour, sugar, baking powder, and salt on low speed until well combined, about 1 minute. Gradually add milk mixture and continue to mix until just incorporated, about 15 seconds. Scrape down bowl and whisk attachment, then continue to whip on medium-low speed until smooth and fully incorporated, 10 to 15 seconds.

4 Using rubber spatula, stir one-third of whipped aquafaba into batter to lighten, then gently fold in remaining aquafaba until no white streaks remain. Divide batter evenly between prepared pans. Bake until cakes are set and spring back when pressed lightly, 25 to 30 minutes, rotating pans halfway through baking. Let cakes cool in pans on wire rack for 10 minutes. Remove cakes from pans, discard parchment, and let cool completely on rack, about 2 hours.

5 Line edges of cake platter with 4 strips of parchment to keep platter clean and place dab of frosting in center to anchor cake. Place 1 cake layer on platter. Spread 1½ cups frosting evenly over top, right to edge of cake. Top with second cake layer, press lightly to adhere, then spread remaining 2½ cups frosting evenly over top and sides of cake. To smooth frosting, run edge of offset spatula around cake sides and over top. Carefully remove parchment strips before serving.

Creamy Chocolate Frosting   makes 4 cups

Why This Recipe Works For a rich, billowy multipurpose chocolate frosting, we melted semisweet chocolate and whisked in coconut milk. Once cooled, we whipped the ganache-like mixture into a mousse-y frosting. The frosting tasted downright decadent, but it looked broken. Using chocolate chips instead of bar chocolate was our fix. Chocolate chips contain emulsifying agents, which stabilized the mixture so it didn't break. Not all semisweet chocolate chips are vegan, so check ingredient lists carefully. Halve this recipe to frost 12 cupcakes. (Use two cans of coconut milk to obtain the ¾ cup cream.) Mixing times won't change. Note that this frosting is made over 2 days.

  3 (14-ounce) cans coconut milk
3⅓ cups (1¼ pounds) semisweet chocolate chips
  ¼ teaspoon salt

1 Refrigerate unopened cans of coconut milk for at least 24 hours to ensure that 2 distinct layers form. Skim cream layer from each can and measure out 1½ cups cream (save any extra cream for another use and discard milky liquid).

2 Microwave coconut cream, chocolate chips, and salt in bowl at 50 percent power, whisking occasionally, until melted and smooth, 2 to 4 minutes; transfer to bowl of stand mixer. Place plastic wrap directly against surface of chocolate mixture and refrigerate until cooled completely and texture resembles firm cream cheese, about 3 hours, stirring halfway through chilling. (If mixture has chilled for longer and is very stiff, let stand at room temperature to soften but still cool.) Using stand mixer fitted with whisk attachment, whip at high speed until fluffy, mousse-like soft peaks form, 2 to 4 minutes, scraping down bowl halfway through whipping.

TESTING NOTES **Dairy-Free Milks**
OUR FAVORITE **Oat Milk**
OTHERS TESTED Coconut milk produces a pale cake with a very fine crumb. Almond milk makes the cake slightly greasy and rubbery. Soy milk creates a slightly dry, spongy, coarse-crumbed cake.

French Apple Tart

serves 8

CRUST

1¾ cups (8¾ ounces) all-purpose
    flour
3 tablespoons organic sugar
    (see page 31)
¼ teaspoon salt
½ cup coconut oil, melted and
    cooled (see page 30)
3 tablespoons water

FILLING

10 Golden Delicious apples,
    (8 ounces each), peeled and cored
3 tablespoons coconut oil
    (see page 30)
1 tablespoon water
½ cup apricot preserves
¼ teaspoon salt

Why This Recipe Works A classic French apple tart is a show-stopping centerpiece dessert—and it's little more than apples and pastry. But such simplicity means that imperfections are hard to hide. First things first: We needed to develop a recipe for a vegan tart shell. While tart crust typically gets its short-bread-like texture from butter, we found we were able to achieve the same effect with coconut oil. We melted the coconut oil and mixed it with the flour and other dry ingredients for a quick-and-easy press-in dough. But our crust was a little crumbly. To fix this, we needed to add some water to account for the moisture lost when we replaced butter with coconut oil. And to achieve an appealing golden color in the absence of butter solids, we baked the shell in a slightly hotter oven than normal—375 degrees rather than 350. For the filling, we cooked half of the 5 pounds of Golden Delicious apples in the recipe into a concentrated puree; we sliced the remaining apples and par-cooked them until they were pliable enough to adorn the top with concentric circles. A thin coat of preserves and a final run under the broiler provided a caramelized finish. You may have extra apple slices after arranging the apples in step 6. If you don't have a potato masher, you can puree the apples in a food processor. To ensure that the outer ring of the pan releases easily from the tart, avoid getting apple puree and apricot glaze on the edge of the crust. The tart is best served the day it is made.

1 FOR THE CRUST Adjust 1 oven rack to lowest position and second rack 6 inches from broiler element. Heat oven to 375 degrees. Whisk flour, sugar, and salt together in bowl. Add melted oil and water and stir with rubber spatula until dough forms. Using your hands, press two-thirds of dough into bottom of 9-inch tart pan with removable bottom. Press remaining dough evenly into fluted sides of pan. Press and smooth dough with bottom of dry measuring cup to even thickness. Place pan on wire rack set in rimmed baking sheet and bake on lower rack until crust is evenly golden brown and firm to touch, 35 to 40 minutes, rotating pan halfway through baking. Set aside until ready to fill. (Crust needn't be cool before filling.)

2 FOR THE FILLING Reduce oven temperature to 350 degrees. Cut 5 apples lengthwise into quarters and cut each quarter lengthwise into 4 slices. Melt 1 tablespoon oil in 12-inch skillet over medium heat. Add apple slices and water and toss to combine. Cover and cook, stirring occasionally, until apples begin to turn translucent and are slightly pliable, 3 to 5 minutes. Transfer apples to large plate, spread into single layer, and set aside to cool. Do not clean skillet.

3 While apples cook, microwave apricot preserves until fluid, about 30 seconds. Strain preserves through fine-mesh strainer into small bowl, reserving solids. Set aside 3 tablespoons strained preserves for brushing tart.

4 Cut remaining 5 apples into ½-inch-thick wedges. Melt remaining 2 tablespoons oil in now-empty skillet over medium heat. Add remaining apricot preserves, reserved apricot solids, apple wedges, and salt. Cover and cook, stirring occasionally, until apples are very soft, about 10 minutes.

5 Mash apples to puree with potato masher, then continue to cook, stirring occasionally, until puree is reduced to 2 cups, about 5 minutes.

6 Transfer apple puree to baked tart shell and smooth surface. Select 5 thinnest slices of sautéed apple and set aside. Starting at outer edge of tart, arrange remaining slices, tightly overlapping, in concentric circles. Bend reserved slices to fit in center. Bake tart, still on wire rack in sheet, on lowest rack, for 30 minutes. Remove tart from oven and heat broiler.

7 While broiler heats, warm reserved preserves in microwave until fluid, about 20 seconds. Brush evenly over surface of apples, avoiding tart crust. Broil tart, checking every 30 seconds and turning as necessary, until apples are browned in spots, 1 to 3 minutes. Let tart cool for at least 1½ hours. Remove outer metal ring of tart pan, slide thin metal spatula between tart and pan bottom, and carefully slide tart onto serving platter. Cut into wedges and serve.

Making the Apple Rosette

1 Starting at outer edge of tart, arrange apple slices, tightly overlapping, in concentric circles.

2 Bend 5 thinnest slices of sautéed apple to fit in center.

Peach-Raspberry Crisp

serves 6

Why This Recipe Works As an homage to the classic dessert known as Peach Melba, we wanted to combine peaches and raspberries in a warm summer crisp. Since fruit fillings are naturally vegan, we tackled the dessert's crowning glory, the crisp topping, first. We liked the chewiness and crunch that a combination of oats, flour, and nuts offered. Typically, we would use butter to hold those ingredients together, but we found that coconut oil worked just as well. A bonus: While butter needs to be chilled and carefully cut into the dry ingredients, we were able to simply melt the coconut oil, saving time and effort. Fruit juiciness varies based on ripeness, so to even the playing field, we macerated and drained the peaches before assembling the crisp, avoiding runny filling and soggy topping. We added back a measured amount of the peach juice, thickened with ground tapioca, to create a gooey, flavorful filling. Layering the raspberries on top of the peaches instead of folding them in prevented them from turning to mush. Topped with our crunchy vegan crisp topping, the soft, warm, bubbling fruit makes for the perfect summer dessert. You can substitute 1¾ pounds frozen peaches for fresh in this recipe; be sure to thaw before using. Do not use quick or instant oats in this recipe. Measure the tapioca, which may be sold as "Minute Tapioca," before grinding it. Grind the tapioca to a powder in a spice grinder or a mini food processor.

FILLING

2½ pounds peaches, peeled, halved, pitted, and cut into ½-inch wedges
¼ cup (1¾ ounces) organic sugar (see page 31)
⅛ teaspoon salt
2 tablespoons instant tapioca, ground
1 tablespoon lemon juice
1 teaspoon vanilla extract
10 ounces (2 cups) raspberries

TOPPING

½ cup (2½ ounces) all-purpose flour
¼ cup packed (1¾ ounces) organic brown sugar (see page 31)
¼ cup (1¾ ounces) organic granulated sugar (see page 31)
¼ teaspoon ground cinnamon
¼ teaspoon ground ginger
¼ teaspoon salt
¼ cup coconut oil, melted and cooled (see page 30)
½ cup (1½ ounces) old-fashioned rolled oats
½ cup pecans, chopped
2 tablespoons water

1 FOR THE FILLING Adjust oven rack to upper-middle position and heat oven to 400 degrees. Gently toss peaches with sugar and salt in bowl and let sit, stirring occasionally, for 30 minutes. Drain peaches in colander set inside bowl; reserve 2 tablespoons juice and discard extra.

2 Return drained peaches to bowl and toss with reserved juice, ground tapioca, lemon juice, and vanilla. Transfer to 8-inch square baking dish, press gently into even layer, then top with raspberries.

3 FOR THE TOPPING Meanwhile, process flour, brown sugar, granulated sugar, cinnamon, ginger, and salt in food processor until combined, about 15 seconds. Add melted oil and pulse until mixture resembles wet sand, about 10 pulses. Add oats, pecans, and water and pulse until mixture forms marble-size clumps and no loose flour remains, about 15 pulses. Refrigerate mixture for at least 15 minutes.

4 Sprinkle topping evenly over fruit, breaking into ½-inch pieces as necessary. Bake until topping is well browned and fruit is bubbling around edges, 30 to 35 minutes, rotating dish halfway through baking. Transfer to wire rack and let cool for at least 30 minutes. Serve warm.

Pie Dough

Why This Recipe Works A tender, flaky, and crisp crust, with a rich baked flavor—this is the not-so-humble aspiration of any budding pie maker. This is why butter so often finds its way into a pie crust recipe: The water in the butter evaporates in the oven to help create pockets of air between layers of pastry. And with flour and chilled cubes of butter (helped only by some sugar, salt, and maybe shortening) being the only key ingredients in pie dough, veganizing this workhorse would be a challenge. Baking with all shortening gave us a tender crust, but it lacked structure and was greasy. Vegetable oil was a failure, delivering a cracker-like crust. We'd hesitated to try coconut oil, because it's very hard when chilled—too hard to roll. But when we substituted room-temperature coconut oil for the chilled butter (and passed on chilling the dough itself), we achieved a flaky, nicely browned, rich crust; however, it crumbled when sliced. For structure we turned to a method used in the test kitchen's standard Foolproof Pie Dough: We mixed only half the flour with the coconut oil; we then pulsed in the remaining flour before folding in our water. The two additions made two grades of dough: one tender and rich due to its flour being coated in fat and one lean to offer structure to hold any filling.

Single-Crust Pie Dough   makes one 9-inch pie crust

1½ cups (7½ ounces) all-purpose flour
 1 tablespoon organic sugar (see page 31)
 ½ teaspoon salt
 ½ cup plus 1 tablespoon coconut oil (see page 30)
 ¼ cup ice water, plus extra as needed

1 Process ¾ cup flour, sugar, and salt in food processor until combined, about 5 seconds. Pinch off ½-inch pieces of oil into flour mixture and pulse until sticky and dough just begins to clump, 10 to 16 pulses. Redistribute dough around workbowl, add remaining ¾ cup flour, and pulse until just incorporated, 3 to 6 pulses; transfer to large bowl.

2 Sprinkle ice water over top of dough, then, using rubber spatula, fold and press dough to fully incorporate water and bring dough together, being careful not to overmix. If dough doesn't come together, add up to 1 tablespoon ice water, 1 teaspoon at a time. Form dough into 4-inch disk. (Dough can be wrapped tightly in plastic wrap and refrigerated for up to 2 days or frozen for up to 1 month. Let dough sit at room temperature to soften completely before rolling out, about 2 hours if refrigerated or 4 hours if frozen.)

3 Roll dough between 2 large sheets parchment paper into 12-inch circle. Remove top parchment and gently flip into 9-inch pie plate; discard second sheet parchment. Ease dough into plate by gently lifting edge of dough with your hand while pressing into plate bottom with your other hand.

4 Trim overhang to ½ inch beyond lip of plate. Tuck overhang under itself; folded edge should be flush with edge of plate. Crimp dough evenly around edge of plate using your fingers. Wrap dough-lined plate loosely in plastic and refrigerate until dough is firm, about 45 minutes. (Dough-lined plate can be refrigerated for up to 24 hours.)

5 TO BAKE Adjust oven rack to lowest position and heat oven to 400 degrees. Set rimmed baking sheet in second rimmed baking sheet. Line chilled pie shell with double layer of aluminum foil, covering edges to prevent burning, and fill with pie weights. Bake on prepared sheet until pie dough looks dry and is pale in color, about 30 minutes, rotating plate halfway through baking. Remove foil and weights and continue to bake crust until light golden brown, 10 to 15 minutes, rotating plate halfway through baking. Let crust cool completely in plate on wire rack. (Cooled crust can be wrapped with plastic wrap and stored at room temperature for up to 24 hours.)

Double-Crust Pie Dough
makes enough for 1 double-crust 9-inch pie

3 cups (15 ounces) all-purpose flour
2 tablespoons organic sugar (see page 31)
1 teaspoon salt
1 cup plus 2 tablespoons coconut oil (see page 30)
½ cup ice water, plus extra as needed

1 Process 1½ cups flour, sugar, and salt in food processor until combined, about 5 seconds. Pinch off ½-inch pieces of oil into flour mixture and pulse until sticky and dough just begins to clump, 12 to 15 pulses. Redistribute dough around workbowl, add remaining 1½ cups flour, and pulse until just incorporated, 3 to 6 pulses; transfer to large bowl.

2 Sprinkle ice water over top of dough, then, using rubber spatula, fold and press dough to fully incorporate water and bring dough together, being careful not to overmix. If dough doesn't come together, add up to 2 tablespoons ice water, 1 teaspoon at a time. Divide dough in half and form each half into 4-inch disk. (Dough can be wrapped tightly in plastic wrap and refrigerated for up to 2 days or frozen for up to 1 month. Let dough sit at room temperature to soften completely before rolling out, about 2 hours if refrigerated or 4 hours if frozen.)

Pecan Pie

serves 8

⅓ cup coconut oil (see page 30)
⅓ cup (1⅔ ounces) all-purpose flour
1¼ cups maple syrup
¾ cup water
⅔ cup packed (4⅔ ounces) organic
   dark brown sugar (see page 31)
½ teaspoon salt
2½ cups (10 ounces) pecans,
   toasted and chopped
4 teaspoons vanilla extract
1 recipe Single-Crust Pie Dough
   (page 292), fully baked and cooled

Why This Recipe Works We knew that hitting the hallmark of a pecan pie in a vegan version might be challenging. The toasty pecans should be enveloped by a sweet, custard-like filling. A classic recipe relies heavily on butter and eggs to get the texture of the filling right, so we really felt the deleterious effects of using standard vegan ingredients such as margarine, flaxseeds, or silken tofu, which contributed unpleasant flavors, or oil, which never fully emulsified into our filling. With these ingredients, we missed the clean, simple flavors of caramel and toasted nuts. Things seemed promising when we tried our favorite recipe and just omitted the dairy and eggs, but it never set up, even long after cooling, and it was more like a sticky caramel-nut pie, not a true pecan pie. It was then that we struck upon using a classic French technique usually reserved for savory sauces: a roux. By cooking a little flour in hot oil and whisking in some maple syrup, sugar, and water, we were able to create a thick emulsion that gave our pie body and cohesion. However, by the time we had incorporated enough roux to hold our pie together after slicing, the filling felt heavy. By baking our already fully cooked pie in a low oven until it puffed, we cooked off some of the extra moisture, and our filling assumed the light custardy texture and glossy sheen we were looking for with less roux. And the low temperature meant the parbaked crust never got too dark.

1 Adjust oven rack to middle position and heat oven to 275 degrees.

2 Heat oil in large saucepan over medium heat until shimmering. Whisk in flour and cook, whisking constantly, until combined and pale honey-colored, about 2 minutes. Whisking constantly, add maple syrup, water, sugar, and salt and cook until combined and sugar is dissolved, about 1 minute. Bring to boil, then reduce heat to medium-low and simmer, stirring occasionally, until rubber spatula leaves trail when dragged across bottom of saucepan, 3 to 5 minutes. Off heat, stir in pecans and vanilla.

3 Transfer pecan mixture to pie shell and spread evenly with rubber spatula. Bake until edges of filling are slightly puffed and a few small bubbles appear around edges, 45 to 55 minutes. Let pie cool completely on wire rack until filling has set, about 4 hours, before serving.

Blueberry Pie

serves 8

30 ounces (6 cups) blueberries

1 recipe Double-Crust Pie Dough (page 293), room temperature

1 Granny Smith apple, peeled, cored, and shredded

¾ cup (5¼ ounces) plus 1 tablespoon organic sugar (see page 31)

2 tablespoons instant tapioca, ground

2 teaspoons grated lemon zest plus 2 teaspoons juice Pinch salt

2 tablespoons coconut oil (see page 30)

⅔ cup water

2 teaspoons cornstarch

Why This Recipe Works We wanted a blueberry pie that had a firm, glistening filling full of fresh, bright flavor and still-plump berries. To thicken the pie, we favored tapioca, which allowed the fresh yet subtle blueberry flavor to shine through. Too much of it, though, and we had a congealed mess. Cooking and reducing half of the berries helped us cut down on the tapioca, but not enough. A second inspiration came when we remembered that apples are high in pectin, a type of carbohydrate that acts as a thickener when cooked. Along with a modest 2 tablespoons of tapioca, a peeled and shredded Granny Smith apple thickened the filling to a soft, even consistency. To vent the steam from the berries, we found a faster, easier alternative to a lattice top: a biscuit cutter, which we used to cut out circles in the top crust. We thought a pie wouldn't be complete without a glistening, bronzed top that comes from an egg wash. To make this pie look blue ribbon–worthy, we first sprinkled sugar over it before baking. Then, we borrowed a technique sometimes used when baking rye breads: We painted a hot cornstarch slurry over our crust when we pulled it from the oven. Once dried, it gave the pie the gleaming, golden finish we wanted. Use a coarse grater to shred the apple. Measure the tapioca, which may be sold as "Minute Tapioca," before grinding it. Grind the tapioca to a powder in a spice grinder or a mini food processor. Make sure your dough is room temperature before rolling out.

1 Place 3 cups blueberries in medium saucepan. Cook over medium heat, stirring and mashing occasionally with potato masher, until half of blueberries are broken down and mixture measures 1½ cups, 7 to 10 minutes. Transfer to large bowl and let cool completely, about 20 minutes.

2 Meanwhile, adjust oven rack to lowest position and heat oven to 400 degrees. Line rimmed baking sheet with aluminum foil. Roll 1 disk of dough between 2 large sheets parchment paper into 12-inch circle. Remove parchment on top of dough round and flip into 9-inch pie plate; peel off second sheet parchment. Ease dough into plate by gently lifting edge of dough with your hand while pressing into plate bottom with your other hand. Roll other disk of dough between 2 large sheets parchment paper into 12-inch circle.

3 Place shredded apple in center of dish towel. Gather ends together and twist tightly to drain as much liquid as possible. Transfer apple to bowl with cooked blueberry mixture and stir in remaining 3 cups uncooked blueberries, ¾ cup sugar, tapioca, lemon zest and juice, and salt until combined. Spread mixture into dough-lined pie plate. Pinch ½-inch pieces of coconut oil and disperse evenly over top of blueberries.

4 Using 1¼-inch round cookie cutter, cut out single round in center of 12-inch dough circle. Cut out 6 more rounds from dough, 1½ inches from edge of center hole and equally spaced around center hole. Loosely roll dough circle around rolling pin and gently unroll it onto filling.

5 Trim overhang to ½ inch beyond lip of plate. Pinch edges of top and bottom crusts firmly together. Tuck overhang under itself; folded edge should be flush with edge of plate. Crimp dough evenly around edge of plate using your fingers. Sprinkle surface evenly with remaining 1 tablespoon sugar.

6 Set pie on prepared baking sheet and bake until crust is light golden brown, about 25 minutes. Reduce oven temperature to 350 degrees, rotate sheet, and continue to bake until juices are bubbling and crust is golden brown, 40 to 50 minutes longer.

7 Whisk water and cornstarch together in small saucepan. Whisking constantly, bring to boil over high heat; remove pot from heat. Working quickly, brush surface of pie with cornstarch mixture, being careful to avoid pooling. Let pie cool completely on wire rack, about 4 hours, before serving.

Pumpkin Cashew Cheesecake

serves 12 to 16

Why This Recipe Works When asked their favorite dessert, many people will say cheesecake—one of the most dairy-heavy treats. Maybe it's this popularity that intrigues so many vegan bakers, despite the obvious hurdles. In pursuing our take on vegan cheesecake, we decided on pumpkin cheesecake, one of our favorite variations on the classic. Without the help of unctuous cream cheese, we'd need to focus our attention on a thick, creamy base. So we looked to our go-to vegan cheese, cashew cheese; once soaked and pureed, the sweet, mild-tasting cashews made a velvety cheesecake base. However, once unmolded, the cake slumped into a mound of pumpkin mousse. Other recipes call for fortifying the base with silken tofu, but this took both the "cheese" and the "cake" out of cheesecake, creating a rubbery, off-tasting confection. Blotting the pumpkin puree with paper towels before mixing it with the rest of the ingredients was a simple way to eliminate moisture, but the cake still lacked the dense, set-up structure of true cheesecake. We tried mixing in agar-agar (an algae-based substitute for gelatin), but this left behind undissolved flakes in our thick filling. Instead, we mixed in our number-one vegan pantry item: melted coconut oil. Because coconut oil is solid at room temperature, the cheesecake set up into a sliceable dessert after 6 hours in the refrigerator. A small amount of nondairy cream cheese provided tang. We had the best luck using Tofutti Better Than Cream Cheese dairy-cheese, as the cheesecake won't set up properly. Not all graham crackers are vegan, so check ingredient lists carefully. For best results, chill the cheesecake for the full 24 hours. Don't let the cheesecake sit at room temperature for more than 1 hour; it will soften too much.

FILLING

- 4 cups (1¼ pounds) raw cashews
- 1 (15-ounce) can unsweetened pumpkin puree
- ⅔ cup coconut oil, melted and hot (see page 30)
- 2 tablespoons lemon juice
- 1½ tablespoons vanilla extract
- 1⅓ cups (10⅓ ounces) organic sugar (see page 31)
- 1 teaspoon ground cinnamon
- ¾ teaspoon salt
- ½ teaspoon ground ginger
- ¼ teaspoon ground nutmeg
- ¼ teaspoon allspice
- 8 ounces dairy-free cream cheese, softened

CRUST

- 8 whole graham crackers, broken into 1-inch pieces
- 1 tablespoon organic sugar (see page 31)
- ⅓ cup coconut oil, melted (see page 30)

1 FOR THE FILLING Place cashews in bowl and add water to cover by 1 inch. Soak at room temperature for at least 12 hours or up to 24 hours.

2 FOR THE CRUST Adjust oven rack to lower-middle position and heat oven to 325 degrees. Spray bottom and sides of 9-inch springform pan with vegetable oil spray. Line pan bottom with parchment paper and grease parchment.

3 Process graham crackers and sugar in food processor to fine, even crumbs, about 30 seconds. Sprinkle melted oil over top and pulse to incorporate, about 5 pulses. Sprinkle crumbs into prepared pan and press into even layer with bottom of dry measuring cup. Bake until fragrant and edges begin to darken, about 13 minutes. Let cool completely on wire rack, about 1 hour.

4 While crust cools, line baking sheet with triple layer of paper towels. Spread pumpkin puree on paper towels into even layer. Cover pumpkin with second triple layer of paper towels and press firmly until paper towels are saturated. Discard top layer of towels, then transfer pumpkin puree to now-empty food processor bowl.

5 Rinse and drain soaked cashews well. Add cashews, hot melted oil, lemon juice, and vanilla to food processor and process until thoroughly combined and cashews are finely chopped, 2 to 3 minutes, scraping down sides of bowl as needed. Add sugar, cinnamon, salt, ginger, nutmeg, and allspice. Continue to process until thoroughly combined, about 1 minute. Add cream cheese and process until very smooth and creamy, about 3 minutes, scraping down sides of bowl as needed (mixture will be grainy like ricotta cheese).

6 Pour filling into cooled crust and, using offset spatula dipped in hot water and wiped dry, smooth top. Refrigerate for at least 6 hours or up to 24 hours.

7 To unmold cheesecake, run thin knife between cake and sides of pan, then remove sides of pan. Slide thin metal spatula between parchment and crust and carefully slide cheesecake onto plate. To slice, dip sharp knife in hot water and wipe dry between cuts. Serve immediately.

COCONUT WHIPPED CREAM

4 (14-ounce) cans coconut milk
2 tablespoons organic sugar
(see page 31)
2 teaspoons vanilla extract

STRAWBERRIES

2 pounds strawberries, hulled and
quartered (6⅓ cups)
6 tablespoons (2⅔ ounces) organic
sugar (see page 31)

SHORTCAKES

2 cups (10 ounces) all-purpose flour
2 tablespoons organic granulated
sugar (see page 31)
2 teaspoons baking powder
½ teaspoon baking soda
½ teaspoon salt
1 cup unsweetened coconut milk
beverage, chilled
½ cup coconut oil, melted and
cooled (see page 30)
1 tablespoon lemon juice
1 tablespoon turbinado sugar

Why This Recipe Works Strawberry shortcakes, with their rustic biscuits, juicy berries, and fluff of whipped cream, capture the casual fun of early summer days. But this special treat is a three-part dessert, and only one—the fruit filling—is vegan. We tested vegan shortcakes with tough, crumbly biscuits and soupy, bland dairy-free cream. We started with our great Savory Drop Biscuits (page 55) and added 2 tablespoons of sugar and a final sprinkling of turbinado sugar. Coconut milk whipped just like heavy cream into velvety billows, and its mild coconut flavor complemented the sweet strawberries and rich biscuits. Chill the unopened cans of coconut milk for at least 24 hours before whipping. Use only the very thick portion of the milk, or the cream won't whip properly. Don't use light canned coconut milk. Use a slotted spoon to portion the berries.

1 FOR THE COCONUT WHIPPED CREAM Refrigerate unopened cans of coconut milk for at least 24 hours to ensure that 2 distinct layers form. Skim top layer of cream from each can and measure out 2 cups of cream (save any extra cream for another use and discard milky liquid). Using stand mixer fitted with whisk, whip coconut cream, sugar, and vanilla on low speed until well combined, about 30 seconds. Increase speed to high and whip until mixture thickens and soft peaks form, about 2 minutes. (Whipped cream can be refrigerated for up to 4 days.)

2 FOR THE STRAWBERRIES Using potato masher, mash one-third of strawberries with sugar in bowl. Stir in remaining strawberries, cover, and let sit while making biscuits, at least 30 minutes or up to 2 hours.

3 FOR THE SHORTCAKES Adjust oven rack to middle position and heat oven to 475 degrees. Set rimmed baking sheet in second baking sheet and line with parchment paper. Whisk flour, granulated sugar, baking powder, baking soda, and salt together in large bowl. Whisk coconut milk, melted oil, and lemon juice together (oil will clump) in second bowl. Stir milk mixture into flour mixture until just incorporated.

4 Using greased ⅓-cup dry measuring cup, drop level scoops of batter 1½ inches apart on prepared sheet. Sprinkle evenly with turbinado sugar. Bake until tops are golden, 12 to 14 minutes, rotating sheet halfway through baking. Transfer biscuits to wire rack and let cool completely, about 30 minutes.

5 Split each biscuit in half and place bottoms on individual plates. Using slotted spoon, portion strawberries over biscuit bottoms, then top with dollop of whipped cream. Top shortcakes and serve immediately.

TESTING NOTES **Dairy-Free Milks**

OUR FAVORITE **Coconut Milk**

OTHERS TESTED Almond milk makes the biscuits tougher and a little salty-tasting. Oat milk produces noticeably sweeter biscuits. Soy milk imparts a distinct soy flavor and a slightly wetter crumb.

Coconut Ice Cream

makes 1 quart

2 (14-ounce) cans coconut milk

2 tablespoons cornstarch

½ cup (3½ ounces) organic sugar (see page 31)

¼ cup light corn syrup

¼ teaspoon salt

1 teaspoon vanilla extract

Why This Recipe Works Developing a recipe for ice cream without milk, cream, or eggs seemed like a tall order, but we were determined to make a thick, creamy vegan frozen treat with the dense texture of the premium ice creams we love. Tasters enjoyed the clean coconut flavor and silky texture of canned coconut milk for the base. In addition to sugar, we added corn syrup, which interfered with ice crystal formation. Including cornstarch also prevented ice crystal formation and acted as a stabilizer. But tasters noticed a persistent grainy, starchy texture—and it wasn't caused by the starch. This graininess, as it turned out, came from unemulsified bits of fat. The solution? We blended our hot mixture after cooking, so the fat became fully emulsified. The lightly coconutty base was the perfect backdrop for flavor variations—we liked one version with lime and another horchata-inspired flavor with warm spices. We prefer to make this recipe in a canister-style ice cream maker; the ice cream was grainy when made in self-refrigerating models. If using a canister-style ice cream maker, be sure to freeze the empty canister for at least 24 hours and preferably for 48 hours before churning. Make sure your blender is only two-thirds full or less, open the lid vent, and hold in place with a dish towel in step 2. Do not use light canned coconut milk in this recipe.

1 Shake unopened cans of coconut milk to form homogeneous mixture. Whisk ¼ cup coconut milk and cornstarch together in small bowl and set aside. Combine remaining coconut milk, sugar, corn syrup, salt, and vanilla in large saucepan. Cook over medium-high heat, whisking often to dissolve sugar and break up any clumps, until small bubbles form around edge of saucepan and mixture registers 190 degrees, 5 to 7 minutes. Reduce heat to medium. Whisk cornstarch mixture to recombine, then whisk into coconut milk mixture in pan. Cook, constantly scraping bottom of pan with rubber spatula, until thickened slightly, about 30 seconds.

2 Carefully transfer mixture to blender, let cool slightly, about 1 minute, then process on high speed for 1 minute. Pour ice cream base into large bowl and let cool until no longer steaming, about 20 minutes. Cover with plastic wrap and refrigerate for at least 6 hours or up to 24 hours. (Alternatively, place bowl over ice bath of 6 cups ice, ½ cup water, and ⅓ cup salt and chill base to 40 degrees, stirring occasionally, about 1½ hours.)

3 Whisk chilled ice cream base until recombined and smooth, then transfer to ice cream machine and churn until mixture has consistency of soft-serve ice cream and registers 22 to 23 degrees. Transfer to airtight container, cover, and freeze until firm, at least 6 hours or up to 24 hours. Serve. (Ice cream is best eaten within 2 weeks).

VARIATIONS

Coconut Horchata Ice Cream

Add ¾ teaspoon ground cinnamon and ⅛ teaspoon ground cloves to coconut milk mixture in saucepan before cooking in step 1. Serve topped with toasted sliced almonds.

Coconut Lime Ice Cream

Substitute 1 tablespoon lime juice for vanilla extract. Add 2 teaspoons grated lime zest to coconut milk mixture with lime juice in step 1.

Raspberry Sorbet
makes 1 quart

1 cup water
1 teaspoon Sure-Jell for Less or
    No Sugar Sugar Needed Recipes
⅛ teaspoon salt
1¼ pounds (4 cups) raspberries
½ cup (3½ ounces) plus
    2 tablespoons organic sugar
    (see page 31)
¼ cup light corn syrup

Why This Recipe Works Raspberry sorbet is refreshing—but it's often too icy to be worth eating. For smooth scoops, we froze a small portion of the base separately, adding it back to the rest before churning. Because this small amount froze so rapidly, there wasn't enough time for large ice crystals to grow; mixing this superchilled mixture into the larger base encouraged the growth of similarly small crystals, for a fine-textured result. We also added pectin in addition to the berries' natural amount to give the sorbet stability in and out of the freezer. If using a canister-style ice cream machine, be sure to freeze the empty canister for at least 24 hours and preferably 48 hours before churning. For self-refrigerating machines, prechill the canister by running the machine for 5 to 10 minutes before pouring in the sorbet mixture. Let the sorbet sit at room temperature for 5 minutes to soften before serving. Fresh or frozen berries may be used. If using frozen berries, thaw them before proceeding.

1 Heat water, pectin, and salt in medium saucepan over medium-high heat, stirring occasionally, until pectin is fully dissolved, about 5 minutes. Remove saucepan from heat and let cool slightly, about 10 minutes.

2 Process raspberries, sugar, corn syrup, and cooled water mixture in food processor until smooth, about 30 seconds. Strain puree through fine-mesh strainer into bowl, pressing on solids to remove seeds and pulp (you should have about 3 cups puree); discard solids. Transfer 1 cup puree to small bowl and place remaining puree in large bowl; cover both bowls with plastic wrap. Place large bowl in refrigerator and small bowl in freezer and chill for at least 4 hours or up to 24 hours. (Small bowl will freeze solid.)

3 Remove puree from refrigerator and freezer. Using tines of fork, scrape frozen puree into large bowl with chilled puree. Stir occasionally until frozen puree has fully dissolved.

4 Transfer mixture to ice cream machine and churn until mixture resembles thick milkshake and lightens in color, 15 to 25 minutes. Transfer to airtight container and freeze until firm, at least 2 hours or up to 5 days. Serve.

VARIATION
Raspberry Sorbet with Ginger and Mint
Substitute ginger beer for water in step 1. Add 2-inch piece of peeled and thinly sliced ginger and ¼ cup mint leaves to food processor with raspberries. Decrease amount of sugar to ½ cup.

desserts

Nutritional Information

Analyzing recipes for their nutritional values is a tricky business, and we did our best to be as accurate as possible. We were strict about measuring when cooking and never resorted to estimating. We also didn't play games when analyzing the recipes to make the numbers look better. To calculate the nutritional values of our recipes per serving, we used The Food Processor SQL by ESHA Research. When using this program, we entered all the ingredients, using weights for important ingredients such as most vegetables. We also used our preferred brands in these analyses. When the recipe called for seasoning with an unspecified amount of salt and pepper, we added ½ teaspoon of salt and ¼ teaspoon of pepper to the analysis. We did not include additional salt or pepper for food that's "seasoned to taste." Unless otherwise indicated, the information applies to a single serving. If there is a range in the serving size, we used the highest number of servings to calculate the nutritional values.

	Serving/ Portion	Cal	Fat (g)	Sat Fat (g)	Chol (mg)	Carb (g)	Protein (g)	Fiber (g)	Sodium (mg)
BREAKFAST AND BRUNCH									
Tofu Frittata with Mushrooms	8	160	10	1	0	7	11	2	370
Tofu Scramble with Bell Pepper, Shallot, and Herbs	4	100	6	0	0	4	8	1	440
Tofu Scramble with Tomato and Scallions	4	100	6	0	0	4	8	1	440
Tofu Ranchero	4	510	25	3	0	61	17	17	1610
Sweet Potato Red Flannel Hash with Tempeh	4	390	20	2	0	39	15	11	820
Black Beans on Toast with Avocado and Tomato	4	280	13	1.5	0	34	8	8	640
Overnight Three-Grain Breakfast Porridge	4	360	4.5	0	0	72	10	10	360
Creamy Breakfast Grits with Chives	6	180	9	1	0	20	3	2	320
Savory Drop Biscuits	per biscuit	250	15	13	0	27	4	1	400
Currant Scones	per scone	260	10	8	0	39	4	2	330
Lemon-Glazed Ginger Scones	per scone	370	10	8	0	66	4	1	330
Maple-Glazed Pecan Scones	per scone	420	15	8	0	68	4	2	330
Blueberry Muffins	1 muffin	290	10	1	0	44	4	1	320
Classic Pancakes	6	300	9	7	0	47	6	2	650
100-Percent Whole-Wheat Pancakes	6	330	12	8	0	52	8	6	590
Belgian Waffles	4	460	16	12	0	66	11	2	740
Banana Bread	per slice	290	9	0.5	0	49	4	2	210
Coffee Cake	10	370	15	10	0	56	4	3	310
All-Morning Energy Bars	per bar	190	12	1.5	0	18	6	3	120
Chia Pudding with Fresh Fruit and Coconut	4	250	12	4	0	31	8	11	190

	Serving/Portion	Cal	Fat (g)	Sat Fat (g)	Chol (mg)	Carb (g)	Protein (g)	Fiber (g)	Sodium (mg)
Mixed Berry Smoothie	2	250	8	2.5	0	47	5	6	150
Green Smoothie	2	270	12	1.5	0	40	6	7	160
Tropical Fruit Smoothie	2	350	7	2.5	0	72	5	7	150
SOUPS, STEWS, AND CHILIS									
Chickpea Noodle Soup	6	200	6	0	0	29	7	5	1000
Creamless Creamy Tomato Soup	8	150	7	1	0	17	3	2	600
Farmhouse Vegetable and Barley Soup	8	220	4	0	0	39	6	6	1120
Classic Croutons	per ¼ cup	20	2.5	0	0	3	1	0	40
Super Greens Soup with Lemon-Tarragon Cream	6	170	8	2	0	20	5	3	970
Creamy Curried Cauliflower Soup	6	180	14	5	0	13	4	5	640
Roasted Eggplant and Tomato Soup	6	230	15	2	0	22	3	6	920
Classic Gazpacho	10	60	0	0	0	11	2	3	810
Spicy Gazpacho with Chipotle Chile and Lime	10	60	0	0	0	12	2	3	810
Tortilla Soup	8	190	6	0	0	29	6	6	1060
Turkish Tomato, Bulgur, and Red Pepper Soup	8	140	4	0.5	0	21	3	4	840
Red Lentil Soup with North African Spices	6	270	11	1.5	0	34	12	8	730
Thai Coconut Soup with Tofu	8	180	12	8	0	10	8	2	1040
Quinoa and Vegetable Stew	8	260	9	1	0	38	7	7	590
Mushroom and Farro Stew	4	450	10	1	0	76	16	10	870
Ultimate Vegan Chili	8	450	13	1	0	69	19	17	1200
Roasted Poblano and White Bean Chili	6	310	9	0.5	0	48	14	12	1120
Butternut Squash Chili with Quinoa and Peanuts	6	610	39	15	0	61	14	12	1380
BURGERS, SANDWICHES, AND PIZZAS									
Lentil and Mushroom Burgers	per Burger	410	17	2	0	54	12	5	520
Black Bean Burgers	per Burger	320	13	1	0	43	10	7	670
Pinto Bean–Beet Burgers	per burger	440	19	2	0	55	12	6	910
Grilled Portobello Burgers	per Burger	450	33	4.5	0	33	7	3	1010
Creamy Chipotle Sauce	per table-spoon	60	6	1	0	1	0	0	70
Pub-Style Burger Sauce	per table-spoon	70	8	1	0	1	0	0	220
Tahini Sauce	per table-spoon	90	8	1	0	4	3	1	5

	Serving/ Portion	Cal	Fat (g)	Sat Fat (g)	Chol (mg)	Carb (g)	Protein (g)	Fiber (g)	Sodium (mg)
Quick Pickled Radishes	per table-spoon	5	0	0	0	1	0	0	75
Quick Sweet-and-Spicy Pickled Red Onions	per table-spoon	20	0	0	0	5	0	0	45
Crispy Onions	per table-spoon	25	2.5	0	0	1	0	0	25
Chickpea Salad Sandwiches	4	340	17	2	0	37	11	7	790
Curried Chickpea Salad Sandwiches	4	380	17	2	0	47	11	8	720
Tofu Banh Mi	4	500	28	3	0	50	15	7	760
Falafel with Tahini Yogurt Sauce	8	300	22	3	0	33	10	15	630
Korean Barbecue Tempeh Wraps	4	750	27	4.5	0	97	31	14	2470
Sizzling Saigon Crêpes (Banh Xeo)	8	290	11	3	0	43	6	4	1170
Baja-Style Cauliflower Tacos	6	470	28	17	0	52	8	9	470
Thin-Crust Pizza Dough	per slice	160	1	0	0	31	5	1	290
Whole-Wheat Pizza Dough	per slice	140	3	0	0	25	4	2	340
Pesto Pizza with Fennel and Cauliflower	per slice	280	13	1.5	0	33	6	2	440
Mushroom Pizza with Cashew Ricotta	per slice	300	14	2	0	34	8	1	630
MAIN DISH SALADS AND BOWLS									
Kale Caesar Salad	6	320	22	2.5	0	24	7	4	620
Green Salad with Crispy Spiced Chickpeas and Mustard Vinaigrette	6	260	22	2	0	11	2	2	550
Garlicky Tofu Tabbouleh	6	210	13	2	0	16	9	4	500
Cauliflower Salad with Chermoula and Carrots	6	240	16	2	0	22	4	5	350
Asparagus and Arugula Salad with Cannellini Beans	6	160	12	1.5	0	11	4	3	330
Quinoa, Black Bean, and Mango Salad with Lime Dressing	6	450	27	3.5	0	45	9	8	740
Farro Salad with Sugar Snap Peas and White Beans	6	310	9	1	0	50	11	8	460
Wheat Berry Salad with Chickpeas, Spinach, and Orange	6	300	8	1	0	50	9	10	450
Freekeh Salad with Butternut Squash, Walnuts, and Raisins	6	420	19	2.5	0	55	9	11	400
Red Rice and Quinoa Salad	6	350	11	1.5	0	59	6	5	100
Chickpea Salad with Carrots, Arugula, and Olives	6	180	11	1.5	0	17	4	4	570
Chickpea Salad with Fennel and Arugula	6	170	11	1.5	0	16	4	4	520
Spiced Lentil Salad with Winter Squash	6	260	13	2	0	29	8	7	220
Cilantro Sauce	per table-spoon	40	4	0.5	0	0	0	0	95
Chile Sauce	per table-spoon	50	3.5	0	0	6	0	0	180

	Serving/Portion	Cal	Fat (g)	Sat Fat (g)	Chol (mg)	Carb (g)	Protein (g)	Fiber (g)	Sodium (mg)
Chile Sauce	per table-spoon	15	0	0	0	2	0	0	440
Curried Peanut Sauce	per table-spoon	45	3.5	0.5	0	3	1	0	180
Miso-Ginger Sauce	per table-spoon	50	4.5	0.5	0	2	0	0	210
Basmati Rice Bowl with Spiced Cauliflower and Pomegranates	6	380	19	3	0	47	7	5	530
Brown Rice Burrito Bowl	6	450	23	3.5	0	54	8	6	630
Farro Bowl with Tofu, Mushrooms, and Spinach	6	480	25	2	0	52	15	6	810
Spicy Peanut Rice Noodle Bowl	6	470	23	3	0	58	12	5	510
Barley Bowl with Roasted Carrots and Snow Peas	6	450	23	3	0	54	13	13	240
Brown Sushi Rice Bowl with Tofu and Vegetables	6	560	17	1	0	87	17	9	800
Korean Rice Bowl with Tempeh (Dolsot Bibimbap)	6	610	21	2	0	88	20	9	2050

NEW DINNER FAVORITES

Creamy Cashew Mac and Cheese	6	610	30	13	0	70	19	6	1050
Mushroom Bolognese	6	460	9	1	0	73	15	5	860
Fettuccine Alfredo	6	520	23	12	0	66	15	5	810
Hearty Vegetable Lasagna	10	410	26	4	0	37	11	5	620
Spaghetti and Meatless Meatballs	6	620	11	1.5	0	98	30	12	1660
Whole-Wheat Spaghetti with Greens, Beans, and Tomatoes	6	440	12	1.5	0	66	17	14	1060
Almost Hands-Free Mushroom Risotto	6	400	11	1.5	0	62	11	3	1130
Almost Hands-Free Fennel Risotto	6	390	11	1.5	0	63	9	4	1160
Vegan Shepherd's Pie	6	350	12	1.5	0	43	17	6	810
Pinto Bean and Swiss Chard Enchiladas	6	470	25	3	0	53	10	12	1380
Cauliflower Steaks with Salsa Verde	4	300	29	4	0	10	4	4	470
Chile-Rubbed Butternut Squash Steaks with Ranch Dressing	4	480	35	4.5	0	44	4	8	1130
Pan-Seared Tempeh Steaks with Chimichurri Sauce	4	490	36	5	0	18	23	13	310
Pan-Seared Tempeh Steaks with Chermoula Sauce	4	500	36	5	0	19	23	13	310
Crispy Orange Seitan	4	490	20	6	0	58	21	2	1470
Teriyaki Tofu	6	220	7	1	0	24	15	2	1550
Thai-Style Tofu and Basil Lettuce Cups	4	270	17	2	0	15	16	4	810
Barbecue Tempeh, Mushroom, and Bell Pepper Skewers	4	490	22	2.5	0	48	25	13	750

nutritional information

	Serving/ Portion	Cal	Fat (g)	Sat Fat (g)	Chol (mg)	Carb (g)	Protein (g)	Fiber (g)	Sodium (mg)
STIR-FRIES, CURRIES, AND NOODLES									
Stir-Fried Tofu, Shiitakes, and Green Beans	4	320	17	1.5	0	28	14	4	890
Stir-Fried Tempeh, Napa Cabbage, and Carrots	4	430	17	2	0	48	20	13	1080
Stir-Fried Eggplant with Garlic-Basil Sauce	4	150	9	0.5	0	19	4	4	970
Thai Red Curry with Cauliflower	4	260	17	9	0	23	9	7	1080
Thai Red Curry with Bell Peppers and Tofu	4	330	21	9	0	21	13	3	840
Saag Tofu (Tofu and Spinach)	6	250	16	2	0	17	12	6	630
Indian-Style Curry with Sweet Potatoes, Eggplant, and Chickpeas	6	250	11	3.5	0	33	8	8	440
Indian-Style Curry with Potatoes, Cauliflower, and Chickpeas	6	250	12	4	0	33	6	9	440
Potato Vindaloo	6	220	6	0	0	38	5	7	590
Shiitake Ramen	6	300	5	0.5	0	54	9	6	1930
Tofu Pad Thai	4	640	26	2.5	0	88	18	8	1000
Udon Noodles with Mustard Greens and Shiitake-Ginger Sauce	6	360	6	0	0	60	17	7	880
Sesame Soba Noodles with Snow Peas, Radishes, and Cilantro	4	540	20	2.5	0	74	19	7	1590
Spicy Basil Noodles with Crispy Tofu, Bok Choy, and Bell Peppers	6	470	16	1	0	72	13	4	1160
SNACKS AND APPS									
Kale Chips	4	70	4.5	0.5	0	7	4	3	310
Ranch-Style Kale Chips	4	80	4.5	0.5	0	9	4	3	310
Spicy Sesame-Ginger Kale Chips	4	80	5	0.5	0	8	4	3	310
Crispy Spiced Chickpeas	6	160	10	1.5	0	14	4	3	400
Whipped Cashew Dip with Roasted Red Peppers and Olives	per ¼ cup	210	17	3	0	10	5	1	290
Whipped Cashew Dip with Chipotle and Lime	per ¼ cup	200	17	3	0	9	5	1	220
Whipped Cashew Dip with Sun-Dried Tomatoes and Rosemary	per ¼ cup	210	18	3	0	10	5	1	240
Hummus with Smoked Paprika	per ¼ cup	140	11	1.5	0	8	4	2	230
Sweet Potato Hummus	per ¼ cup	140	9	1.5	0	12	2	2	250
Muhammara	per ¼ cup	150	13	1.5	0	9	2	1	370
Pita Chips	8	210	14	2	0	17	3	1	300
Guacamole with Habanero and Mango	per ¼ cup	90	7	1	0	6	1	4	150

	Serving/Portion	Cal	Fat (g)	Sat Fat (g)	Chol (mg)	Carb (g)	Protein (g)	Fiber (g)	Sodium (mg)
Nacho Dip	per ¼ cup	90	5	0	0	9	2	1	300
Loaded Nachos	6	440	20	2	0	59	10	7	1100
Buffalo Cauliflower Bites	6	410	34	14	0	26	3	2	570
Ranch Dressing	per tablespoon	90	10	1	0	0	0	0	120
Marinated Cauliflower with Chickpeas and Saffron	8	110	7	1	0	9	3	2	310
Socca with Swiss Chard, Pistachios, and Apricots	8	240	15	2	0	22	6	6	320
Polenta Fries with Creamy Chipotle Sauce	4	390	27	3	0	34	4	4	730
DESSERTS									
Chocolate Chip Cookies	per cookie	280	14	9	0	39	4	2	150
Chocolate Chip Oatmeal Cookies	per cookie	280	13	8	0	40	4	2	150
Peanut Butter Cookies	per cookie	190	10	3.5	0	24	4	1	160
Aquafaba Meringues	per cookie	15	0	0	0	3	0	0	5
Almond Aquafaba Meringues	per cookie	15	0	0	0	3	0	0	5
Fudgy Brownies	per bar	210	8	2.5	0	34	2	2	90
Raspberry Streusel Bars	per bar	200	10	7	0	27	2	1	50
Dark Chocolate Cupcakes	per cupcake (with frosting)	330	16	12	0	46	4	3	180
Yellow Layer Cake	12 (with frosting)	640	30	22	0	93	6	4	380
Creamy Chocolate Frosting	12	280	20	14	0	31	3	3	55
Creamy Chocolate Frosting for Cupcakes	12	140	10	7	0	15	1	2	30
French Apple Tart	8	500	20	17	0	79	4	8	160
Peach-Raspberry Crisp	6	410	17	9	0	67	5	8	150
Single-Crust Pie Dough	8	230	16	14	0	21	3	1	150
Double-Crust Pie Dough	8	470	32	27	0	42	5	1	290
Pecan Pie	8	780	51	24	0	80	7	4	300
Blueberry Pie	8	660	35	30	0	83	6	4	310
Pumpkin Cashew Cheesecake	16	440	32	16	0	35	8	2	180
Strawberry Shortcakes with Coconut Whipped Cream	8	470	27	23	0	54	6	4	340
Coconut Ice Cream	8	280	21	19	0	25	2	1	95
Coconut Horchata Ice Cream	8	280	21	19	0	26	2	1	95
Coconut Lime Ice Cream	8	280	21	19	0	26	2	1	95
Raspberry Sorbet	8	130	0	0	0	33	1	5	50
Raspberry Sorbet with Ginger and Mint	8	130	0.5	0	0	33	1	5	55

Conversions and Equivalents

Some say cooking is a science and an art. We would say that geography has a hand in it, too. Flours and sugars manufactured in the United Kingdom and elsewhere will feel and taste different from those manufactured in the United States. So we cannot promise that the pie crust you bake in Canada or England will taste the same as a pie crust baked in the States, but we can offer guidelines for converting weights and measures. We also recommend that you rely on your instincts when making our recipes. Refer to the visual cues provided. If the pie dough hasn't "come together," as described, you may need to add more water—even if the recipe doesn't tell you to. You be the judge. The recipes in this book were developed using standard U.S. measures following U.S. government guidelines. The charts below offer equivalents for U.S. and metric measures. All conversions are approximate and have been rounded up or down to the nearest whole number.

Example
1 teaspoon = 4.9292 milliliters, rounded up to 5 milliliters
1 ounce = 28.3495 grams, rounded down to 28 grams

VOLUME CONVERSIONS	
U.S.	**Metric**
1 teaspoon	5 milliliters
2 teaspoons	10 milliliters
1 tablespoon	15 milliliters
2 tablespoons	30 milliliters
¼ cup	59 milliliters
⅓ cup	79 milliliters
½ cup	118 milliliters
¾ cup	177 milliliters
1 cup	237 milliliters
1¼ cups	296 milliliters
1½ cups	355 milliliters
2 cups (1 pint)	473 milliliters
2½ cups	591 milliliters
3 cups	710 milliliters
4 cups (1 quart)	0.946 liter
1.06 quarts	1 liter
4 quarts (1 gallon)	3.8 liters

WEIGHT CONVERSIONS	
Ounces	**Grams**
½	14
¾	21
1	28
1½	43
2	57
2½	71
3	85
3½	99
4	113
4½	128
5	142
6	170
7	198
8	227
9	255
10	283
12	340
16 (1 pound)	454

CONVERTING TEMPERATURES FROM AN INSTANT-READ THERMOMETER

When a recipe includes a doneness temperature, we recommend an instant-read thermometer for the job. Refer to the table above to convert Fahrenheit degrees to Celsius. Or, for temperatures not represented in the chart, use this simple formula:

Subtract 32 degrees from the Fahrenheit reading, then divide the result by 1.8 to find the Celsius reading.

Example
"Churn until mixture has consistency of soft-serve ice cream and registers 22 to 23 degrees."

To convert:
$22°F - 32 = -10°$
$-10° ÷ 1.8 = -5.56°C$, rounded to $-6°C$

CONVERSION FOR COMMON BAKING INGREDIENTS

Baking is an exacting science. Because measuring by weight is far more accurate than measuring by volume, and thus more likely to produce reliable results, in our recipes we provide ounce measures in addition to cup measures for many ingredients. Refer to the chart below to convert these measures into grams.

OVEN TEMPERATURES		
Fahrenheit	**Celsius**	**Gas Mark**
225	105	¼
250	120	½
275	135	1
300	150	2
325	165	3
350	180	4
375	190	5
400	200	6
425	220	7
450	230	8
475	245	9

INGREDIENT	OUNCES	GRAMS
Flour		
1 cup all-purpose flour*	5	142
1 cup cake flour	4	113
1 cup whole-wheat flour	5½	156
Sugar		
1 cup granulated (white) sugar	7	198
1 cup packed brown sugar (light or dark)	7	198
1 cup confectioners' sugar	4	113
Cocoa Powder		
1 cup cocoa powder	3	85

* U.S. all-purpose flour, the most frequently used flour in this book, does not contain leaveners, as some European flours do. These leavened flours are called self-rising or self-raising. If you are using self-rising flour, take this into consideration before adding leavening to a recipe.

Index